"I believe nutritional medicine to be the mandatory medicine of the next century. It is extremely effective, particularly in the early stages of disease, where modern orthodoxy fails miserably. Its preventive approach is a guaranteed benefit; and last but not least, it is economically effective."

—*Derrick Lonsdale, M.D.*

Why I Left
ORTHODOX
MEDICINE

Healing for the 21st Century

Derrick Lonsdale, M.D.

With a Foreword by James P. Frackleton, M.D.

HAMPTON ROADS
PUBLISHING COMPANY, INC.

Cover design by Marjoram Productions

For information write:

Hampton Roads Publishing Company, Inc.
134 Burgess Lane
Charlottesville, VA 22902

Or call: (804) 296-2772
FAX: (804) 296-5096
e-mail: hrpc@mail.hamptonroadspub.com
Internet: http://www.hamptonroadspub.com

If you are unable to order this book from your local
bookseller, you may order directly from the publisher.
Quantity discounts for organizations are available.
Call 1-800-766-8009, toll-free.

ISBN 1-878901-98-2

10 9 8 7 6 5 4 3 2

Printed on acid-free paper in the United States of America

To my wife
Adèle

Table of Contents

Foreword

This book is *must* reading for this period of time of great confusion in the delivery of medical care. It takes the reader through the changes in philosophy experienced by a physician in an academic setting, based on his discovery of the logic of natural self-healing.

In this chemically polluted world, drugs in general only add to the body's burden of poisons. The "new medicine" of the 21st century must be a paradigm shift from what was done in the 20th century under the title of "scientific medicine."

The presently accepted traditional or orthodox medicine has taken on all the characteristics of a religion, and any threat to its status quo is unfortunately treated as heresy. Our present course will bankrupt our country without having the desired results of *good, effective medicine*. Though the developing science of nutritional treatment may appear, at first sight, to be an oversimplification, it actually influences body repair at the cellular level. Nutrition works, and this book provides a foundation for understanding why.

James P. Frackelton, M.D.
Past President,
The American College for
Advancement in Medicine

Introduction

This is not a do-it-yourself book. It does not tell the reader what nutrient supplement to purchase from the health food store. Hundreds of books like that are in existence. This book is different because it tells you *why* nutrition and nutrient supplementation represent a *paradigm shift* in *concept*. It describes why I believe that nutritional medicine *is* a paradigm shift. The last one occurred when germs were discovered as a common cause of many different disease conditions.

In order to understand the nature of this book, it is necessary to review recent history in the development of medical science. Hippocrates, generally conceded to be the father of modern medicine, actually operated on principles which were far removed from our present approach. The foundation of his treatment was based upon rest and diet. One of his most important tenets was the simple statement "Thou shalt do no harm," essentially meaning that if the attending physician does anything at all for the sick patient, it must never be actively harmful. In this statement is implicitly the concession that the approach used by a physician might fail, but that it must not make things worse.

This tenet would appear to be something which is so obvious that it barely needs stating, but we shall see why this approach may easily be lost with our present attitude in modern medicine. Hippocrates also said, "Let your medicine be your food and your food be your medicine." In the modern era, that remarkable piece of wisdom has been almost totally lost, and it is worth examining why this is so.

Consider the development of medical thought over the centuries. The ancient Chinese people proposed and used advanced techniques for centuries, but by language and geography they were necessarily isolated, and their wisdom was never easily accessible to the Western world. In the meantime, development of scientific thought was proceeding at a painfully slow pace in Europe.

For example, we think of Harvey as the genius who discovered the circulation of the blood. Obviously, Harvey was indeed a genius, for his discovery was brought to light in a time when current thought in Europe had no idea of the functions of the complex machinery now known as the cardiovascular system. Yet this concept was understood fairly well by the Chinese for as long as 4000 years before and was incorporated into their techniques as a matter of course.

The real problem is the accumulation of collective wisdom in a cohesive and retrievable form. This is seen sharply with the obvious background of the short human life span. Consider the vast quantities of literature that has ever been written; it is impossible for any one individual to grasp even the smallest part of it. Hence, we develop our concepts in relatively small groups and easily become convinced that our own is the "only truth."

It is a painful reiteration of the story of the blind men and the elephant. A group of blind men were asked to describe an elephant that each had examined to the best of his ability. One described the animal as a "long tube"; another as a "flat piece of material," and so on. Of course, each was describing a very limited view, depending upon whether he had touched the trunk, the ear, or other organ of the whole animal. It is paramountly human that each of these blind men was equally convinced that he had described the whole elephant. Of even greater importance, each was convinced that the others had made fundamental mistakes in their ability to observe the animal. It is also obvious that each was making an accurate assessment of his observation. The failure to perceive the big picture was the error common to all of them.

This universal problem of mankind creates the collective failure to see the big picture. So we must now examine the development of our own particular "blind man" concept. That is, we must look at the mechanisms that led to our present views of the medical science that has come to be known as allopathy. The medieval period in Europe was associated with such nebulous things as evil spirits and witchcraft. There was no particular plan which referred to medical thought. No really good or practical ideas came until relatively recently when microorganisms were discovered to be a cause of a great many different diseases. Allopathy is defined as a medical technique which deliberately induces inflammation. This approach arose from the fact that research showed that a fundamental response of the body to infection was inflammation. What was more natural than to attempt to find ways and means of inducing inflammation as a defensive response? Physicians no longer do this, but the concept of killing the enemy has remained as the dominant theme that guides our collective thought patterns.

Every effort was then made to find ways and means of killing the germs without killing the human being who was attacked. Penicillin did two things. It gave doctors a useful and practical approach to infections for the first time ever, at least with reasonable safety. But it also reinforced the "game plan," which was to kill the enemy.

Nobody will contest the fact that the discovery of penicillin was dramatic, perhaps the most dramatic moment in the history of modern medicine. Like so many things, however, it had its "flip" side, unfortunately. It gave us the idea that Mother Nature had provided an inexhaustible supply of harmless germ killers. A vast research program was initiated to find other substances that had the same kind of effect as penicillin. Now we have a very large number of antibiotics, as they all came to be called. But not all of them were benign: far from it. Indeed, some of them were so toxic to our own cells that they were diverted to the treatment of various forms of cancer.

In fact, the idea of antibiotics was so transparently supportive of collective modern medical wisdom that it blinded us to a whole array of associated factors. It is remarkably akin to the error that has been made in agriculture, in attempting to find ways and means of killing insect pests. Everyone, including the farmers, knows now that this approach perpetrated an ecologic phenomenon which threatens our very existence. The insects became resistant to insecticides and bred resistant strains in their progeny. As quickly as the ingenious chemist found a new chemical, the insect population adapted and became resistant to the lethal attack. Now we have hundreds or thousands of chemical substances and whole generations of insects that are unaffected by the array of chemicals. Ironically, however, *our* cells have not adapted to these chemicals, and we are the organisms that are feeling the effect of this barrage of chemical brinkmanship. Our water is heavily polluted, and our food is tainted with them. Nobody is yet able to assess the amount of disease in humans which is directly related to this use of pesticides.

The idea of "kill the enemy" spread to the treatment of cancer. If the maverick cells that represent the cancer could be killed, then the disease would be cured. We are faced with the same problem. Can we kill the cancer without killing its owner? We are back at the conundrum that faced us when we were trying to find agents to kill germs. Unfortunately, we had forgotten that the body has its own defensive machinery, and no thought was given to finding means to improve or support it. In fact, our therapy often damages the situation to such a degree that we offend that fundamental rule preached by Hippocrates: Thou shalt do no harm.

We have run into a very distinct and important mistake which permeates the whole range of crisis disease. We have become arrogant since we have come to believe that the modern era of medicine is the scientific bonanza of all time. Physicians are trained, and patients are taught, that this modern medicine is fantastic and dramatic and can produce miracles of healing that have never been dreamed of before. So gulled are we that it is sometimes extremely difficult for a physician to observe that his treatment is making things worse. In the excitement of the intensive care unit (terminology which glorifies the active participation of the physician as a healer), he sees the clinical decay of a patient and says to himself: "What a devastating disease this is. Even with the powerful medicines that I have at my disposal, I do not seem to be able to correct this inevitable decline. I must add yet another pharmaceutical miracle drug."

He (the male gender is used for convenience only) has been duped. He has forgotten that he is *not* a healer. He is the servant of a "machine" that is able to heal itself, and he needs humility, not aggression. His training is against him, for the power of the drug companies teaches him constantly that he is in charge of a battery of miracle makers that must be used with increasingly honed skill. It is difficult for him to see that each drug compounds the clinical situation and that it is not the natural course of the disease that is the problem.

This attitude has also given way to the idea that clinical observation is old-fashioned and of no value in the presence of modern technology. The diagnosis is made by finding evidence of structural changes in the body and this is the work-up which must be set in motion in every case. When no evidence of disease is found from this work-up, the patient is placed in a classification of "functional disease," tantamount to an accusation of fraud. This judgment has infiltrated into the patient's consciousness in the form of "the doctor said that it was all in my head." It is not particularly surprising that this classification, rightly or wrongly, has given rise to latent or explicit resentment, since the patient is convinced that the physician considers him to be a fake. Unfortunately, this is often exactly the opinion of the physician who believes that the physical symptoms are some kind of psychological protection for the patient, who is unwilling to face the world.

If this is the model that we have set up and it is wrong, then we have to replace it with a better model. This book is to introduce the reader to such a model. It demonstrates why preventive medicine, which uses nutrition as its core therapy, has to be the medicine of the 21st century. Although a relatively simple model, it is built upon basic science which is well-known and understood. It is only a matter of moving this knowledge out of the laboratory into the clinic, a procedure which can take many years unless the physician is willing and able to be conversant with the patient's problem in both clinical and biochemical terms. It will show the reader that health can be maintained remarkably easily if the human machine is properly serviced and that the fuel that it receives is the most important of all health measures.

I have tried to trace my own development as a physician. I was educated in the most orthodox and austere atmosphere, in a famous London teaching hospital. My early training is remembered with gratitude because it taught me how people tick. Progressing through family practice to the heady atmosphere of a major American subspecialty clinic, I became deeply involved with the fascinating complexities of biochemistry. It was there, in the mill race of hard-won experience, that I began to see the body as a biochemical machine which can repair itself when provided with its nutritional needs. I found that this principle applied to all illness, not just rare and exotic conditions.

To make such a change in personal perspective is just as difficult as changing from one religion to another and demands repeated self-examination and confirmation. In a thousand different ways, I have put my model to the test in my own mind. It has yet to become unglued. I hope that, by tracing a personal event of such magnitude, as I see it, that I have provided the reader with a blueprint that enables that perspective to become visible to others.

Chapter 1

What Is Wrong With Orthodox Medicine?

I grew up in England. I was educated at an English public school and received my medical training at a London medical school. I graduated with a degree given by the University of London and set out to prepare myself for family practice. During my residency, the English health service became law and my pay went up from nine to sixteen pounds a month.

The health service altered the way in which a young physician entered a practice. Buying and selling of "goodwill" was the previous method, and a practice would be purchased from a retiring physician. This method was abolished by the Labor government, and a method known as "assistantship with view to partnership" was instigated. A "principal" physician would take on a salaried assistant for a one-year or two-year trial. If the assistant performed properly, he would be given a partnership on termination of his apprenticeship.

Since the principal physician obtained tax relief from the salary that was paid to the assistant, and giving a partnership meant sharing the income from the practice, it was hardly surprising that assistants would be retained for the terms of the contract and were then told that they were "not really compatible."

Assistantships were advertised through an agency run by the British Medical Association (BMA), and a physician looking for such a position would have to apply. Often, arriving at a prospective assistantship post for interview, the first person that one would meet would be the outgoing assistant, a recurrent experience which would be quite disheartening.

The first job for which I applied was in a country practice in Suffolk. The village population was 5000, and three physicians who were in partnership "ruled" the town and the surrounding country for miles. They required a fourth partner and advertised through the

BMA agency. There were 150 applicants, giving a perspective on the difficulty of entering medical practice at that time, even in the most modest position. We were short-listed to twenty-five and interviewed in a London hotel. There were three of us on the short-short-list, and we were invited to have lunch in the village in Suffolk, where we would be looked over by the partners and their wives. One of the applicants was not able to attend, so I found myself eyeing my one and only rival over the lunch table.

Again, the fact that I got the job really had little to do with my education. All the applicants were more or less equally qualified. I was hired because the senior partner's wife liked me, I was newly engaged to be married, and I was age 27! I reminded the senior partner of himself when he entered the practice. There was no organized work for me to do because the three partners had divided the practice into three segments and continued to see their patients. I was supposed to cover for them when they went on their separate vacations, but there were relatively long periods when none of them were on vacation and I had nothing to do. For a young and willing-to-work physician, it was a sad experience and I soon left.

After a few years of the English health service, I began to become restless for more excitement and an opportunity to use my skills. The health service was set up in such a way that the family doctor was regarded as one who had failed to climb the specialty ladder. He was merely a first encounter with the patient, and if anything was "really wrong" the patient had to be passed on to the specialist in the hospital. The apparently "free" service made many people very unappreciative of their primary care, and they often took little notice of what their family doctor said, insisting upon being referred to a specialist. There was a kind of blackmail in which a patient would ask for something and threaten to leave the physician who did not comply. It has never been a surprise to me that British physicians left their native country in droves. They became part of the so-called brain drain.

A Transition To Pediatric Oncology

I emigrated to Canada and thence to the United States, where I became a board-certified pediatrician in a large multi-specialty clinic. This background was important in my later career development. First, I came to appreciate fully that I had received what I regard to be the best medical training in the world because it was a clinical training which forced me to consider the problems voiced by the patient. That is perhaps a little strange to say, since it might be expected that all medical training would be aimed at that purpose. Unfortunately, I believe that medical training in the United States has been aimed at giving the student a pervasive knowledge of the erudite and arcane manifestations of disease which he does not see in real-life practice.

Having reached a pinnacle of intellectual achievement which has been hard-won, the graduate is equipped with two false concepts. He believes himself to "know it all" and is often unteachable during his residency years, and, secondly, he becomes quickly bored with the reality of practice. Perhaps it is not surprising then that many physicians turn their attention to the stock market, regarding their daily work load as something to be suffered rather than enjoyed. There is little glamor, continuous pressure from an increasingly demanding public, and boredom.

I was lucky, for my job as a pediatrician in this large referral clinic was filled with challenge and excitement. We received referred patients from all over the Midwest, and they were selected, of course, because of their complexity. I can honestly say that there are indeed very few conditions in children that I have not experienced.

During the Nixon era, it will be remembered that enormous amounts of money were set aside for research into the cause and treatment of cancer. The physicians had said, "Give us the money and we will solve the problem of cancer." Alas, we now know that the millions of dollars devoted to this research gave only relatively small returns and the problem is far from solved.

Anyway, there was a need, and it is surprising to many people to learn that there are many forms of highly malignant cancers which affect children. So, I became a pediatric oncologist. *Oncologist* is the fancy word that is used to describe a physician who studies and treats cancer. For six years I took care of all the cancer problems in children that were referred to our clinic for treatment. I became a member of one of the study groups that were being formed all over the country, the idea obviously being that our information would grow faster with a large number of physicians pooling their experiences and resources. I became the pediatric representative on the executive committee and quickly came into contact with the politics.

Each child, after a given diagnosis was made, was logged into a protocol study according to the type of cancer. The idea was simple. All the children from the various institutions that contributed membership to this particular study group were treated by the individual investigators in exactly the same way. Their clinical course, blood counts, and various results were entered on forms. When a given child had completed a protocol study, the forms were mailed to one of the study members who was designated to collate all the data collected for that particular protocol. The results were then passed to the group statistician, who would assess the results in statistical terms. We had to try to assess whether the chosen treatment was beneficial or made things worse.

The only dramatic treatment responses were extraordinarily temporary, and the outcome was almost inevitably death. A physician either becomes case-hardened under these conditions, or he begins to look in other directions to see if there is a better way. This reflects on medical treatment as a whole. We tend to accept the status quo, particularly if a treatment is directed by some large and influential university. After all, we say, surely these are the top researchers who know where they are going. We will obey them and hope that we can gradually improve on the treatment until we have conquered the problem.

To continue the story—as an oncologist, I was engaged in trying to find ways and means of killing the cancer cell—the enemy. It introduced what has been called "brinkmanship," that fine point where the poisonous effect of the drug threatens the cells of the host. After all, it is easy to cure cancer. You simply kill the patient. What transfixed me and made me curious was the occasional child who lived and appeared to be cured. (It should be mentioned that "cure" in cancer at that time was in terms of a five-year survival.)

"Go, Thy Faith Hath Made Thee Whole"

What was different about the children who survived? To this day, I do not know exactly what it was. I can only tell one or two stories that illustrate the wonder that I experienced. One day, a ten-year-old girl was brought in by her mother. She had had a Wilm's tumor removed two years before. A Wilm's tumor is a highly malignant cancer of the kidney and, in this case, it had recurred and metastasized throughout the entire abdominal cavity. It was easy to see that the child was in the last stages of her illness, a state known as cachexia. She looked "old," with dry, parchment-like skin; the facial tissue had atrophied, and her abdomen was filled with hard visible lumps of tissue that could only be the metastatic tumors.

I faced the mother as honestly as I could, telling her that I had no treatment available. I suggested that she should take her home and allow her to die in peace. They were members of a religious splinter group, and the mother said in reply, "Doctor, if God will not work through you, then I will find another person with whom He will work."

She took the child to Oral Roberts, who laid on the healing hands. Soon after, I received a letter from the family doctor, telling me that the tumors had disappeared and that the child was healthy and well again. I received letters from that doctor for a number of years, and each reported the fact that she had remained well.

Another case that stands out involved a six-year-old boy. He had a tumor in his cheek that had been classified as a fibrosarcoma, a rare tumor that occurs in the soft tissues and is highly invasive and malignant. He was treated with poisonous drugs, or chemotherapy as it is called, and cobalt irradiation. The tumor never even hesitated—it just grew steadily, for nothing that we did showed the slightest hint of halting it. One day the parents brought in a faith healer and requested my permission for him to visit the child in the hospital and pray for him. Of course, this permission was given.

After the child was discharged from the hospital, he continued to see me as an out-patient. Unbeknown to me, the family was also seeking treatment in another hospital in Detroit. On one of these journeys, the car hit the guardrail on the freeway and rolled down an embankment, killing all except my patient, who still had his tumor. He was adopted by an aunt. One day, he went to his adoptive aunt with a piece of tissue in his hand. The aunt asked him where it came from and he told her that it had appeared in his mouth and he had scooped it out with his hand. The tissue was taken to a hospital, where it was sectioned and placed under a microscope. It proved to be necrotic, or dead, tumor.

The theory was that the rapidly growing tumor had outstripped its own blood supply, thus choking off its ability to survive as live tissue. The elusive factors were, of course, in reference to why, how, and what was the cause of this dramatic, sudden change. What was the difference between this tumor and others?

An Innovative Approach

In those days, the medical staff knew each other pretty well and were all on a first-name basis with each other. The fearsome powers of the FDA had not become an obtrusive and pernicious foe to imaginative progress. Doctors were still trusted by government and by their patients. So it was that I sat down to lunch with a friend of mine one day. He was the chief of radiotherapy and wielded the cobalt bomb with the precision of a sewing machine. An extraordinary conversation took place.

My friend said, "Do you ever see any patients with leukemia?"

21

"Funny that you should ask," I replied. "What have you in mind?"

It transpired that he had had a patient with a cancer known as Hodgkin's disease. This produces huge, swollen cancerous glands in many different parts of the body. He had treated an enlarged neck gland with cobalt irradiation. To his surprise, a large gland in the groin, which had not been irradiated itself, had disappeared. He had concluded that something had been released from the neck gland when it was treated. This substance, whatever it was, had traveled in the bloodstream, he thought, and affected the gland in the groin.

"I want to irradiate the blood from a patient with leukemia," he continued. "Perhaps this mechanism would apply in leukemia. It is worth trying."

"Well, it so happens that I have an eighteen-year-old girl in the ward who is in the last stages of acute myelogenous leukemia," I replied. "If you can take her blood, irradiate it and put it back into her before she dies, please be my guest."

Acute myelogenous leukemia is one of the most acutely lethal forms of leukemia. It did not respond well to what treatment we had available. In this girl, the platelets in the blood were virtually nonexistent, the white cells were in short supply, and she had begun to develop gangrene in the mouth tissues. She was not a good candidate for any form of treatment, and I did not expect her to survive for long. It seemed to be hopeless as things stood.

My friend took a unit of blood from my patient and placed it under the cobalt bomb. He turned on the machine and went for lunch. When he returned, the machine had delivered 13,000 rads to the unit of blood. This dose of irradiation, if given to a person, would be uniformly lethal, but it was given to the patient's blood outside the body. He then ran it back into the patient.

I continued to give the treatment that I had been using, but I did not expect to see any change and I was extremely skeptical about the irradiated blood. To my surprise, she made a spectacular recovery and went into remission. Remission is the "apparent cure" that is seen in acute leukemia in children and adolescents. It is relatively easy to produce this temporary state, but the disease quickly returns in all its previous violence. Furthermore, this particular form of the disease does occasionally temporarily respond to treatment. Therefore, although pleased to see a remission that was not expected, I was not particularly impressed and did not think the results called for a celebration.

About a month later, this girl returned for her scheduled visit. To my surprise she was using crutches, for she had developed paralysis of certain nerves in the wrist and foot, caused by an unusually toxic response to one of the chemotherapeutic agents that she was receiving. This was far from the usual response; this represented what would be the effect of an overdose of the drug, which she had not received. It meant that something had happened to make her more sensitive to the effects of the drug. Her scalp hair had fallen out, also a common effect of chemotherapy.

When I examined her, I found that the spleen and liver were both very severely enlarged, in fact huge. I thought that the disease had returned and that she was in relapse. Further study soon showed that this was not so. She actually had developed a process known as a balanced hemolysis.

This is how it works. Blood is made in the bone marrow, the blood factory, and put into the circulation. Old blood cells are always being destroyed as they age because they outlive their usefulness. There is therefore a creative supply of cells that goes on all the time and it is balanced against the destructive process. Something had caused the blood to become destroyed at a greatly accelerated rate. But the extraordinary thing was that the bone marrow was keeping up with the destruction—an absolutely amazing finding. In leukemia, the bone marrow becomes defective and fails to put out the required blood cells. But in this case, its activity was positively accelerated.

Since she was not in relapse as far as the leukemia was concerned, there was nothing to be done but to wait and see how Mother Nature would proceed. I gave her a very small dose of a standard drug used to maintain cases of leukemia when they are in remission and sent her home.

Gradually the spleen and liver decreased to normal size and the hemolytic process ceased. Amazingly, she grew back a head of hair which was positively beautiful and had a sheen which almost glowed. The paralysis completely resolved, and she became completely well—for a time only! To my profound regret, she relapsed about a year later and died from her disease.

Of course, we had no idea what the mechanism was but we knew that we had seen something that was truly startling and that we had to pursue it further. We assumed that the original hypothesis was correct, that the irradiation of the blood outside the body caused the release of some kind of immunological factor that went to work against the leukemia.

We treated a total of six cases in this manner, all of them end-stage leukemia. Each had quite startling and even dramatic remissions, but each was short-lived. One day a pediatrician called me to refer a patient of his. He had been treating this twelve-year-old girl for acute lymphatic leukemia for two years, a very long time in those days. She was at the end of her rope, in relapse, and it was unlikely that we would be able to get her into any more remissions. We gave her the irradiation treatment, repeating it about six times. Each time, she had a rather dramatic but short period of remission and lived for about another year. It must be remembered that after two years of conventional treatment, the disease in most cases had ravaged the blood-producing system and the patient could expect little further response to any treatment at all.

We did, for this girl, the "impossible" as it was defined at that time. We were able to induce a remission when the cards were estimated to be 100 percent stacked against her. Of course, we did not achieve a cure in any of these children. We merely borrowed a little more time for each of them. But that was the state of research at that time. Each method that was used appeared to induce remission, but one which could not be maintained. This was merely another method, and it certainly needed further research.

It was decided that we must bring our work to the attention of the department that was most concerned with treatment of blood malignancy, the department of hematology. A formal conference was organized and we gave our presentation. Naturally, I was anticipating a surge of interest from our colleagues. It must be remembered that treatment of these disorders were at best not very effective in adults; in children, the diseases were almost uniformly lethal. So a treatment as relatively simple as this should have produced at least a modicum of interest, if not excitement.

Once again, I learned that when a physician strays from the "usual and customary," he seems almost destined to cause hostility among his peers. The presentation was received with scorn; worse yet, I was unable to generate interest in anyone in the research division. I knew, of course, that this was not going to go anywhere in the medical literature unless we could provide basic science evidence to support it. I was told bluntly to get back to my "usual and customary" approach, in spite of the fact that I had come to the conclusion that it was only a Band-Aid at best and often the acme of cruelty at worst.

To my eternal shame, we dropped the pursuit of this potential benefit. In any clinic where a large number of physicians are cooperating, medical politics become very important. Careers can be advanced or broken by politics' pervasive influence, and one is judged by the standards of the majority. This judgment represents a continued block to progress because there are really very few innovators in medicine, and they are treated as pariahs by their peers. History is replete with stories of this nature. I began to be aware that the people who had stuck to their guns and followed through with their discoveries were extremely brave, often risking complete ruin and despair.

One of the best examples of this kind of irrational response is the story of an Austrian physician named Semmelweiss, in the time before germs had been discovered. This physician noted that, when doctors delivered babies, the mothers frequently died if the physicians had entered the ward from the morgue where they had been performing autopsies. He concluded that the physicians brought something in on their hands from the autopsies and that this was in some way lethal to the mothers. He arranged a very simple experiment which required no equipment and no expenditure. He divided the big open ward into two halves. On one side, all the attending physicians simply washed their hands before attending a woman in childbirth. On the other side, physicians carried on as before, without any hand washing. As Semmelweiss kept the score, the incidence of disease fell dramatically in those women whose physicians washed their hands. Of course, we now know that germs were the cause of the problem and resulted in what came to be known as puerperal sepsis. Semmelweiss had conducted one of the earliest known examples of a "controlled experiment."

What was his reward? He was treated with scorn, and his colleagues literally drummed him out of the hospital. He eventually died a pauper. Irrational? Certainly it was irrational, but it is the predictable behavior of all scientists when innovations are introduced. It is, of course, true that many so-called quack remedies are introduced as innovations, so up to a point the behavior is understandable; but what is irrational is the refusal to consider the studies that have already indicated their worth by the personal observations of the innovator. Apparently, as a species we resist change, since it appears to make us uncomfortable. The vast majority of mankind prefer the status quo.

By this time, I was becoming disenchanted with oncology. It was very stressful to see patients go through such disastrous experiences and to be able to do so little for them. It so happened that a physician who was being considered for a staff position in our department was a pediatric hematologist. I agreed to relinquish the oncology to his care after he joined the staff, leaving me free to develop my interests in the biochemical changes which I had come to believe to be the real problems to solve.

I have described this background of experience which was changing my approach to disease so that the reader might perceive the fact that I represent a growing number of physicians who are questioning the "usual and customary." Many more similar experiences were to come later, of course, and I shall describe them in subsequent chapters. However, at this stage of my career, I had decided that the medical model was constructed in an artificial way that distorted the reality of the situation. In short, there was something disastrously wrong with the model that all physicians use today in approaching disease. In order to understand the model and what is wrong with it, it is necessary to briefly trace the history of medicine.

A Brief Look at Medical History

Thousands of years ago, the ancient Chinese proposed that the world, and indeed the universe, had to be in balance. They gave the name *Yin* to one extreme and *Yang* to the other, proposing that neither were "good" or "bad," but that both were needed to be mixed at some indefinable point of equilibrium. The simplest example would be hot and cold environmental temperatures. A moderate temperature would be a mix of "not too hot" and "not too cold."

This principle was applied to the body, and we are finding more and more that this was an admirable way of thinking about health and its loss. There needs to be balance in so many different things within body function that examples become absurd, but I will give just one. The blood cholesterol, as everyone now knows, should not be too high. Fewer people know that it should not be too low either; there is a point of balance. The ancient Chinese people had noted that the patient's pulse rate and rhythm were distorted by any sort of illness and they were able to detect the nature of the illness by simply feeling the pulse. Only when we understand the function of the primitive part of the brain can we make sense of this. (This will be discussed further in Chapter 6.) These astute people had been able to observe a quality to the pulse rate, involving its rhythm, its regularity, and the nature of its rise and fall as it was palpated at the wrist. Recently, electronic equipment has confirmed that there are many qualities to the pulse that were precisely described by these ancient observers. Perhaps we have lost something of incredible importance that might come under the heading of collected wisdom.

Hippocrates, often referred to as the father of modern medicine, used "low-tech" medical approaches which involved rest, tranquility and diet. He said, "Let medicine be your food and let food be your medicine." Above all, he emphasized that the physician should not harm the patient. The treatment must always be something that would assist the natural healing properties of the body.

It is common in this day and age to say that Hippocrates could do this only because there was nothing else available. He did not have the technical wonders that we have today, and so there was no way that he could detect serious disease that needed aggressive treatment, such as the eradication of a tumor. As we shall see later, the movement toward so-called holistic medicine is a marked return to the philosophical teachings of Hippocrates.

During the Dark Ages, there was a drift away from these early philosophical approaches and a lot of disease was considered to be the work of evil spirits. Lack of hygiene and proper sewage treatment was not associated with fleas from rats that carried bubonic plague and, apart from a few voices in the wilderness, there was no cohesive policy toward the treatment of disease and no basic knowledge of its causes.

Pasteur and others led the way in identifying unseen microorganisms as the main cause of disease, but for a long time it remained a source of frustration. Any attempts to kill the infection endangered the patient. The discovery of penicillin changed all that. It was a dramatic event which changed the medical world overnight. But, like so many events in history that have been beneficial, there was a flip side. The microorganisms that were originally sensitive to the drug learned to become resistant and passed their mechanism of resistance on to their progeny through gene mutations. A massive research began to try to identify drugs that were similar to penicillin but killed the resistant germs. As the world knows, the antibiotic era had begun.

However, few people are aware that many of these later antibiotics are highly toxic. (Even though there are still several hundred deaths a year from penicillin, it is not highly toxic.) Some of these antibiotics were found to be so toxic that they were diverted to treatment of cancer.

It is relatively easy to see the thrust of this disease model. Human beings are attacked by infectious microorganisms that cause illness, so—kill the germs. So pervasive has this mind-set become that doctors even use antibiotics to treat viral illness, even though viruses do not respond to the antibiotics used to kill bacteria. Bacteria are just as smart as they were in developing resistance to penicillin, so we have a vast array of microorganisms that have become genetically resistant to the drugs that are being used to attempt to kill them.

We have to keep on looking for more and more of these compounds to treat the increasing numbers of resistant bacteria. It is hardly surprising that many of them are toxic to our own cells. Also, there are many bacteria that live inside our own bowels. They perform a valuable service to us, but antibiotics kill them as well, seriously damaging our digestive mechanisms that are so dependent upon the presence of these friendly germs. The result is that we are producing drastic changes in the normal equilibrium between ourselves and the environment in which we must live and survive. There is much evidence that there is an ecology in the populations of microorganisms also. The possibility exists that the antibiotic era is responsible for changing this balance also, so that we may well be breeding more and more virulent strains of both bacteria and viruses.

The idea of "kill the enemy" has spread to the treatment of cancer. Cancer has long been regarded as a collection of maverick cells in the body which, like germs, must be destroyed in order to cure the disease. It is remarkably similar to the approach of the farmer and fruit grower. Powerful poisons have been developed to kill the pests that destroy the crops. As the pests develop genetically-determined resistance to the chemicals, the chemists must keep coming up with new chemicals. We now have hundreds of chemical substances to which we ourselves are sensitive but which leave the pests untouched.

These developments have created the 20th-century system of what has come to be called allopathic scientific medicine. To a large extent, it ignores the natural healing mechanisms that exist in the body. Take a very simple example. Why do we have an elevation of body temperature when we have an infection? Basically, it is nature's way of helping us to defend ourselves from the bacterial or viral enemy that has attacked us. A higher body temperature creates an environment which makes germs less efficient in their production of biochemical weapons. The question that has been asked many times is this: Is it rational to use a drug that lowers body temperature if that is part of the body's defense?

Another aspect of modern medicine is the idea that treatment must be "aggressive." We must use all the scientific weapons that we possess, as we are arrayed in battle against an unseen foe. This has given rise to a paradoxical situation which is very hard to attack in reality, even though it is quite obvious in theory. A patient who is being treated for an infection gets worse. The physician may not consider that it is an effect of a drug that he is using and adds another one. The patient gets worse again, and the physician draws the conclusion: "What a virulent disease this is! I must find the right wonder drug to stop the process."

It has been published in a prestigious medical journal that 36 percent of admissions to a major university hospital were due to iatrogenic (doctor-produced) diseases. That is a truly incredible fact, since the public expects to gain benefit from the attentions of physicians. Patients should certainly not expect to become worse and, moreover, most people in America are under the impression that their medical care is among the best in the world. For a crisis disease, particularly one that requires surgery, modern medicine *is* good; but for vast numbers of chemically sick individuals, it is painfully inadequate and even might be called bankrupt. It is ironic that the mortality in any given area always decreases when the doctors in that area are on strike.

Is There a Better Model for Disease?

Earlier, I mentioned the "medical model," a foundation for considering what disease represents. As we have traced the history of medicine, it becomes clear that disease is regarded largely as an enemy to be defeated in a battle. Our present model has documented thousands of different diseases, regarding each one as having a specific cause and a predictable course. For each one, research is aimed at finding *the cure* and we have foundations that have been set up around many of them to finance research in finding this cure.

This model is so deeply ingrained that we immediately label an agent that helps many different conditions as a "cure-all." Such an agent is equated almost automatically with quackery, and this attitude has been instrumental in preventing nutrient substances from being acceptable. The difficulty is that if they actually help sick people, then the model is wrong because the benefit is felt in many different diseases. Hence the agent becomes a "cure-all."

Each disease, having been initially described by an observant clinician, is reported in medical literature. When it becomes sufficiently well-known, it goes into a textbook which is read by medical students as they try to memorize all the different conditions, a herculean task. For each disease, a treatment section explains the drugs that have been used and what effect they have produced. In most cases, the drugs have simply been attempted on a trial-and-error basis. Even when a given drug is found to work, its action is often obscure.

The Physicians' Desk Reference (PDR) is a mighty tome that is updated each year and published by Medical Economics Data. Each drug is listed under a Product Name Index, a Product Category Index, a Generic Index, and a Chemical Name Index. When a given drug listed in the *PDR* is described, whatever is known about its clinical pharmacology is outlined and its indications and uses given. Although this information may be covered in one page, or even a half-page, the warnings of its dangers often cover several pages. In some cases, patients will look up the drugs that have been prescribed for them and be so frightened by the warnings that they refuse to obtain the drugs.

This model necessarily means that a physician is in active control of the disease and treating it. It is *his* responsibility to *heal* the patient— an entirely erroneous and absurd concept. For example, orthopedists do not heal bones; they are technicians who bring the broken ends of the bones into contact. Healing is within the tissue itself. Likewise, using a pharmaceutical which is, by definition, a poisonous or foreign substance cannot induce healing. It merely controls the symptoms. This use of substances to induce changes in symptoms has led to the expectation of a "quick fix" by the public—instant relief from the pain or any other symptom, in many instances without any real effort to address the underlying cause and eradicate it.

If this disease model is to be discarded, there must be a replacement for it, and this is what this book is about. The new model which is to be described makes the physician a much less important figure, whose job is to find ways and means of providing nutrients to be used by the body so that healing can proceed. The word "doctor" comes from the Latin verb *doceo—I teach—*and so the original meaning in English was "a teacher." The teacher's wisdom has to be brought to bear upon the needs of the patient in providing a "quiet harbor," where mental and physical rest is possible, as Hippocrates taught us.

Surely, the modern hospital, with its noise, impersonality, and loss of dignity experienced by the patient is hardly the best atmosphere to encourage any sort of healing process to occur. Surgical cleverness is a remarkable feat of skill, and any one of us may be only too glad at some time to benefit from its lifesaving advances. But surgeons are all too often technicians whose view is purely mechanistic. Not infrequently, they seem to be quite unaware of the enormous stresses that are imposed upon surgical patients. Complications are seen as inevitable risks, and rarely is nutrition considered in relation to the increased demands on physiology. Indeed, who has not complained about hospital food when unlucky enough to be a patient in one?

For years, a very small minority of physicians have been helping their patients through critical illnesses by the use of carefully chosen nutrients. They give nutrients in doses which have caused them to be accused of fraud and quackery by their peers. They have been persecuted and pilloried without the slightest attempt to ascertain what kind of results they are able to get their patients to achieve. These physicians are all disenchanted with much that modern medicine has to offer, but they are not "throwing the baby out with the bath water." They are better doctors because they respect the healing properties of the body and treat it with the utmost respect. Therefore, they use those drugs that are helpful and often lifesaving with discretion and care, because they have come to understand the power that many of these substances have for both good and ill.

I will describe a typical example of the kind of thing that happens in this period of transition where nutrient therapy has emerged. Two physicians each had a case of pneumonia in adjacent beds in a hospital. Both were severe and distinctly life-threatening, and both physicians knew it. One of them used intravenous vitamin C in addition to the antimicrobial drug or drugs that he had prescribed. The patient improved rapidly and became well. This physician went to his colleague who was caring for the other patient and suggested that he do the same, since his own patient was doing so well. The other physician was a traditional practitioner who was firmly under the impression that the use of vitamin C in this manner was fraudulent. He told the physician who had been successful in helping the recovery of his patient to "mind his own business" and refused to give the vitamin C. His patient died.

Of course, it must be emphasized that there could be no proof that the vitamin C had made the difference, since there are always a number of variables to be considered. However, the basic point is this: the administration of vitamin C under these circumstances is completely and absolutely harmless. It carries no risk, and its potential for benefit has been shown thousands of times by practitioners who treat their patients in this way. They are literally shouted down by the traditional physicians when they proclaim their observations. The result is that for years and years there can be pure stalemate between the two groups of doctors. One gets on with his work independently of the other, and a gulf develops between them which ensures that communication between them is impossible.

The model to be described is more like that used in horticulture where a sick plant is provided with sources of nitrogen and phosphate to heal itself. It is a kinder way of viewing illness, because the physician cannot afford to be arrogant. He must listen to his patient carefully for appropriate clues. A clinical diagnosis is unnecessary because it is an artificial and meaningless classification based upon a constellation of symptoms that are both "physical" and "mental" in nature.

As we proceed, we shall see that the hallmark of all disease is the adaptive chemistry in the tissues of the body. The symptoms are merely the "code" by which the sickness is expressed. These symptoms are, in a sense, very misleading since they tend to focus attention on the site of the symptom as the seat of the disease process. They actually indicate that "something is wrong" somewhere in the complex machinery of the body, not necessarily in the area of the body where the brain places the site of the symptom such as pain. Perhaps a simple example will suffice.

Low backache is one of the commonest of all symptoms and has been a source of frustration to both the physician and the afflicted patient. To understand it requires a little knowledge of human evolution. Not so very long ago, in the millions of years of our evolution, we walked on all fours like some of our ape cousins still do. In order to assume our present upright posture, the spinal column had to bend backwards just above the tailbone, producing a very steep lumbar curve, or lordosis, as it is called. In order to bring the center of gravity over the feet, the spinal column had to bend forward again at the neck, thus resulting in two compensatory curves in the whole column.

It is easy to understand that this development, arising relatively recently in our evolution, has created two distinct points of structural weakness. We shall see later that both physical and mental stress is an inevitable fact which is never, in itself, abnormal. It is less or more in degree, that is all. Mental stress is merely one form of stress and may reflect itself by producing low backache. The body "remembers" its sites of physical stress and explains the appearance of low backache appearing as a result of unhappiness or other form of mental pressure.

At this stage, the reader may find that this explanation is incomprehensible. Our present attitude toward the use of the word "stress" needs to be better defined, and this will be discussed in much greater detail in a later chapter.

It is such an important consideration in defining a new disease model that I have introduced the subject early. It is a constant hurdle in patients' understanding of themselves and the conditions that affect their health, and it is suggested that the reader merely places the word "stress" at the back of his mind until the subject is reintroduced later in the book.

In the next chapter, I shall discuss my apprenticeship in body chemistry and its important relationship with diet. It reinforced the notion that there was something deeply wrong with the disease model upon which I had been trained, and it was the next step in my re-education.

Chapter 2

Inborn Errors of Metabolism

At the turn of the century, Sir Archibald Garrod coined the phrase *inborn error of metabolism* to explain the cause of some diseases which were, at that time, inexplicable. It is interesting that this idea occurred to him before human genetic mechanisms had been discovered, because these diseases are invariably inherited.

In order to understand a condition of this nature, it is necessary to give a brief review of some of the basics of body chemistry. In a later chapter we shall be dealing with the subject of oxidation, how the body burns fuel to provide energy. Nothing happens in any machine without energy, and the body is really a machine because it burns fuel just like an automobile, except that the mechanisms are infinitely more complex.

As we all know, food that we consume is digested in the intestine. This is a process by which the complex substances that make up our organic food are broken down into molecules which are much simpler so that they can pass through the intestinal wall into the bloodstream. Protein is built up from chains of molecules called amino acids and it is broken down into these individual constituents, somewhat like knocking down a wall into bricks. They are then absorbed through the bowel wall into the bloodstream and are conveyed to the liver where they may be used as fuel, or they may be diverted to be rebuilt into body protein.

We are going to consider an example of an inborn error involving the processing of an amino acid called phenylalanine, and in order to do that we must describe the principles behind the way a relatively simple substance like an amino acid is built up into an ever-increasingly complex substance such as a hormone.

Phenylalanine is known as an essential amino acid. It is essential because we die if we do not get it in our diet; the body has to have it and is unable to make it from other components of the diet. In this respect, it is just like a vitamin, any and all of which are essential to life. So the word "essential" means exactly that—life-sustaining. It is truly amazing how many substances we require from our diet that are essential, and it is not too far-fetched to ask how much of any one of these dietary components is enough.

What does the body do with phenylalanine or any other molecule of a similar nature? It enters into a series of chemical reactions, each of which makes it a more and more complex substance. For example, phenylalanine is the primary building block for constructing thyroid hormone, which is the final product.

A sequence of this nature is known as a biochemical pathway. Each reaction in the sequence is governed by an enzyme which is under genetic control, and one can easily see how complex this becomes. What is an enzyme? It is a catalyst, a substance which encourages a chemical reaction but does not itself become part of that reaction. This action can be illustrated by turning to a machine which is less sophisticated than the human body, an automobile. Although this comparison may seem to be an insult to ourselves as human beings, it is important in our consideration of nutrition to be aware that food is fuel. We tend to forget this fact all too often.

In an internal combustion engine, the fuel is gasoline. As we all learned in school, combustion is a process by which a fuel combines with oxygen, and the energy so formed is used to drive a series of levers that connect with the wheels. Without a spark plug, this process cannot happen, as we have all learned from experiencing worn-out spark plugs that have to be changed periodically. A spark plug is a catalyst. It causes the explosion by igniting gasoline in the cylinder. I shall return to the internal combustion engine analogy in a later chapter which discusses how our cells use oxygen to provide energy, a process known as oxidation.

Using this simple analogy, these principles apply to ourselves as living machines. Our food is equivalent to gasoline, and the spark plugs are represented by vitamins and minerals. We shall be considering this in more detail later because it is a fundamental message in this book. For the present, we now have a working idea about the function of enzymes in our body chemistry.

Each biochemical reaction in a pathway is governed by the same principle. Substance A is converted to substance B, which is in turn converted to substance C, and so on until the end of the pathway which was designed for the purpose of yielding a very complex material such as a hormone. Each of these steps requires the presence of an enzyme which acts as a catalyst to bring about the reaction. Each enzyme is inherited from our parents, and it is indeed easy to begin to see how very complex the functions of the body are. This is not the end of the story either, because each enzyme has to have exactly the right conditions to work properly. These conditions include the presence of one or more vitamins or minerals, known as *cofactors*. In a sense, the cofactors are like spark plugs to the spark plugs. They provide energy for the catalyst to ignite the reaction.

Now let us see what happens to phenylalanine. As already indicated, it is a normal component of all animal protein, and the digestive process releases the amino acid into the bowel. It is absorbed into the bloodstream and conveyed to the liver. Here, one of these vital enzymes acts on it to convert it to the next substance in the biochemical pathway on its journey to become thyroid hormone.

An infant born with this particular enzyme defective will develop an exceedingly destructive condition which has a difficult name, shortened to PKU. The defective enzyme is inherited from the parents, who are never affected themselves by the disease, which is therefore called a *recessive*. Genes are threaded, so to speak, on rod-like structures called chromosomes, and in each cell of the human body there are twenty-six pairs of chromosomes. In each pair, one chromosome is inherited from the father and the other from the mother. There are therefore two genes for the enzyme that converts phenylalanine, one on each of a pair of chromosomes. In the case of PKU, both parents have a defective gene on one chromosome but not on the other, and for them one gene is enough to make the enzyme even though it is in lower amounts than one finds in perfectly normal people. Both parents are known as carriers of the disease because they are unaffected but capable of passing on the defective gene. If both parents pass chromosomes with defective genes, their baby inherits a double dose of the defective gene and will thereby develop the disease. Each time the parents conceive another infant, they have a one-in-four chance of that infant being affected. There is no way of identifying a PKU carrier easily, and such individuals appear to be perfectly normal in every way. It is obviously a shock to find that an infant turns up with a disease like PKU when there is absolutely no family history of such a state. The carrier state can be handed down through generation after generation without the disease ever turning up. Only if a carrier marries another carrier will the mechanism be set in motion. (It is for this reason that marriage to a close relative is forbidden, because family members are more likely to be carriers of the same conditions, such as PKU.) Even with a first-cousin marriage, which is legal in some places, the danger is greater than marrying someone who is totally unrelated.

Now we must briefly look at how the disease works, so that we can see how a preventive treatment is possible through diet. We are using this example of preventive nutrition as an illustration, and, although PKU is an extremely rare disease, occurring only once in 10,000 births, the principles can be applied to other less rare conditions. Because of the absence of this critical enzyme, phenylalanine accumulates in the bloodstream of the affected individual. All animal protein and a lot of vegetable protein contain phenylalanine. It is present in mother's milk also, so as soon as the infant is fed the amino acid is released from the protein, and the accumulation starts. This accumulation of phenylalanine in the body causes brain damage to occur, although the exact mechanism is not completely understood. However, we do know that keeping this substance at a relatively normal level in the blood prevents the brain damage. Recognizing the presence of the disease is relatively simple. A test known as the PKU test detects the rise in phenylalanine and is now done on all newborn infants after a minimum of twenty-four and preferably forty-eight hours of feeding. Because of the mechanism that we have already discussed, the blood level of phenylalanine does not rise until the infant has received some protein in the diet; therefore, if the test is done too early it will miss the diagnosis.

This test, invented by a man named Guthrie, is known as a screening test. It was the first of its kind to be introduced. There are many similar tests now performed on that small piece of blotting paper which is used to soak up a tiny amount of an infant's blood. It is sent to a central laboratory in each state, and a positive test is reported to the family doctor by telephone. Speed in reporting the results is important because if the infant starts immediately on milk diet containing very low phenylalanine, maintaining the blood level of the amino acid at near normal, he grows up normally. If it is not detected by this means, development will be retarded; and, by the time that it becomes obvious that the baby is abnormal, it is too late. The damage cannot be repaired; it can only be prevented. Since there are no specific clinical symptoms, and the infant appears to be relatively normal, it is imperative to detect PKU before damage occurs. I say "relatively normal" because these babies, if the disease is undetected, are fussy and irritable, cry a lot, and are inconsolable, but, as every mother knows, many infants display that behavior for different and much less serious reasons.

When I first joined the private clinic as a pediatrician, another pediatrician was deeply interested in PKU. It was still being researched, and the cause of the disease had just been discovered. However, nobody knew what the effect would be if a special diet were introduced, and no screening tests had yet been devised. This pediatrician had devised a special formula that was made in the clinic pharmacy because no commercial supply of formula was available as it is today. However, although we were able to see that treated infants became calmer, it did nothing to reverse the mental retardation that had already developed. Because there were no screening tests available at that time, these infants were never recognized until they were older and the damage had already been done.

It was an exciting time in this field of medicine. I learned a great deal from this pediatrician and took over her practice after she left the clinic. I became fascinated by the fact that severe mental retardation could be prevented by such a relatively simple method as a special diet. Could it be applied to other, more common conditions? Was diet a common cause of diseases which we had ascribed to other less mundane phenomena?

I quickly developed an attitude of looking much more closely at all the brain-damaged infants that I saw daily. Even the condition that is usually called cerebral palsy was, I realized, usually *assumed* to be due to birth injury. Perhaps some of these cases were due to faulty chemistry. I helped to run a special clinic that was known as the cerebral palsy clinic. I saw these children on a weekly basis with another physician who was a specialist in physical medicine because most children with cerebral palsy have significant physical crippling which benefits from physical therapy. This physician was regarded as much more important than I was because the focus was on the children's inability to move. Nothing else could be done for them. I can remember that she became irritated with me because I was always looking for phenomena that she regarded as very rare, whereas cerebral palsy was seen as common without considering the primary cause as anything but brain injury from birth.

I became more and more interested in what happens when one of these enzymatic errors occurred. One of the very puzzling features was that most of these defective genetic disturbances had an effect upon the brain. It did not seem to matter which of the many damaged biochemical sequences occurred; each gave rise to another disease, the most important result being profound mental retardation. I concluded that the failed sequence gave rise to an excess of the dammed-up substance—the phenylalanine—or perhaps caused a deficiency of the substance or substances that would be formed later in the biochemical pathway.

I began to read the biochemistry textbooks, trying to understand the complex inter-relationships. I became a consultant for the north-eastern part of the state and helped to bring into being the screening tests for Ohio. I attended the pediatric research meetings where new conditions of this type were being reported one after the other. It required a much better understanding of biochemistry. It was not sufficient to be a clinician. Having spotted one of these diseases, a physician had to see it as failed chemical mechanisms, for there was only one hope of influencing it, and that was through diet and nutritional elements.

Most of the infants that were detected by the newborn screening program were referred to me if the family lived in the northeastern part of the state, so I had a PKU clinic in which I was regulating the well-being of about twenty or more children with the condition. It must be remembered that we knew very little about the preventive approach until enough of these children had been followed for long enough.

An extremely important finding was that it was wrong to try to keep the blood phenylalanine in the range of normal. Here is the problem. Phenylalanine is, as I have noted, essential for life. If it was provided in excess in the diet, the child would become retarded. And if it was insufficient, the child would be retarded because of lack of brain development and growth. Again we are reminded of the ancient Chinese philosophy in which Yin and Yang are extremes to be avoided, though both are necessary.

I remember, in particular, an infant in my care with PKU. One day I went into the consulting room where this infant was lying on the examination bed waiting for me. As the door opened, he jumped visibly, indicating that his nervous system was in a state of ir-ritability. When the blood test came back from the laboratory, the phenylalanine was very high, and I drastically reduced his intake of the amino acid. His blood level fell into the normal range, and I believed that he was in the safe zone of treatment. I discovered, however, that his head circumference was not increasing. Brain growth was delayed, a very serious situation for the future. I con-cluded that this situation was the result of phenylalanine starvation and increased it in the diet. To my surprise, he became irritable again, and the blood level of phenylalanine had increased dramatically.

There was an obvious conclusion: the supply of phenylalanine had to be enough, but not too much and not too little. But how did a physician know how much was enough? When this infant's blood level had been normal, he had failed to develop. I discovered that the blood level had to be above the normal range, but that it was obviously a fine point of balance.

In the early stages of this research, a number of infants had been treated at many institutions by depriving them of enough phenylalanine to enable their brains to grow. This had been achieved by keeping their blood levels in the range that is seen in normal children, instead of a little above it. Naturally, many pediatricians concluded that the dietary treatment was a failure and a great deal of controversy existed for a number of years. I published my results, and this helped to enable us to see that the point of balance could be obtained by a reasonable approach to the blood test, instead of insisting upon its remaining strictly in the normal range. My ideas were being observed by others at the same time, so I was not instrumental in guiding this research into safe harbor solely on my own efforts. However, it was interesting that I had made these observations independently and not as a result of being told about it by others.

The approach became so efficient that I found PKU a very easy condition to manage. One child, I remember, achieved an Intelligence Quotient of 128, a pretty high I.Q. for anyone, with or without PKU. In addition to the satisfaction of knowing that I was really helping these children, I found the intellectual stimulation exciting. The *preventive* mechanisms were the most important lessons that I was learning. It was truly remarkable that such a serious threat to the brain could be prevented by such a simple and relatively "low-tech" treatment with diet.

A number of these inborn errors of metabolism were recognizable by the odor that emanated from the patient. The PKU children smelled of mice, for example. The odors were a result of the production of chemical substances in the body because of the primary defect. Of course, such a smell does not occur unless the chemistry has become fully developed and brain damage has already begun. So it is not something that can be used to spot the disease early enough to prevent brain damage; the stable door has been shut after the horse has bolted. But some of these diseases are initially recognized by a peculiar odor arising from an obviously sick child. The advantage of identification even at this stage is that it enables an alert physician to spot a potentially new disorder of this type. I say new because, in theory, a genetic mutation can occur at any time within a family inheritance pattern.

There is a condition known as Oasthouse Disease because the affected child smells like an oasthouse, a kiln used to bake hops in the making of beer. Another one is maple syrup urine disease, called by that name because the urine smells exactly like maple syrup (not because it tastes like it!). My experience with this disease is worth reviewing, because it is another stage in my development toward the use of nutrition and vitamin therapy.

One day a child was referred to one of the pediatricians with a peculiar history. He "had not been doing too well" but he fell out of his baby buggy onto a wooden floor. No one was particularly surprised that he became unconscious, but what was peculiar was that he would recover consciousness in the hospital, only to lapse back into a coma. This happened repeatedly, and he was referred to us for further study. We found that he had maple syrup urine disease as the primary problem, and this had been triggered into activity by the head injury. This situation illustrates an exceedingly important point. Many diseases of this nature may appear in the newborn infant in the most nonspecific terms. In other words, the symptoms may be those which occur in infections such as meningitis. In fact, even though the beginning of the disease is produced by the biochemical changes, infection often supervenes. If the infant should die, an autopsy might reveal only the evidence of infection. The primary condition is not revealed. We shall see in the next chapter that a biochemical condition may be only marginal and become active under stress such as a head injury or an attack from an infection.

The case just described was my first introduction to the fact that physical stress could trigger an underlying condition. Since we equate a head injury to a state of unconsciousness in a healthy person, we may well explain the unconsciousness as being due to an injury that was more severe than it was originally thought to be. The underlying condition is never even suspected. We will see other examples of this later. My next experience with maple syrup urine disease was equally instructive. A seven-day-old infant was admitted to the ward because of seizures. An alert nurse noted the characteristic smell and she was right on course, for the infant did indeed have the disease. It was in the very early stages of research, and little was known about it. Most of the scientific studies had been done in a university hospital in New York, and I referred the baby to the doctors in that institution. This was a much greater problem than in PKU, because no less than three essential amino acids are blocked in their metabolism in this condition. Juggling the diet demanded an extremely expensive laboratory evaluation of repeated blood tests, and it demanded a research situation. I took care of this child for many years; although she returned from New York in pretty good condition, the parents were unable to carry out the very difficult dietary program, and she gradually became more retarded.

By this time I was known as the pediatrician on the staff who was interested in diseases associated with peculiar odors. One day, a pediatrician called from the southern part of the state to refer a newborn infant who was having seizures and who "smelled peculiar." The physician did not refer the infant to anyone in particular, and the department secretary who took the message assigned the case to me and put down an admitting diagnosis of maple syrup urine disease, which it proved to be. When one considers that this condition is likely to occur only once in 200,000 births, the diagnosis by a secretary over the telephone makes it a little comical.

This infant came from Appalachia, and since little was then known about its inheritance I went to the home of the family and studied it. As is often seen in that part of America, there were more first-cousin marriages in the family than there were non-consanguineous marriages. The disease had erupted a number of times and not been recognized. In some cases, children had survived but were seriously retarded. The main benefit of this study was that the disease was shown to be recessively inherited by the pattern of the occurrence, and I reported it in a medical journal.

All of these children, even though they had a rare disease whose mechanism was fairly well understood in biochemical terms, were easily made very much worse by any superimposition of virtually any form of stress involving injury or infection, and this was to be an important lesson for me as we shall see later. The question then was: what is the role of this stress? How does it make things worse in an established disease? How does it affect normal, "healthy" people?

This relationship between stress and disease was brought home to me by studying a child who had PKU. This child had been diagnosed before the screening tests had come into being and was already retarded by the time that the condition had been recognized. He developed a cold, just as any child might. But I was concerned about what it might do to his primary condition, the PKU. I performed daily blood tests on him throughout his illness and found something that I found to be profoundly important. His blood phenylalanine increased a little more each day until it reached a pinnacle and began to decrease until it reached the level that it had been before his cold started. I could not alter this by changing the amount of phenylalanine in his daily diet.

I now realize what this meant. The virus that caused his cold was acting as a general stressor to his body chemistry. Because he had a genetically-determined weakness, the enzyme that was called upon to process phenylalanine was "weighed in the balance and found wanting." The substance that was blocked in its normal processing increased in concentration in the blood until the effect of the virus ceased. Perhaps another way of thinking about it is to return to our view of the human body as a machine. Any form of stress will call the whole system to an increased state of activity. Just as an automobile will use more fuel in climbing a hill, so the machinery of response in the body is mobilized under any form of stress, including an infection. The strength of a chain is in its weakest link. In this child the weakest link was the missing enzyme.

I became aware of the influence of stress through this kind of experience, and it is so important that I shall be devoting a complete chapter to it later on. I believe that the following story will illustrate it better than anything, for it reveals how a disease can be so heavily influenced by emotional stress, even in an infant.

It is not clear exactly what is the cause of the condition that I am about to describe. It occurs quite rarely and exclusively in infants and is best thought of as a "disease of maturation." There is a certain type of cell that exists in the body that is highly specialized, called a mast cell. Its job is to produce a chemical called histamine which is used to carry out some important functions. As we mentioned earlier, the body requires enough of this, not too little and not too much, but the right balance. The most common presentation of the disease is called urticaria pigmentosa. Mast cells become overactive in the skin and an affected infant is covered with brown pigmented spots that look somewhat like hives. These may last some months and gradually clear up. Rarely, the mast cells go wild and behave like cancer. They grow rapidly and infiltrate into various organs in the body. One of the indications of this disease is the brown spots on the skin of an obviously ill infant. If, on examination of the infant's abdomen, an enlarged liver is found, it would increase the suspicion. However, the only way that this dangerous condition can be confirmed is by a surgical biopsy of the enlarged liver; finding the massive infiltration of mast cells there would confirm the diagnosis.

One day, a pediatrician, whom I knew quite well as a very observant and unusually knowledgeable physician, called me to refer an infant who was obviously ill and showed these clinical characteristics. He suspected that the child had the rarer manifestation of the disease described above, known as generalized mastocytosis. He also knew that it would require biopsy of the liver and that was the reason for the referral.

When I saw this black infant, who was about six months of age, it was immediately obvious that he was ill and that the liver was very much enlarged. There was an interval of several days before the surgical operation for biopsy could be scheduled; as I saw this infant each day on my daily rounds, I began to observe some truly extraordinary changes in the baby. He was a particularly attractive little fellow, and the nurses had taken a fancy to him, giving him a great deal of attention. It was quite amazing to see him respond. He began to smile and, to my great surprise, quickly began to sit up by himself, something that he could not do when he was admitted to the hospital.

Even more surprising was the fact that the enlarged liver began to decrease in size on a daily basis. Although I had no idea what was really going on, a liver biopsy in a young patient like this is always extremely stressful and should not be undertaken unless it is absolutely needed for guiding the physician in the treatment plan. I postponed the biopsy in order to see what would ultimately happen with the tender loving care that he was receiving. When the skin cleared up and the liver enlargement disappeared completely, I naturally thought that the provisional diagnosis was wrong and discharged the baby to the care of his mother. At the time of discharge, I sat down with the mother and explained the situation as I saw it. I said that urticaria pigmentosa, the appearance on the skin, which was undoubtedly present, was a rare condition that cleared up spontaneously in most instances. The main reason for the admission to hospital was the question of whether the even rarer manifestation of the disease was present. I explained that the liver, which had been so enlarged, had reduced to a normal size and that we could afford to wait and see whether the effect of "maturation" was unusually rapid. Perhaps the disease, if it were present, was undergoing a natural remission. I instructed her to bring the baby back for review in one month.

When I next saw the patient, I was horrified to find that the liver was again enlarged and he was again sick, though perhaps not as alarmingly as he had been originally. I again explained to the mother that we should wait a while longer to see how Mother Nature was handling the situation. I tried to indicate to her the fact that, because the liver had reduced in size spontaneously, the process of "maturation" might be accelerated, and that it was far safer to wait.

Few Americans are patient. Most people desire an immediate answer, and I had a difficult time with this mother. One of the most curious experiences that I have ever had took place in a matter of a few seconds while I was talking to her. I was describing to her how her baby had responded to TLC in the ward, and her facial expression suddenly changed dramatically. The appearance of her eyes was quite frightening and I felt that, for an instant in time, I had witnessed the presence of a potential psychosis.

Madness is a very curious phenomenon, because it can be covered up and the person can be as charming and normal as anyone else. It is this kind of thing that makes it difficult for most people to understand the mind of a killer like Jeffrey Daumer and other significantly disturbed people. At any rate, I was so sure that I had seen something dangerous in this woman that my letter to the referring pediatrician reflected my impression. When I look back on this incident, it seems just as fantastic today as when I originally experienced it. My letter suggested that this mother was capable of doing harm to her own baby, that she was a potential child abuser.

Can you imagine the effect that this had on the pediatrician? Remember the fact that he had referred a sick baby with a potential cancer-like disease, and that there was no question but that the child was sick. How could I be so cruel as to infer that there was anything but concern and worry for this poor mother? The pediatrician was appalled and thought that I must be some kind of monster even to think this way.

A few weeks later this infant was taken into a local emergency room "because he had fallen off a table and landed on his head." His head was subjected to x-ray and a fractured skull was found. The pediatrician attended the case and knew that indications of child abuse can be very subtle, often presenting at an emergency room with a false story. He remembered my letter about the mother, so he referred her to a psychiatrist.

I was to see the report of the psychiatrist later, but this situation was at that time unfolding without my participation. He reported that the mother was a perfectly normal person and had absolutely no trace of a psychotic tendency. She was concerned about her infant as she would be expected to be under extremely trying conditions. The consulting pediatrician who had suggested the possibility of child abuse must be some kind of unusually cruel person.

My next contact with this case was one that I can never forget. It came in the form of a letter from the referring pediatrician who had, of course, continued to care for the child. He told me that the child had been found in the bathtub, drowned, and that it was a clear situation of classic child abuse. One of his remarks was very poignant. He said, "I wonder how I could have prevented this?" Of course, the answer is that he could not. With major suspicions generated in this manner, he had done his best and could not have done any more. This case, an illustration of the difficulty in understanding child abuse, also tells us something about how the human brain works. Child abusers love their children, but they are almost always psychological cripples who have been abused themselves in their own childhood. They are programmed by their parents and the act of child abuse that they perpetrate on their own children is a compulsion that they cannot avoid except by an extreme effort of will.

This concept introduces the subject of the brain, or at least an important part of it—its similarity to a computer. It is programmed by the people who have first contact with a newly born infant. These are most frequently the parents, of course, but not necessarily. We shall be discussing this idea of the brain as a computer a great deal in this book, because it is an extremely important concept that enables us to understand a lot of otherwise incomprehensible human behavior. It enables us to understand a great deal of physical illness as well.

I told this story because I wanted to illustrate the effect of stress on all forms of illness, both physical and mental. Some people may have difficulty accepting the fact that this infant had a potentially serious disease that could be affected by how he was being handled by his own mother. "Doctor, are you suggesting that a six-month-old baby can be so severely affected physically by a psychologically adverse relationship with his own mother?" I am afraid that I have to answer yes to that question.

My work with inborn errors of metabolism was an opportunity for me to begin to understand things that I had not been taught in medical school. No physician is totally equipped with the necessary knowledge when he comes out of his official training. He does not become a wise physician except by seeing life as it really exists in its infinitely variable nature. He actually learns from his patients and that is perhaps why it is called "the practice of medicine." My subsequent experiences as I came into contact with human beings of every variety have confirmed for me that there are only three things that we have to be concerned about in our approach to disease. These are genetics, stress, and nutrition. I will be discussing this concept in further detail later because it has become the core of my philosophy.

I have gradually come to see that our concept of ourselves as human beings is often terribly misguided. One of the greatest delusions that we have is the notion that we always have what we are pleased to call "free will." This means that we *always* have a choice when we make a decision, that we are always in control of our own destiny. Consequently, many human actions surprise us constantly because they are not "reasonable actions." We have added to the confusion by adding incomprehensible words like "soul" and "spirit" and many people become extremely hostile if it is ever suggested that the body, together with the brain that controls it, is a fantastically complex *machine.* The idea that we are "less than gods in our own right" is offensive, so we are blind to our real place in the animal kingdom.

I remember talking to a gentleman once. As I recall it, I was discussing the state of health of his child who was under my care. I happened to refer to humans as animals, and he became quite irate. "How dare you refer to my child as an animal!" he exploded. His ingrained perspective blinded him to the simple truth, and he had never thought it out in the light of reality, as indeed very few do. It is unfortunate that our communication is almost completely confined to words that merely carry symbolic meaning. Subtle shades of meaning are very difficult to introduce, but we really need an understanding of them to be able to communicate with precision. Because of this lack, there is often misunderstanding, particularly when a new idea is introduced.

I find it virtually impossible to practice medicine without a consideration of philosophy, for the infinite variety of mental play of which the brain is capable makes it extremely difficult to believe that it is really a machine. But consider it from a strictly practical point of view. What *is* an emotion, a thought, or other mental process? It is, in reality, a very complex electro-chemical reaction. Obviously, if the chemical reaction is exaggerated or abnormal in some way, so will its effect be abnormal. If the brain chemistry is destroyed, as in PKU, it is obvious that this function is impaired and it will reflect itself in its owner being what we call retarded. The machine does not work properly.

This is by no means a new idea at all. The French philosopher Descartes was very concerned about the machinery of the human body in these very pragmatic terms. He regarded it as just that, a machine. The idea is distasteful to many because it appears, at first sight, to deny religious views, and psychologists may not like it at all because they are trained to try to change the way people behave. They may not see the behavior in chemical terms and the idea of nutrition changing such behavior is largely foreign to many of them.

I hope that this book will acknowledge that each of the various disciplines that contribute to health are part of a much bigger picture and that we must not continue to be blind men describing an elephant. I hope that we might be able to see the elephant if we follow through with the ideas that I am introducing here.

I want to end this chapter by telling two more stories which again illustrate how the brain is a machine. A woman came to see me because she was under the impression that she was standing at a forty-five-degree angle. Part of her brain told her that this was completely incorrect because she knew that it was impossible and that she would fall over. But her brain chemistry was distorted, and her perception of reality was consequently distorted.

It is worth remembering that we have absolutely no idea whether our world even exists except by how we perceive it through our brains. Each message that comes into the brain is initiated by an outside stimulus such as a light ray, a sound wave, a contact with some chemical that gives rise to a sense of smell, or physical contact with an object that gives rise to a sense of touch. Each of these stimuli must be processed by the brain and interpreted in the light of our continuing experience. We take it for granted that the stimulus is arising from a "real" situation, and therefore the thing that gives rise to that stimulus exists.

Consider that this "reality" is nothing more than an interpretation which is itself chemical in nature. If the stimulus gives rise to a distorted chemical reaction, the interpretation will be distorted too. Hence, my patient's problem was a biochemical change in her ability to interpret a particular form of reality which gives us the sense of standing upright instead of at an angle. With a few changes in her diet and some supplementary vitamins, this curious anomaly disappeared.

The second story was published in a book which was entitled *Sexual Abnormalities in the Male*. A case was reported of a man who would begin to laugh whenever he had sexual intercourse with his wife. The laughter would crescendo until he was helpless, and the act could not be completed appropriately. There would be two ways of seeing this. You could say that the man was psychologically abnormal, which he certainly was, or you could interpret it in a chemical sense.

Sexual intercourse is a prime example of a computer at work. As the sensory impulses come into the brain, there is a crescendo of "excitement" that finally gives rise to orgasm, which is completely automated. It is a very complex process, involving many parts of the "computer" and, of course, it requires an integration of many chemical reactions which form the interpretation of what is going on and the sensual experiences of the act.

Suppose that this chemistry is abnormal. Instead of causing a motor mechanism that we call orgasm, the motor mechanism that is initiated is one that is usually fired by something that we find funny. Laughter is nothing more than a series of explosive exhalations with an accompanying noise, and it is associated with specific stimuli which are generally humorous. If the connections were distorted, then instead of giving rise to the usual motor effect that results from sex, another unusual motor effect results, in this case laughter.

The fact that this case naturally led to divorce is by no means unexpected and constitutes predictable behavior of the species. The question remains. Was this unfortunate man sick? Everyone would say yes, but nearly everyone would think of it as a "mental" illness and not consider it as an abnormal chemical reaction in the brain. I am pretty sure that he would not want this particular reaction to take place in this manner any more than anyone else. However, we have a mind-set in explaining it as "mental," and it would matter very little what kind of explanation the man offered himself. He would be stamped, and if he did not believe that he was a "mental case" in the first place, he would certainly wind up with that concept because it would be forced upon him by the current beliefs of society as a whole.

I strongly believe that this is an important problem in certain criminal acts, as I shall illustrate later. So I can only say again that my work with these inborn errors, that everyone acknowledged to be biochemical in nature, was my training ground for a major change in my perspective of my own species and its illnesses and diseases. It enabled me to think in a different way and thereby has made me more effective in helping my patients.

Chapter 3

Intermittent and Vitamin-Responsive Disorders

History

Throughout the '60s and '70s, there was an enormous interest in body chemistry as technological improvements in the laboratory were made. PKU was representative of a whole string of conditions that came to be known as amino acid disorders. All these diseases seemed to have two things in common. They all resulted in severe mental retardation, and they were all recognizable only by special tests that would identify an excess of amino acid in the blood and urine, as we have discussed.

It is important to point out that until relatively recently, nobody had the faintest idea what caused mental retardation. Any form of mental change in the Middle Ages was considered to be related to such phenomena as evil spirits haunting the patient. Mad people were put into dungeons and often were chained to the wall if they were violent. So conditions like PKU had significance which was disproportionate to their rarity, for it started physicians thinking about the human brain as an electro-chemical machine.

Pediatricians in the rarified academic atmosphere of the universities spent a lot of time examining urine from children who exhibited evidence of severe retardation. They were looking for other amino acid disorders similar to that represented in PKU, the prototype. Many such conditions were detected and, one by one, they were reported in the pediatric scientific literature. It was almost like panning for gold, and in most instances it involved the work of a team made up of a clinical pediatrician, a biochemist, and a variable number of technicians who ran the machines that performed the necessary complex analyses.

Because of my increasing interest in body chemistry as the

"bottom line" in diagnosis of a variety of neurologic disorders whose cause was totally unknown, I became gradually more familiar with the complex biochemistry involved in understanding the mechanism of each of the disorders as they were reported.

After some years of this frenzied search for amino acid disorders, in which each disease became a sort of collector's item, a new set of similar conditions began to appear. These diseases were brought about by a genetic defect in processing complex substances, known as organic acids. Some of these organic acids, which were spilled through the kidney into urine in the same way as amino acids, had most peculiar odors, sometimes quite obnoxious. For example, one of them was similar to the characteristic odor of cat's urine. These organic acids are caused by genetically determined mechanisms similar to those that were found to cause the amino acid disorders.

It was not that these conditions were really new; they were being recognized because of the improvement in laboratory technology. Neither were they of immense importance to humanity as a whole, merely as diseases. They are exceedingly rare and, as we have discussed, they are usually not even recognized before the infant or young child dies from an overwhelming infection such as meningitis, unless the attending physician is unusually knowledgeable and suspects the possibility. Thus meningitis, for example, is the diagnosis on the death certificate, even though the real underlying cause of the disease was severely disrupted body chemistry.

On the other hand, we get some surprises from nature, as one might expect. There is a condition called alcaptonuria which occurs rarely in infants, a genetically determined phenomenon. These infants excrete an organic acid called homogentisic acid. Its peculiarity is that it is not associated with mental retardation, and there is apparently no disease in the affected infant or child. The urine turns brown when exposed to the air in an alkaline medium. This brown pigment is also formed in the body over the years and, in the later years of life, bone cartilage becomes brown and causes a form of arthritis known as ochronosis. An interesting side note is that Dalmatian dogs excrete homogentisic acid in their urine and presumably this is more embarrassing to the owner because of the peculiar brown color that accrues when the dog urinates.

This condition in infants reminds me of an amusing tale. A pediatrician was examining a male infant in his consulting room. The infant was lying on an examination bed naked and, as infants do, urinated. The stream hit the newly plastered wall of the doctor's room and, to the great surprise of the physician, quickly traced a pretzel-like pattern of brown coloration on the wall. His knowledge enabled him instantly to recognize that the infant had alcaptonuria. The newly plastered wall had provided the alkaline medium for the reaction to take place quickly.

The importance of these diseases lies in the fact that through them Mother Nature exposes the secrets of body chemistry. We are able to see how the human body behaves when it is completely intact by learning what happens when there is a breakdown in the chemical machinery. I became acutely aware of the incredible complexity involved in the body. I found my involvement in this search to be thrilling and exciting because it had to bring me closer to the true nature of human disease.

Perhaps the curious thing about these diseases, all so different in their biochemical abnormalities, is that they are all extraordinarily similar from a clinical standpoint, with the occasional exception as just discussed. If the infant manages to survive, he will inevitably be severely mentally retarded. It is simply impossible to recognize any one of them by their purely clinical expression unless the urine contains a substance with a characteristic odor. Infants are always extremely sick by the time they develop such diseases in their classic, full-blown form.

Intermittent Disease

Now we come to discuss a much more important aspect of this subject, the occurrence of intermittent disorders. They are more important because they are more closely related to many common conditions which physicians see every day. A biochemical disorder that affects a child suddenly at intervals, from which the child recovers spontaneously, and which leaves the child relatively normal between each incident of disease, is a diagnostic challenge, to say the least. How can this kind of thing occur?

In the previous chapter, I described how a defective genetic mechanism gives rise to a deficiency of an enzyme which participates in a biochemical pathway. Remember also that each enzyme must have special conditions to make it work properly. It requires the proper physical environment such as appropriate temperature and pH, and it has to have a proper association with vitamins and minerals that serve as cofactors.

A number of possibilities can occur. The genetically determined defect may be in the production of the enzyme in sufficient quantity, a fault in the structure of the protein from which it is made, or a defect in the way in which that enzyme is able to cooperate with its cofactors. Perhaps an analogy is in order. Imagine a space ship which is scheduled to dock with an orbiting satellite. There is a docking device on the satellite into which the space ship must fit for the two to be properly linked. If something is wrong with the docking mechanism, the union is impossible. An enzyme represents the satellite, and there is a sort of docking mechanism known as a receptor site. The vitamin and/or mineral cofactor must fit into this receptor in order to provide the enzyme with its services. If for some reason it does not fit properly, the chemical reaction which it governs will be less effective.

It is important to emphasize that the cofactors are obtained from food, and vitamin or mineral deficiencies will result in loss of activity in the particular enzyme that requires that cofactor. Thus, it becomes of extreme importance to understand that nutritional deficiency of vitamins and minerals can produce a biochemically determined disorder identical to that which can occur if there is a genetic abnormality of the enzymatic machinery itself.

Let us summarize these facts:

1. The enzyme is produced in the body by mechanisms that are inherited. Loss of its activity is usually a function of inheritance, although it may result from poor diet if the deficiency is marginal and prolonged over a period of years.

2. Each enzyme must cooperate with a vitamin or mineral which is derived from diet.

3. If there is something structurally wrong with the ability of the enzyme to cooperate with the cofactor, this is a defect with which the person is born and it is governed by a genetically determined fault in the mechanism itself.

4. If there is a dietary deficiency of cofactor, the result is the same as when the enzyme mechanism is damaged by genetically determined fault.

Thus, it is not too complex to understand that each enzyme in the body is dependent upon a proper combination of inheritance and nutrition. To understand the nature of an intermittent disorder, let us turn to the time when this kind of condition was first described.

The reader will remember that I described a disease which goes by the imaginative name of maple syrup urine disease. Urine and sweat from an affected person smells exactly like New England maple syrup. On one occasion, when we had a child in the hospital with this disease, we placed a cup of urine and a cup of maple syrup on the nurse's desk. We invited any physician, student or nurse who might be passing by to guess which was urine and which was syrup by smelling each cup. No one was able to detect which was which. This particular child taught me another important lesson. I was able to keep her pretty healthy on a carefully controlled diet; but, if she developed a cold or viral infection, her disease would become very much more severe and would even threaten her life. I can still remember vividly an occasion when I had admitted her to the hospital with one of her occasional viral illnesses. She was about four years of age at the time, and there was an enormous increase in the maple syrup smell in association with the infectious illness. I remember picking up one of her tiny bedroom slippers that had fallen off her bed; the odor of maple syrup from it was overwhelming. Not only did the smell increase in urine, but also in her sweat.

What was more important, however, was the fact that this inter-current infection had made her biochemical condition very much more severe. It was precisely the same phenomenon as the child described in the last chapter whose PKU became worse when he developed an infection.

What did these two children have in common? Only the fact that the respective disease in each one became worse under the stress of a viral or other kind of infectious illness. How did the infection have its effect? We shall see in the next chapter how I describe a child whose disease could be brought on by inoculation, infection, or even a head injury! The importance of this is great because we are now introducing that component of life which we put under the deceptive heading of—*stress!* We shall be giving this a much harder look later on in the book. In the meantime, it should merely be emphasized that the viral infection in my patient was a source of stress. Her response to it, involving an increase in her metabolism to meet that stress, was "weighed in the balance and found wanting" at the point in her body chemistry which was the point of weakness.

What frequently happens in medical science is that a classic disease becomes described and is reported in a medical journal. After some years, we begin to see reports of variants. So did it happen with this curious condition called maple syrup urine disease. A professor of pediatrics in a major hospital in New York reported a child whose maple syrup urine disease operated only if and when she had an infection. She was ostensibly normal between her occasional infections, though she would develop a little bit more damage to her nervous system with each episode of infection. This is not too difficult to understand, because the biochemical abnormality, each time it was induced by the stress of infection, would carry out a little more erosion of nervous function, leaving a permanent effect.

Having been exposed to three cases of maple syrup urine disease, my pediatric colleague and I were very conversant with the condition. Our knowledge led to an experience which was so utterly bizarre that I can remember it as though it happened yesterday. The name of the child who was the central character was called Deidre, and the story went somewhat like this.

Our clinic, as all major clinics, consisted of many different departments of specialists. The idea of specialization is that each specialist is conversant with the diseases that affect the body within the interest of each specialist. The neurologist is an expert in disease of the nervous system, the gastroenterologist focuses on the bowel, and so on. At the time of this particular case, we had not developed a whole series of specialists in the various diseases of children. Consequently, my colleague and I were classified merely as generalists in all the conditions of children. We would be responsible for all the children in the pediatric ward, no matter what specialty their disease represented. We were able to tap the expertise of the various specialists within the clinic, but all of them were conversant with only adults for the most part, and few were familiar with the special problems of children.

Medicine has grown up around the specialist in the past 100 years, and each specialist is generally regarded as the guru who always knows the answer within his specialty. The only problem with this perception is that the body does not understand the manmade classification of diseases within these convenient boundaries. We shall be discussing a model that relies on chemistry and which indicates that making a what is called a clinical diagnosis is largely irrelevant. In the future, diseases will be classified in biochemical terms, and the expert will be the biochemist who is also a physician.

So it transpired one day that a neurologist in another state called one of the neurologists in our clinic, whose name was Tom. The outside neurologist had worked with Tom in previous years and wished to refer Deidre to him because of her extremely bizarre history.

At the age of two years, she had struck her head and was reportedly unconscious for a short time but recovered spontaneously. Throughout childhood she had experienced frequent high fevers associated with ear infections, a very notable part of the history in terms of explaining some very common modern phenomena in children which we shall be discussing later. At the age of nine years she developed an ear infection and then, one week later, she had been struck on the head with a baseball bat. She had not lost consciousness, but complained of a headache which lasted only a brief period. On the following morning she complained of headache, blurred and double vision, and dizziness which lasted only briefly. She continued to have similar incidents, especially in the morning, and her mother noted that she occasionally slurred her speech. A few days before she was transferred to our clinic, the child's teacher had reported that her speech was thick and she walked unsteadily. Her gait became increasingly unsteady, and she began to experience incontinence of urination. Her mother noted teeth-grinding during sleep. We shall be mentioning this later in the book when we consider what happens to children who have a junk diet. In this case, however, the teeth-grinding was part of an unusually active and abnormal function because of an inherited abnormality.

A few days later she was observed to have episodes of staring, and her vision seemed to be impaired since she groped for food at the table and missed her mouth when eating. She began to have periods of lethargy and would suddenly shoot out an arm or leg involuntarily. She had been admitted to the local hospital after the neurologist had found abnormalities in her nervous system. I have a strong feeling that her peculiar behavior was regarded as "psychological" and that this attitude had probably resulted in the relatively prolonged period of observation before her symptoms were taken seriously. She was transferred to the care of Tom in our clinic and many abnormalities were observed in the examination of her nervous system. A brain-wave test (electroencephalogram) was also found to be abnormal.

It was our custom as pediatricians to supervise the care of all children in the pediatric ward, no matter who was the primary physician. So, it came to pass that my colleague in the pediatric department was making his rounds and came to Deidre's bed. He was an astute clinician, and during the course of his physical examination he noted whiffs of an odor which reminded him of maple syrup. I was the doctor who was considered to be interested in strange odors, and I can well remember my colleague fetching me excitedly from another part of the ward. Laboratory tests did indeed prove that she was an example of intermittent maple syrup urine disease.

Why does the brain become toxic in this disease? Three amino acids are blocked by the absence of an enzyme that is common to the three of them. Toxic products called keto acids are formed, and it is believed that these substances which accumulate are responsible for interfering with normal brain function. In Deidre's case, we reasoned that these substances should be flushed out of her system as quickly as possible.

She was treated by means of an artificial kidney, which is used usually when a person's kidney has failed and the waste products of metabolism have collected in the blood. The machine did get rid of the accumulated abnormal acids that had formed in Deidre's body and she gradually recovered from her drastic illness.

Why did this child become sick in the first place? By means of special studies, we found that the enzyme that was necessary for processing the three amino acids was defective. It was present, but in only half the normal concentration. When Deidre became stressed in any way whatsoever, her metabolic machinery would have to accelerate as it does in everyone. In her case the particular machinery which deals with the three amino acids in question would also attempt to accelerate. Because of the partial block in the enzyme mechanism, the condition which was usually latent would light up and express itself clinically.

Vitamin Dependency

Within a few years, researchers found that a number of diseases of this nature could be treated by giving the patient huge doses of a cofactor to the enzyme. They came to be known as vitamin-dependent diseases. Several cases of maple syrup urine disease were found to be dependent upon vitamin B_1. Such people can be treated preventively by recognizing this anomaly and providing them with the necessary vitamin.

The fact that vitamin-dependent maple syrup urine disease had been described in the prestigious medical literature did not mean that it would be readily accepted, as is illustrated by the following story.

Because of my experience with this disease, I was known by several physicians at the local university. An infant was born in the local area and, because of the typical odor that came from her, she was recognized as having the disease. She was transferred to the university, and I was asked to see her. I suggested that she might have the vitamin B_1 dependent variety of the disease and obtained a specimen of her urine that was sent for a special test. Although this test suggested that vitamin B_1 dependency might be present, it was by no means proof, and my university colleagues did not have much faith in it anyway. However, I pointed out that giving the infant the vitamin could not possibly do any harm and was worth trying. The physician in charge of the case was dead against it, but after some discussion he eventually permitted me to give the infant a trial for about a month.

Even in an acceptably proven case of dependency of this nature, a month of treatment would be insufficient to provide evidence of benefit. The body chemistry did not change perceptibly, and the vitamin was discontinued. Several years went by, and the mother brought the child to see me again. I reinstated the vitamin and it did seem to help her in that it seemed to calm her.

The point is this: here we had a child whose biochemical abnormality was known. We knew that the enzyme responsible for carrying out the metabolic processing of three amino acids was defective. We also knew that this enzyme required vitamin B_1 as a cofactor. It seems reasonable that if you recognize a cripple, you should at least offer him a cane to help him walk. There was no reason to withhold the vitamin since it is a water-soluble vitamin that can be given to anyone with complete safety. The prejudice against vitamins in general is so great in the scientific world of medicine that it would be regarded as an "unscientific approach," so its use was frowned upon at the university.

Generally speaking, we think of a biochemical loss of a vitamin as a vitamin-deficient disease. The three best known of these are scurvy, pellagra, and beriberi. But with a vitamin-dependency state the patient will not respond to ordinary doses of the requisite vitamin. It requires megadoses and even then the response will be slow as the machinery begins to revive. The disease will appear exactly the same as a dietary deficiency. If a physician were to recognize it as such, he might provide the patient with the correct vitamin but decide that he was wrong in the diagnosis when the patient failed to respond to the doses of vitamin that would be expected in a normal person. He has to depend upon biochemical tests that are highly specialized if he is to obtain the truth. Alternatively, he might be so concerned that the clinical characteristics of the disease fit for a particular vitamin-deficiency disease that he might go on increasing the dose. By trial and error, he might well find that his patient eventually responds if he has the courage and the perception to pursue that course.

The reader will readily perceive that an illness of this nature might well be a tremendous puzzle to any physician. There is a catch to the whole thing, based upon the fact that modern medicine believes collectively that the diseases considered to be those of malnutrition have been conquered in advanced societies. Thus, few physicians are knowledgeable about the clinical manifestations of vitamin-deficiency diseases. They are considered exceedingly rare and are seldom considered as possibilities of diagnosis.

Since we have a tremendous preoccupation with infection as a major cause of illness, an obscure brain disease might easily be classified as a form of encephalitis or "brain inflammation," and the vital chemistry which is the real cause not even considered. Imagine an intermittent disease in a child. He is perfectly well in his infancy and early childhood. After an infection he develops an illness which is obviously affecting the brain or nervous system. Many tests are carried out, perhaps in a very sophisticated hospital setting, and no cause is determined. Since it clears up spontaneously, the subject is put aside. Perhaps the next thing is a mild head injury and the same thing happens. Even an inoculation produces the same effect. We shall see in the next chapter how I was confronted with such a situation and how it was solved to the benefit of the child and his family.

From an everyday point of view, the important thing about something of this nature is whether it is rare or relatively common. The fact is that each of us comes into the world with a set of genes which govern our personal characteristics. The genes are inherited from our ancestors, and we obviously have no control over them. Since absolutely nothing is perfect, even in nature, we must inherit the risks of gene imperfection as well as their strengths. If it is true that a gene causes a particular enzyme mechanism to be unusually weak in its complex duties, it may be the point of weakness in our general response to virtually any form of stress. We shall be dealing with this in much more detail in a later chapter, but I wish to introduce the idea here because it is important in understanding how nutrient prevention and therapy are rapidly rising to a lofty position in medicine.

Many vitamin-dependency states have now been reported, some of which operate intermittently as we have described. A number of these are mental diseases. I remember an adolescent girl who developed her psychosis only in the spring. Although I did not know the mechanism at the time, I would now assume that her metabolic processes were adequate for her except at the time of the vernal equinox, a time of stress for some people for reasons that are unknown. Some people who have psychotic disorders have responded to folic acid, a B vitamin. Others have been helped by injections of vitamin B_{12}. In a subsequent chapter I shall be describing a number of individuals who benefited from vitamin B_1.

I should like to describe a patient who was vitamin-dependent and who gave me a rich introduction to the problem. A female infant was referred because of a serious delay in both her physical and mental development. She had a facial expression which is usually seen in severely retarded infants. Her arms and legs were stiff and obviously highly abnormal. She fitted the picture which has been found to be related to defective chromosome balance. As many people know, a child with Down's syndrome is known to have an imbalance in the chromosomes inherited from his father as compared with those that come from his mother. Many conditions have been found to be produced by variations on this theme, and the referring physician in this case had sent the child for a chromosome analysis.

During our studies, I found that a test for vitamin B_1 deficiency was positive; I thought that this was strange since she certainly did not have a condition which could be even remotely compared with that which would normally be expected from this kind of deficiency. However, her chromosome analysis was normal, and I decided to treat her with vitamin B_1 in large doses. The referring pediatrician was furious because I was using a vitamin, a thing which "good doctors are not supposed to do because it is quackery." Within a few months, the infant had shown a remarkable acceleration in her development. What particularly pleased the mother was that her grotesque irritability and constant crying had stopped, and she was beginning to develop personality. Her mother began to read everything that she could find on the subject of vitamin therapy and has become more knowledgeable than most physicians on the subject. She found that as the child became older she could reverse her setbacks by increasing the dose of the vitamin, presumably as her growth demand increased. She is now an adolescent, obtaining normal grades in school and playing an instrument in the school band. She takes 2,250 milligrams of vitamin B_1 three times a day in order to maintain her mental and physical health (the recommended daily allowance for vitamin B_1 is about 1.5 milligrams), and she takes a number of other vitamins as well.

Some of the obvious questions that many people ask are "Does she really need that huge dose of vitamin?" and "How do you know that it was the stuff that she needed? Could she have grown up normally without it?" There is no way of knowing the answers, but one can say that an infant with such physical appearance and disastrous physical findings on the initial examination would be predictably abnormal for life, based upon previous experience with such an infant. Furthermore, neither she nor her mother are about to risk her trying to do without it. If she forgets to take the vitamin, she immediately feels the effect and this gives her a constant reminder of its assumed need.

This experience taught me many things. First, if I had listened to the conventional approach of my peers, this child may not have grown up normally. The use of vitamins in therapy is still, at the time of this writing, regarded as a form of malpractice. I have lost virtually all my former medical friends because I have strayed from the conventional, and it is surprising how much anger is showered upon the maverick. More importantly, I learned that the dose of a therapeutic vitamin could be ascertained only by trial and error, by experiment with the individual. I learned also that vitamins and minerals are the most powerful therapeutic weapons that we possess in medicine today.

I would like to briefly touch again on the subject of stress—something that we all live with as a necessary part of life's journey. Consider a motor car that has a good engine but which has been improperly fueled. It might be in a good enough state to run on level ground. If it should come to a hill, however, it might have much more trouble. The problem would present itself to the owner by means of symptoms. A smart mechanic might first ask whether the owner has read his owner's manual and if he knows which fuel to order. It is, of course, obvious that the car might just as easily fail if it has something wrong with the motor that has been caused at the time of its manufacture. The hill is to the car what stress is to the human being living in a hostile world. We all have to cope with it and must adapt to the changes that occur on a day-to-day basis.

Another factor which complicates the picture in the diagnosis of disease is the relatively recent discovery that microorganisms give rise to illnesses which we refer to as infections. When I say "relatively recently" I am referring, of course, to historical time, because a hundred years or so is nothing in history. Because physicians have been taught to think of the body's defense reactions as responses to invading germs, we see certain phenomena as only the result of such an infection. For example, a sore throat, accompanied by swollen glands in the neck and fever, is automatically considered to be an infection. Because we live in the age of antibiotics, we do not think it out any further. If we cannot find evidence of a bacterial cause such as a streptococcus, we assume that the cause is from a virus. The patient receives an antibiotic, regardless of whether it is potentially harmful as a drug in its own right.

The point that I am trying to make is one that I shall return to again and again. Each of us lives in a dangerous world, surrounded by all kinds of invisible stressors, many of which are indeed bacteria and viruses. The defense reaction to a stressor, however, regardless of the nature of the stressor, is much the same.

Let me provide a simple example. I was asked to see a lady in her sixties. She had experienced many episodes of fever in which her body temperature would be as high as 104°F. She had been investigated repeatedly for evidence of obscure infections, none of which had ever been shown to be present. I assumed that her fever was really a form of stress response to a nonexistent stressor. I believed that her brain was deceiving her insofar as it was under the impression that she was in some way being attacked by a stressor. The body temperature is controlled by the brain computer and I therefore prescribed a medication called diphenylhydantoin, which is usually used to treat epilepsy. Her fever disappeared, and she has not had another attack now in several years.

Here is another example. I was asked to see a six-year-old child who had a remarkable but not a particularly unusual story. For about two years, he had been affected by repeated episodes that always started in the same way. First he would become irritable and pale. His mother would take his temperature and find that it was 103° or 104°F. He would also complain of a sore throat, and enlarged glands would be visible in his neck. It was, of course, predictable that it would be diagnosed as a throat infection and that his pediatrician would administer an antibiotic.

The fever would gradually subside and the glands would disappear, and in a week or so he would return to school. Within a short period of time another episode would occur. His mother wanted to know whether there was an alternative to this approach. At this time in my career we were making a diagnosis of "fever of unknown cause," and it was customary to admit such a child to the hospital and study him with a multitude of tests. When I explained this to the mother, she said, "Doctor, when you do the tests, would you please measure the level of folic acid and B_{12} in his blood?" Both of these are B vitamins, and it was a most unusual request, so I naturally asked her why.

She replied that they had been tested at another hospital where he had been investigated and the doctors had told her that they were increased and that she must have been giving him too many vitamins. She said that she did not understand that because she had not been giving him any vitamins. Sure enough, they were indeed increased in concentration and I was intrigued about the reason. I found that he had definite evidence of vitamin B_1 deficiency and started giving him this vitamin. He was sent home from the hospital, and when I saw him again in a month or so he had not had any more of his attacks and was well in every way. I measured the two B vitamins in the blood again; they were now in the normal range.

I then asked the mother whether she would be willing to stop giving him vitamin B_1. Naturally, she was not very willing, but we still did not know whether the vitamin had been instrumental in his improvement or whether it was coincidence, and in the interests of science she agreed. About three weeks later the child had a recurrence of his fever and swollen glands. During the illness he walked in his sleep and descended the stairs, urinating as he walked.

When I saw him, he had a huge swollen gland in his neck, and I readmitted him to the hospital. Blood levels of folic acid and B_{12} were again elevated and I repeated the large doses of vitamin B_1. The swollen gland disappeared and he was well again within five days. I did not give him an antibiotic. The blood was once more tested for the two vitamins previously elevated, and they were close to being normal again.

He continued on the vitamin B_1 for a year and I heard nothing from his mother until she called me to say that the episodes had started again. I simply directed her to start giving him a multi-vitamin/mineral complex in addition to the vitamin B_1. I later heard from her that the child was again well.

What was the explanation of his increased vitamin B_{12} and folic acid in the blood? We do not know for sure, but there is evidence from published research. These two vitamins are part of a network of nutrients that must be taken in with diet as we have discussed. They must then be activated in the body, a complex biochemical process which requires energy. Since his requirement for vitamin B_1 had not been met, he was deficient in this energy and the two vitamins were not being activated. They were present but not biologically active and were simply piling up in the blood. This phenomenon has been observed in infants dying from crib death, a phenomenon that we shall be discussing later.

It must be pointed out that this child's diet was typical of the average menu consumed by American children. It was loaded with calories and, in particular, there was an enormous amount of sugar and "junk" in it. In addition to the vitamin supplement that he received, this diet was corrected in no uncertain terms. We shall be discussing the role of diet later on, for it is quite a complex subject and it is obviously not easy for people to understand this seemingly obscure relationship.

What had I learned from this case? Once more I was confronted with a situation which was completely foreign to my teaching and was certainly not "usual and customary," the formula that guides so much medical action. It seemed to me that the brain computer was being deceived. It was receiving input from the child's environment which was triggering off behavior that would be normally a way of combating an infection, whether the stressor was actually an infection or not! Few people ever stop to think what sore throat, fever, and swollen glands really means. It is a defense reaction made by the human organism to an invading germ—usually!

What I am saying is this: it is invariably assumed that a reaction of this nature is automatically due to an infection. Since it is tacitly accepted that germs or viruses cause infections of this nature, an antibiotic is given because it is the only treatment generally accepted as appropriate for such a phenomenon. I was able to show that this child's problem was solved by giving him a vitamin instead of an antibiotic.

Was he vitamin-dependent? What had diet to do with this? Was there really a germ involved? Suffice it to say at this stage of the book that investigation of this child at another hospital had involved the removal of a swollen gland from the neck during one of his illnesses. It had been examined under the microscope, and it had shown what pathologists easily recognize as the normal reaction of such a gland to infection!

I would like to defer the explanation of this mystery to a later chapter because we shall be examining the mechanism in some detail. In the meantime, this was not the only child that I had seen with this kind of problem. I would like to describe another case because it is similar but even more dramatic.

A six-year-old child was referred to our clinic because he had been taken to his family doctor for a cold and cough. The doctor had subjected the child to a chest x-ray and, to the doctor's surprise, it showed the presence of a huge tumor. There was nothing to do but to take him to surgery and open his chest to see what the tumor was. I was present at the operation and knew the surgeon pretty well. We saw a mass which was about the size of a golf ball, and since it was not obvious what kind of tumor it was, the surgeon took a small piece out of it and we took it down to a pathologist. I shall always remember the pathologist looking through his microscope at the slide and saying to the surgeon, "Larry, since when have you been removing normal lymph glands?"

We could not believe it and thought that the tissue had been taken from a tumor which contained some normal lymph gland. So we went back to the operating room and took another piece of tissue. To our surprise, the pathologist gave us the same answer, that it was normal tissue. There was nothing more to be done; the wound was closed and the child sent back to his hospital bed. Evidently, for some reason, this lymph gland had become enlarged but was not strictly a tumor. The situation was much the same as the child described earlier, although I had forgotten about the possibility of increased concentrations of folic acid and B_{12} and did not measure it in this child.

The next day I called the parents to my office to tell them the good news of what had happened. In our conversation I asked them about the child's diet, since by this time it had become an important subject for me. I discovered that it was full of junk food, sugar, ice cream, and so forth, the "usual and customary" childhood diet in America. So I did some biochemical testing and proved that this child was in fact deficient in vitamin B_1. I started giving him the vitamin and made sure that his diet was corrected.

It is still amazing to me that it only took about one month for this chest tumor to disappear completely. I see the situation in the same way as I saw the case described above. It was no longer possible for me to see children with serious organic disease without at least thinking along these lines. Above all, I began to ask parents what their children were eating and drinking and have been repeatedly startled at some of the dietary indiscretion that I have witnessed. I hope that this will be made more credible in later chapters.

The subject matter of this chapter is vitamin dependency and intermittent biochemical disease. What have these two cases to do with this? Am I trying to say that any disease at all can be a varying degree of deficiency of a vital nutrient? If so, can it be that a dietary deficiency can affect a normal person in this way or does it have to be a vitamin-dependency state in which the person requires much more of the vitamin than is usual? Although it may stretch the credibility of the reader, either of these possibilities exists. If the diet is bad enough, it can produce devastating changes in the brain/body relationships in a genetically normal person. In a dependency state it would occur much more easily because the vitamin need would be so much more than is normally found in even a good diet.

If a dietary deficiency exists long enough in a genetically normal person, it can become an acquired state of dependency because the enzyme system becomes damaged and requires prolonged nutritional support in order to repair itself. Thus, it can be seen that nutritional disorder is invariably related to inheritance factors and is heavily influenced by the shifting state of stress that is experienced by each one of us as we live our lives.

Are intermittent vitamin-dependent diseases common? We have no real idea whether this is so or not. We have discussed the fact that the classic and recognized vitamin-dependent states are rare. But the exact needs of any one vitamin or other nutrient for any one individual is not known. Therefore, there are probably plenty of people who become chronically sick, sometimes for entire lifetimes, and never know that their sicknesses are simply because they are eternally short of given nutrients. They are born with this need and nobody ever suspects it, just like the infant that I described above who had to have enormous doses of vitamin B_1 in order to survive. In her case, she was fortunate because it was recognized, but the state of medical thinking at the moment would almost guarantee that her chances of her need being discovered would be very bleak indeed.

Why is this so? Surely, the rational person would say, if something is so relatively simple, the treatment so readily available and cheap, why do doctors not jump on the idea? Either it is an approach which works or some physicians are foisting the idea on the public merely to make money out of them. It is simply because it does not fit into the present training of physicians. It is too new. The small number of doctors and nutritionists who advocate the general use of vitamins as therapeutic agents are still regarded as mavericks. The resistance is quite amazing.

I remember treating a child with rheumatoid arthritis by nutritional means; the treatment proved to be successful, whereas the conventional approach of the rheumatologist had not. The father of the child went back to the rheumatologist to tell him that this had happened. In a very informal way, he wished to get him to realize that there was a different approach of which he may not be aware. He expected the rheumatologist to be pleased to receive this information. What actually happened was that the physician turned his back on the child's father and walked out of the room.

This is not new in the annals of medicine. It takes a generation to make a paradigm shift, and this is what nutritional medicine is, a paradigm shift. The history of medicine is crammed with such stories. Virtually all the major benefits that we accept today such as anesthesia and sterile surgery have been fought over and the proponents have had to prove their cases, invariably receiving some form of persecution similar to that endured by religious converts throughout history.

The surprising thing is that a doctor may be confronted with the facts very forcibly and refuse to recognize them because they do not fit in with his training and the current thought of the majority. Peer pressure is also a very powerful force, and to escape from it can be dangerous to the livelihood of the escapee. Official forces come into play that might never have been suspected, such as licensing boards and county medical societies. Persecution may follow, and I often think of the early Christians who used to meet in secret. They would put a crude drawing of a fish outside the meeting place so that their colleagues could recognize the meeting place.

I am a member of a national organization known as the American College of Advancement in Medicine (ACAM). This is a group of physicians that number fewer than 500, contrasting with the thousands of physicians who are members of the monolithic American Medical Association. In the early days of its organization, the pioneers who were forging the group together from scratch would meet secretly in a hotel room, sometimes extending their meetings into the early hours of the morning. They had been persecuted in their individual practices and were always fearful of their discussions being overheard by officialdom. People do not go to these lengths unless they really are committed to a principle. The fact that they had seen something that their colleagues had either not seen or refused to recognize does not mean that their observations were false. They were and still are true pioneers, and, like pioneers throughout history, they will be forgotten. The "pioneers" that will move into history will be the people that were the greatest detractors.

There will be some exceptions. Linus Pauling is being recognized for his leadership in the field of nutritional and vitamin therapy. Other great pioneers will be those who researched the effects of stress on disease, notably Dr. Hans Selye, whose writings have been largely ignored by organized medicine to date. Interestingly enough, neither of these great men were practicing physicians. Linus Pauling is a doctor of philosophy and one of the great chemists of the century. Hans Selye carried out his research on animals in a research institute in Montreal and, although he was trained as a medical doctor, he did not practice.

This may appear to be a diversion from the title subject of this chapter, intermittent and vitamin-dependent disease. However, I wanted to point out the fact that there is good scientific evidence for the use of megavitamin doses in classic diseases that are known to be rare. I have pointed out that Mother Nature does not deal in totally "black" and "white" areas. There are the "grey" areas, where the need of a given vitamin or mineral in an individual is greater than the usual requirement. Such people are relatively common and create a great challenge to the development of a proper therapeutic approach. In fact, it can be said that the proper nutrient, given in sufficient dose for a long enough period of time, is actually the *only* way that such a sick person can be treated successfully.

I will end this chapter with the story of a family that I came to know very well and in which tragedy struck with unmitigated ferocity. My first contact was with six-month-old David. He had experienced repeated episodes in which he stopped breathing. There were also repeated attacks of vomiting and diarrhea, and the infant's life had been severely threatened many times. We found that he had a metabolic dysfunction which was identified by a special test which suggested that the disease would respond to vitamin B_1. Both parents had the same test done, and each was positive, but in much less a degree. It strongly suggested that they were genetic carriers of the disease that David had, particularly as his older sister had the same but much less severe condition. The parents were carriers of a recessively inherited genetic principle in exactly the same way as I described the inheritance of PKU.

David and his sister grew up with mental retardation, and both of them had to be in a residential care facility. They responded only partially to vitamin B_1, but another factor entered into the picture. Absolutely no one, other than the parents, believed that this was a metabolic disease, and vitamin therapy was regarded as unnecessary if not downright fraudulent. The children never have had a consistent vitamin program.

Now we come to the crux of the story. The father was involved in a serious accident. He was hit by a car and was somersaulted over its roof. Although he had no broken bones, he was never again the same person. He suffered from severe stiffness and pain in many muscles; this had been described as fibromyositis and was treated with aspirin.

About two months after the accident, he played a game of solitary squash as part of his attempt to rehabilitate himself through exercise. Evidently he had gone to the bathroom after leaving the squash court, for he was later found there dead. At autopsy he was found to have some narrowing of the main blood vessel as it leaves the heart to carry blood to the body. This condition, known as aortic stenosis, is known to be associated with sudden death for no apparent reason.

He had an insurance policy that provided double accident indemnity, but the insurance company refused to pay because it was believed that his death had no relationship with the accident some two months previously. I argued on behalf of his widow, saying that the stress of the accident was extremely important since it had had a significant effect on his metabolism. I strongly believed that his death would not have occurred if he had:

1. Not had the accident.
2. Not had the carrier state described.
3. Not had aortic stenosis.

In my view, the accident stimulated his body chemistry to meet the demand of the trauma. The genetic weakness in vitamin B_1 chemistry made this much more difficult and made him much more fragile and susceptible to sudden death related to the aortic stenosis. There were, therefore, three separate factors which contributed to this man's death. The only one that was superimposed was the accident; he was therefore, in my opinion, entitled to double accident indemnity.

The insurance company won the day because my concept is definitely not the "usual and customary" formula that all insurance companies use, even though it was the truth. The carrier-state concept is strengthened by the fact that I have continued to see the widow as a patient. She has had repeated episodes of fibromyositis, which is clearly stress-related. Her stress, of course, has been more closely related to her struggles to find a job to support herself and her two retarded children. Although her stress is usually "mental" in character, on at least one occasion she had a severe attack after a skiing injury. The effect of stress is the same, whether the force is a mentally appreciated one or a physical act of trauma.

Now we are ready for the next chapter, which tells the story of another family who changed my professional thinking even more. It is discussed in some detail because it led me to some more important discoveries which will be outlined in chapter 5.

Chapter 4

The Case of J.V.

Having become conversant with the possibility of abnormal body chemistry as a cause of many different conditions in children, I was always on the lookout for something of this nature, particularly if there was any form of mental interference, including retardation.

One morning, I was making rounds with a group of residents. Teaching rounds in any major hospital where residents work is always regarded as an important major part of their training, so we were not concerned solely with the patients whom I was attending. We came to a crib in which sat a six-year-old boy named J.V. who was under the care of another physician. He was sitting bolt-upright and I shall never forget his striking appearance, which I can still see in my mind to this day.

His face was bright red and he had a look of fear that was poignant. His eyes seemed to be staring at nothing and one had an instant reaction of sympathy for him. The story told to me by the resident remains as one of the most incredible ones of my career. On more occasions than his mother could remember, he had suffered from bouts of a condition called cerebellar ataxia. The cerebellum in the brain has much to do with our poise and balance, and *ataxia* is the word used by doctors to describe the state of someone who has lost his balance in a pathologic manner. Each episode was invariably triggered by some form of stressful stimulus. A simple infection such as the flu or even a cold, a protective inoculation as given to most children preventively, and on one occasion a head injury, had resulted in onset of a series of frightening symptoms.

J.V.'s speech would become thick and slurred, like that of someone who had too much alcohol. His balance would become seriously impaired to the point where he was unable to stand. He would begin to experience delusions—also like an alcoholic—and this would cause tremendous fear as one would expect. Each episode lasted for a week or so and gradually cleared up spontaneously, without any treatment whatsoever.

A severe neurological impairment of this nature is always treated as a potentially serious phenomenon, and he had been examined by a number of neurologists. At the time that I first saw him, he was in the care of a neurosurgeon who was performing a number of high-tech studies to rule out a space-occupying lesion in the brain such as a cyst or brain tumor. In fact, he had had such studies repeatedly and none of them had revealed any structural cause. In order to identify a biochemical disorder of the sort that was discussed in the last chapter, the physician has to think in biochemical terms, and no one had approached it from this angle. Of some importance and urgency was the fact that he had been examined by an ophthalmologist, and optic neuritis had been seen in both his eyes. This is a condition in which the optic nerve begins to deteriorate and, if progressive, will eventually threaten sight. As would not be unexpected, the child's school work was rapidly deteriorating, and his psychological assessment revealed that his I.Q. was in the high range of mental retardation.

I pointed out to the residents that this story fitted exceedingly well a newly described condition known as intermittent maple syrup urine disease. The reader will remember that this curious condition received its name from the fact that urine from an affected child smelled exactly like maple syrup. It too is a biochemical disorder where the enzymatic machinery in the brain does its job until it is stressed by one of the factors that triggered the disorder in J.V.

There is a relatively simple way of making this diagnosis, and that is, of course, to smell the child's urine. But urine from J.V. did not smell like maple syrup, so the next stage was to perform a test known as a two-dimensional amino acid chromatogram. The principle behind the test is quite simple. When one of these biochemical disorders exist, the disturbance gives rise to either a deficiency of a vital compound that should be made for normal function, or an excess of something which is being dammed up by the failed reaction. This substance may be present in the urine and this technique acts as a screening test.

Urine is placed in a solvent system that will dissolve the compounds that are being sought and then allowed to soak up into a special piece of paper that is like blotting paper. Running it through two dimensions and two different solvent systems tends to separate out the huge number of compounds that exist in urine. We were looking for an unusual presence of amino acids which are the building blocks that enzymes use in performing their jobs.

To my surprise, the chromatogram showed a vast amount of an amino acid called alanine. It was otherwise normal. After his current episode of ataxia was over, the alanine disappeared from the urine of J.V.

This situation presented a scientific conundrum, or riddle, and began the most exciting and productive two years of my entire medical career. In the first place, no one had described in the world literature any condition that was characterized by an excess of alanine in human urine. This does not mean, of course, that it had never existed previously; it had just not been detected. As already mentioned, it requires a special technique to identify it, and physicians will not do the test too readily because it is not a common way of evaluating human disease in everyday practice.

I remember going to my office and hanging a biochemical chart on the wall and studying it to see how alanine could be blocked in its natural processing within the body. It seemed to be impossible to do this blockage to occur without killing the living cell, and yet here we were with a sick child, not a dead one, in whom alanine was a huge waste product in the urine when he was sick.

I was struck by the discovery that each of these episodes experienced by J.V was an exact facsimile of the disease known as beriberi. Beriberi is a very complex disease, appearing mostly in relationship to a deficiency in the diet of vitamin B_1, or thiamin. It is a vitamin that stands astride the most important reaction in the body in developing energy metabolism by which all our body cells survive.

Beriberi varies in its symptoms in an astonishing manner, depending upon the age of the individual who is affected. It is extremely lethal to an infant, very damaging in a five-to-eight-year-old child, and quite chronic or drawn out in the adult. Even in the adult, the disease can become acutely lethal, producing an agonizing death that was called *shoshin* by the Japanese when the disease was common. Hence, the disease has long been classified as infancy-type, childhood-type, and adult-type beriberi. There are two forms of chronic beriberi in the adult, one known as "wet" and the other as "dry," depending upon how much fluid (edema) has collected in the tissues.

After years of study and research, I know now that this disease represents the absolute prototype for the clinical appearance that is observed as a result of severely damaged energy metabolism. If we use the analogy of an automobile, we can envisage a constriction in the fuel line from the tank to the engine. If the accelerator is pressed under such circumstances, the fuel requirement of the engine is increased, but it cannot be delivered, and the performance of the engine becomes more severely compromised. The engine is obviously more likely to stall.

It still remained to be seen whether this understanding could explain the mysterious illness in J.V. I had to wait and see if he would develop another attack of ataxia so that I could test my theory and carry out more studies to support the idea. Up to this point, every moment that I had free from seeing patients was spent in the medical library. I quickly discovered that beriberi literature was very old; much of it was written in the late 1930s after thiamin had been synthesized for the first time. Literally nothing had been written about it in the English literature after the 1950s. I believe that this lack reflects a basic flaw in medical thinking. We were convinced that the disease, which was considered to be a pure nutritional disease, was conquered, and we could go on to other things.

At this point it is important to take note of an intellectual quirk in modern medicine. A manuscript that offers references that date back more than a few years is considered to be written by someone who has not "researched the most recent literature where all the modern advances are reported." It is also worth reflecting that scientists are often far from being altruistic searchers of truth. I felt very much alone in my preoccupation with the problem surrounding J.V. I did not think of it as solving a problem for one single child with a rare and extremely exotic disease. I believed that solving his problem would reflect itself in throwing light on the broader issue of energy metabolism. I believed that energy deficiency was the secret to many of the obscure neurological conditions seen in a pediatric ward of a major hospital. Most of these are described in Latin, further discouraging searches for the underlying biochemical cause.

So, I remember going into the office of the head of my department. I wanted a sympathetic ear to hear my theory and the flood of unanswered questions. I told him that I was of the opinion that J.V. had a metabolic disease which exactly imitated childhood beriberi and I wished to research it in reference to defining it further and exploring the use of an appropriate vitamin. I was told that I was "getting too big for my boots," and it was clear that no help would be forthcoming from that quarter.

One cold February night, J.V. was brought in by his parents and I was presented with one of the strangest aspects of his extraordinary case. He had begun another episode of ataxia. I told the parents of

73

some of my theories and that I needed to have him in the hospital for some detailed studies. To my great surprise, they were most reluctant to let the child come into the hospital at all and demurred at every suggestion that I made. After more than two hours, after the clinic was long since silent and deserted, I managed to extract a grudging permission. I was allowed to take blood and urine, and nothing more. I was not allowed to extract a sample of spinal fluid, a relatively simple and necessary way of evaluating a critical biochemical balance in the brain.

In spite of the fact that I described the problem scientifically and in spite of the fact that he has had treatment that has protected him from further attacks, this peculiar antagonism has persisted through more than twenty years. Although the family lives in an area close to my present office, I have never seen the father from that day to this. Recently, when J.V. had some illness, the mother took him to another physician and then called me to provide the required "advice" to the physician, who was himself ignorant of the problem.

Whether this attitude resulted from blaming me as the bearer of ill tidings or not is a moot point. Human psychology seems to have virtually endless anachronisms, but it is certainly a most disheartening thing to experience when the search is for the pure benefit of the patient. In fact, J.V., who is now an adult, has never consulted me since the original studies.

Anyway, J.V. was admitted to the hospital, and it was extremely fortunate that I ordered urine to be collected continuously, in twelve-hour segments, throughout the entire illness. The day urine was then recorded from 8AM to 8PM, and the night urine from 8PM to 8AM. As it turned out, this was the best order that I gave, for it revealed something that I had never even slightly suspected.

In a multi-specialty clinic, it is customary to share a complicated case with a specialist, so a neurologist helped me supervise the child's stay in hospital. I mention this because it also helped to reveal an unsuspected factor. The neurologist would see J.V. earlier in the morning than I and, since he would be unable to find anything seriously wrong clinically, he would sign his discharge. When I saw him later, I would cancel his discharge, simply because he was manifestly ataxic. I would think to myself that the neurologist had "gone off his head" because he had not seen what I had seen. By the same evening, when the parents visited him, his balance was completely off and he had the thick, slurred speech. For the first three or four days, this performance was repeated and he was getting worse each day. Then, to our amazement, he began to improve and finally, after ten days, he was back to normal again.

The complexities of the studies were tremendous and were reported in an important pediatric medical journal. I will not try to put them into anything more than a relatively simple terms to illustrate the points that I wish to make in using this case for the benefit of others. Each twelve-hour urine sample was subjected to the test mentioned earlier, a chromatogram. We finally wound up with about twenty-two separate specimens of urine, numbered consecutively. Thus, odd numbers represented night urine specimens and even numbers indicated the day specimens.

One morning, I was sitting in the laboratory having my morning coffee and chatting with the technician. I had worked with this particular technician for years and we were good friends. She told me that the urine specimens had all been passed through the first dimension. The technique is that a small amount of the specimen is pipetted onto a strip of the special blotting paper which is placed in a tank and subjected to what is called high-voltage electrophoresis. The various compounds in the specimen separate according to their individual electric charge and migrate along the strip which is bathed in a solvent. This process is known as the first dimension. Each strip is dried and then sewn with a machine to the edge of another larger piece of the blotting paper. Each piece is now stapled in the form of a cylinder and placed in jars, where the lower edge is bathed in another solvent. As the solvent is soaked up by the paper, it dissolves the various organic substances and they are distributed over the paper. This is the second dimension; thus the name two-dimensional chromatography. After drying, the paper is sprayed with a substance known as ninhydrin which stains amino acids a bright purple color. They are recognized by their geographical location on the paper when the chromatogram is read.

The technician had stained the first-dimension strips, and we had laid them on the floor in sequence. This method had two advantages. It gave lots of room and we were able to stare down at them while we sipped our coffee. As I looked at them I gradually became aware that chromatogram number 1 was lighter than number 2, which was darker than number 3, a sequence that went through the entire series of specimens. However, another curious observation was that these features became progressively more marked up until about the sixth day and then gradually became less marked. I had never heard of such a phenomenon, and we pursued it with interest.

It turned out that the amino acid alanine was always in heavier concentration in the day than in the night specimen, rising to its heaviest concentration on the sixth day and then gradually receding until it reached normal levels, after which this night/day seesawing ceased. This proved to be vital information which has been instrumental in my understanding the machinery of human adaptation.

It turned out that these chromatograms exactly mirrored the daytime clinical worsening that was observable in the child. He became gradually worse until the sixth day of his illness, after which a gradual spontaneous improvement took place. I later deduced that this extraordinary phenomenon represented circadian rhythm (which we will be considering in Chapter 6). This is a day/night rhythm that is maintained by the brain in its overall control of the physical mechanisms of the body. When we drive the family car into the garage at night we shut off the engine. This saves fuel, of course, and the car "gets a rest." Our bodies are governed by the same principles. The brain shuts us down partially during the night and "revs us up" by day. Obviously we cannot shut off the "engine" completely at night because we would die, but circadian rhythm enables us to conserve energy while the energy stores are being rebuilt for the next day.

Thus, I was able to interpret the peculiarity of J.V.'s illness. He was prone to having a maladaptive response to virtually any form of physical stress. His brain computer was energy-deficient, although it was able to cope with most of everyday living. However, when "weighed in the balance," his adaptive machinery was found to be wanting. Subsequent actions of this computerized mechanism would go awry if the stress was too great for adaptive machinery to make the proper adjustments. Since the brain is the most oxygen-hungry part of the whole body, the energy deficiency was quickly reflected in dysfunction of the normal control mechanisms, resulting in ataxia and delusions.

The recommended daily allowance (RDA) for thiamin is about 1.5 milligrams (mg) a day. This child required 600 mg on a regular basis and, if stressed by an infection or trauma, would have to increase his dose automatically to 1200 or 1800 mg, the so-called megadose. It is obviously important to emphasize that this dose was necessary for this particular child because his inherited defect had made him thiamin-dependent. For him it was a *normal* dose—an extremely important principle.

To illustrate the importance of this discovery, let me describe what happened when J.V. went to Florida on vacation. This was before I had him stabilized on the required dose of thiamin. The

ambient temperature was 90°F and the family entered an air-conditioned store. Almost immediately, J.V. became unconscious and
started to wheeze as though he had asthma. He was taken at once to
a local emergency room, by which time he had recovered and the
physician could find nothing wrong with him. He was discharged.
The same thing happened a day or so later when the air conditioning
in the family car was turned on.

It is relatively easy to see what happens in these situations if we
know and understand how the underlying biochemical problem has
affected the adaptive response. The computer, which controls all
these adaptive responses, sends out exaggerated signals to body
organs. In the case of J.V., the bronchial tubes were reacting abnormally and going into spasm, resulting in the wheezing noise that we
call asthma. Although reflex signals of this nature are a normal
adaptive response in themselves, they were improperly organized by
a sick nervous system. Hence, the reaction could be summed up as
a maladaptive reaction to a normal stress stimulus. The stress of the
change in environmental temperature is obviously one that the
normal human being takes in stride. In J.V., the effort was too great
for the brain computer and unconsciousness ensued because it had
insufficient energy to respond appropriately. It was overwhelmed by
lack of oxidative metabolic function, the equivalent of stalling in an
automobile engine. (This concept will be made clearer in a later
chapter.)

It is often stated that truth is stranger than fiction. Our development as a species has led us to a rather arrogant concept of our place
in the universe. Many cultural and religious tenets have emphasized
on humans' soul and spirit. Focusing on this aspect, we give little
thought to how this machinery that houses the spirit is fueled and
maintained. It is extremely difficult for most physicians to see J.V.
as a machine which is kept at a marginal level of physiologic
function by an engine which has difficulty in processing fuel. We
see behavior as a purely voluntary function, and "bad behavior" is
"wilful" and therefore to be punished rather than understood. Our
present medical model insists that J.V. must have some kind of
structural problem such as a brain tumor to explain his symptoms.
Thus, this child had been subjected repeatedly to highly sophisticated studies by neurologists and brain specialists. When a structural
abnormality was not revealed, the thinking was directed toward the
possibility that the tumor was too small, or that the particular test
had missed it. Abnormal brain chemistry had not even been considered by anyone previously, and the idea that it was an illness

representing a deviant stress response was considered to be an absurd idea, not even worth considering by scholarly medical minds.

To illustrate the complexities with which the family have had to contend, the official name of this disorder is pyruvic dehydrogenase deficiency (thiamin-dependent). So consider what happens under the following conditions. J.V. had a brother, T.V., and it was found that he had inherited the same unstable mechanism as J.V. In at least the early days of this child's life, the defect did not seem to be as bad as that of J.V. so his parents had not sought any medical advice, as far as I know. As he grew up, he refused to recognize that his diet was inherently important in giving disadvantage to his unfortunate inheritance. Junk food is bad for healthy kids, but for these children it is a potential death sentence. Anyone with this defect would have a very hard time burning any form of sugar in the diet. Oddly enough, marginal malnutrition, about which much more will be said in a subsequent chapter, makes children irritable and difficult to handle from a disciplinary point of view. They become progressively more difficult to reason with and are totally unable to see themselves as others see them. They are beyond an ability to reason properly. So I have little doubt that T.V. was not very cooperative in terms of diet.

One day T.V., then an adolescent, was walking in the park with a friend. As he was crossing a stream, he slipped on a rock, apparently striking his head, though it was later reported that this did not appear to be a serious injury. He immediately became unconscious and lay with his head in the water, requiring quick rescue by his friend. He was taken to the nearest emergency room and his mother was called in. In her predictable frenzy of concern she told the physician that her son was known to have pyruvic dehydrogenase deficiency, and that thiamin was highly necessary in large doses. She not surprisingly encountered total skepticism. Imagine a mother going into a strange emergency room where her son has been brought following an injury. The story given to the physician is that this boy had fallen and struck his head on a rock. He had suffered near-drowning and there seemed more than ample explanation for his trip to the emergency room. Now his mother comes into the room and pleads with the physician to believe her. She tells him that the boy has a condition which is excessively rare and that he may not even have heard of. Rather naturally, even though it should not work this way when it comes to a physician's care for his patient, she is treated as being crazy. The physician never called me for confirmation.

He recovered, and his mother brought him to see me in my office. I recognized some of the outward signs of malnutrition which are

78

common in modern adolescents. I placed him on a regimen of appropriate vitamins, including thiamin, of course. I tried to explain to him that his near-disaster was not just a simple head injury, that it was far more complex than that, and that it linked up with all the very erudite studies that had shown the underlying and potentially dangerous genetic defect in his ability to produce energy for his brain and nervous system. I emphasized that his body engines required absolutely the best fuel that he could obtain and that so-called junk food was a potential danger to him. It was clear, even at the time, that he did not believe me. Whether he followed the prescription or not is unknown, because he never came back. I learned a year or so later that he had drowned. I never learned the details, but I have always suspected that it was some kind of mechanism related to his primary genetic problem. His mother never took me into her confidence.

This lack of confidence, or whatever it was that prevented a dialogue between the family and me, has concerned me greatly over the years. I have concluded that the bizarre biochemical problem that the boys had inherited from their parents was, in some way, affecting the mother also. This, hypothetically, made it difficult for her to comprehend with sufficient impact what a dangerous situation existed for her sons. The father never called me or visited me and I have had absolutely no communication with him since the very first time that I saw J.V.

It must be remembered that, if there is an important genetic change in a human being, that is reflected in *every single cell in the body*—and each of us has about 100 trillion cells. Each cell has to make its own way in helping to run the total system. It takes in oxygen and nutrients through the cell membrane, which is its surrounding wall, and uses them in an energy-consuming process to carry out that function to which it has become specialized. Brain cells are exceedingly demanding of oxygen, and the defect in both of these children created a difficulty in using oxygen efficiently.

It is an interesting reflection on the case of this family that I met such skepticism from virtually all physicians. As I was preparing all the biochemical data to publish my findings, I tried to get guidance from at least one "expert." I found out about the politics of pediatric research meetings in a hurry. In those days I was young, vigorous—and naive!

Throughout my professional career I had always preferred to attend the research meetings rather than the clinical symposia. I believed that it was the forum for exchange of information that would generally develop better means of helping our patients. The papers were presented formally, usually by the "young Turks," the investigators who were looking for promotion to the august state of professorship in a university. Their professors would then get up at question time and discuss the work of their protégés, before going elsewhere to pursue their own political interests with their peers in the lobby.

There was a club-like atmosphere, and a physician's membership depended upon whom he knew and whether he pleased them or not. I did not come from one of these university "clubs" and so there was no entry to the hierarchy. Merit in science is seldom sufficient, on its own, to be heard. I still believed, however, that there was enough altruism that a case of this nature would raise the interest of one of the senior scientists, even though I did not know him personally.

He was one of the professors of pediatrics whom I knew to be in the forefront of metabolic disease in children, so I sought him out. While I was seriously trying to present my data to him, I noticed that he was looking over my shoulder, trying to spot his important colleagues. A wave, a smile and "I'll be with you in a moment, George," was the formula that kept intervening. Finally, I was given the weighty answer to my question. The professor said, "Well, you are wrong, boy [in my explanation of the facts], and I'll tell you why! If the patient had this problem, he would be dead!"

How often have scientists made this fundamental error in pronouncing judgment on natural phenomena? We develop a preconceived notion from a discovery of only part of the picture. That picture governs our reactions, sometimes for decades, before Mother Nature proves to us that we were wrong in drawing that particular conclusion.

So, I was really on my own as I wrestled with the problem of J.V., but the patient kept giving me the clues that made it all gradually come together. This case was indeed a turning point in my career. I felt humbled by the complex nature of the many facets of the problem that had to be considered. It was more than obvious that this illness was a disorder affecting the computerized mechanisms by which we adapt automatically to the changes in our environment that I define as environmental stress.

The astonishing thing was the simplicity of the treatment. The choice of a single, relatively cheap and readily available vitamin had, to all intents and purposes, solved the problem. I say "to all intents and purposes" because we now know that when a given vitamin is used in this manner, it does not operate in a vacuum. We shall see, in the next chapter, how therapeutic vitamins must act as a team of integrated nutrients. Using a solitary nutrient in this manner is never a complete answer because it alters the balance of the vitamin/mineral intake. Therefore, there had to be some defects in the metabolic balance of J.V. that remained. To be sure, he should have been under my continuous care and study for years to come, but too often humans do not act together to try to solve problems, and besides, there is always the economic factor, which is heaped upon the skepticism. Perhaps the most destructive factor is the credibility gap, the thing that separates human minds the most.

Of great interest to me is why J.V. had a recent illness, the facts about which I am totally ignorant. Perhaps it was because he had been delinquent in taking his supplementary thiamin, under the impression that his condition had "gone away." Or perhaps it was because his nutritional intake was unbalanced with reference to the nutrient supplements of his diet. Why did the mother (or the patient himself, since he is now an adult) consult a physician who was totally ignorant of the underlying problem? Even more curious was the fact that she called me and asked me to advise the physician in charge. For a number of reasons, I was not allowed to see the patient when he was in a local hospital, and I do not know what the outcome of the illness was or what the state of the patient is to this day.

There is still so much to be learned about the physiology of complete nutrition, and we can ill afford to treat problems of this nature in a cavalier fashion when the foundation of the basic cause has been already ascertained. The sufferings of this child, the premature death of his similarly affected brother, and the stress imposed upon the whole family should serve as a beacon to guide us in the continued quest for the ultimate truth. There is no room for petty jealousies and political bias, though it is unfortunately true that we seem unable to discard these confounding factors. As a species, we have become enormously clever, and knowledge should make us wiser and bring us closer; the very opposite, however, seems to be happening. Wisdom is a rare commodity in today's world, as indeed it always was.

In the next chapter we shall examine the effect that J.V.'s illness had upon my development as a physician and see how some of the curious cases that I encountered could be understood because of this newly acquired knowledge. In many respects, I see our medical machinery grinding away in an archaic and much-too-narrow path. We have to learn to see illness as a breakdown in homeostatic adaptive responses and be less concerned with the "enemy" in the form of the dangerous world in which each one of us lives. We all live under stress. It is an inescapable component of being alive. Indeed, it is an inescapable force that acts on inanimate objects as well. For example, metal expands and contracts in response to temperature change. What J.V. taught was how the essential automatic machinery by which we adapt to these stresses functions. Even more important, I was able to understand what happens when it breaks down. Stress is not the cause of illness. It is our ability to make the necessary physical and mental adaptive adjustments that must be examined.

Chapter 5

Where This Experience Led

My experience with J.V. and his brother was a very sobering one. It made me aware that a six-year-old child could have repeated illnesses involving his brain and nervous system which defied attempts to diagnose them by conventional means. When an intermittent disease of this nature is presented to physicians, their training has taught them to think in structural terms. They use more and more highly sophisticated techniques to attempt to identify the changes in tissues, known as pathology. If none is found, the disease is considered to be psychologic in nature, a word that is synonymous with the term "functional."

My own experience has taught me that this is an erroneous approach, and I use another analogy to explain it. Imagine an aeroplane in which the occupants have heard of hurricanes but do not know anything about their nature. They fly over a Caribbean island that has been devastated by a hurricane, and they see the widespread damage. Because they do not understand the fact that the storm has long since gone, they are under the impression that they are actually looking at the hurricane, rather than the damage left in its wake.

We can compare disease to the hurricane. Disease is bad chemistry in the cells of the body. The bad chemistry results in damage which is visible when the cells are viewed with a microscope. The pathologist identifies the damage and calls it the disease, whereas he is really looking at the effect of the disease. (Like all analogies, this one can only take the perspective so far, for a "hurricane" in the tissues can strike without causing visible damage. This particularly applies to mental conditions such as schizophrenia, a phenomenon whose cause has eluded discovery for years. In a later chapter it may become much clearer why conditions like schizophrenia can occur without causing visible damage. For now, I would like to describe some of my exciting discoveries which occurred in the wake of studying J.V.)

My library research over a period of several years had been a voyage of discovery. It is, of course, obvious that a medical paper (or any other paper for that matter) is useless unless it is read. The person who writes a paper hopefully knows what he is talking about, but his knowledge is disseminated via the readership. Thus, our world libraries are crammed with information which does nothing more than gather dust.

When one embarks on a library search, it is indeed like a voyage. New facts are discovered like undiscovered islands and they begin to fit into a kind of map which gives a big picture of the terrain. So my quest for knowledge regarding the discovery and research of vitamin B_1 opened up corridors of understanding of which I had never even dreamed. It is amazing what can be found in a library if you start looking.

Consequently, I developed an unusual knowledge of beriberi, the classic condition which is most associated with vitamin B_1 deficiency. More importantly for my own development, I became very knowledgeable about energy metabolism. What do I mean by this technicality? The fact is that comprehending the principles of energy metabolism is the equivalent of a motor mechanic understanding details about what makes an engine work. Because, in human metabolism, this is so very complex, it is not often that a physician becomes familiar with the principles. It is left to the biochemist or the research worker, neither of whom generally treat patients.

This give rise to a paradox. The physician, who is trained to take care of sick people, receives basic training in energy metabolism and biochemistry. However, when he graduates, he is more or less told to forget all that learning because, although it instructs him in the principles of body function, it is not considered that it can be used to treat illness. The drug manufacturer becomes his professor, and the detail man who peddles the drugs to him in his office becomes his teacher. It is, of course, quite incongruous that we should develop medicine in this manner, but we must be aware that so-called scientific allopathic medicine is an authoritarian discipline that preaches an aggressive, drug-oriented approach to influencing diseases in an active and controlling manner. Little thought is given to how to help the body heal itself.

My professional approach to illness was forever changed, and I began to see things quite differently. At this time, I was also deeply involved in certain aspects of laboratory diagnosis and research, particularly related to the biochemical conditions described in previous chapters. I had become very interested in amino acid analysis, using the technique already discussed, known as chromatography. After the urine has been soaked up on the paper, the individual amino acids are recognized by their location on the paper and are made visible by spraying the paper with a chemical known as ninhydrin. It has a most characteristic odor and whenever I notice its presence in a laboratory it still conjures up memories of those years.

Many physicians within the clinic would send samples of urine to this laboratory for amino acid analysis. In addition to identifying rare disorders of the type that we have been discussing, the analysis gives some information about many different conditions which are much more common, including the effects of malnutrition.

I would review these chromatograms with the technician, a highly skilled woman with whom I worked for a great number of years. Her work was always meticulous, and she was always as interested in our findings as I was. We would write the reports as we viewed the chromatograms and send them to the individual doctors, telling them what we saw and whether it was considered to be normal or not. As in most laboratory tests, most of them would be normal, but in many instances it could throw light on the nature of the disease that the physician was trying to identify. In many cases, when the pattern was abnormal, I would go and visit the patient in the hospital ward to see what kind of clinical situation existed.

I had little hope of changing the current attitude of most of the physicians toward the diseases that their patients had, even though I had begun to be aware that so many of them had an obvious biochemical underpinning. It seemed to me that there could be only one basic way of influencing a biochemical disorder—by correcting the biochemistry. This can be done only by providing the body with nutrients, by means of which it can do its own repair. Let me provide an example. One day, we saw a strange chromatogram and I went to see the patient. It turned out that she was a middle-aged woman who had paralysis of the bowel. She had been investigated to the hilt and represented an unsolved puzzle. What was so interesting to me was that she had what was described by her attending physicians as a horrible personality. She had been sustained on intravenously administered nutrition because her bowel was out of commission, and there was every reason to believe that such nutrition was incomplete. Because of my special knowledge, I was easily able to recognize the pattern of choline deficiency. Choline, sometimes classified as a vitamin in the B group, is a nutrient from which the body makes a vital compound known as a neurotransmitter. Called acetyl choline, it is necessary for the appropriate nervous function of the whole bowel. Without it, the bowel is in a state of paralysis. Even more interesting, absence of this neurotransmitter in the brain alters the personality radically. The original problem, whatever it was, was almost certainly nutritional in character. It was the treatment that was compounding the situation because of nutritional deficiency in the intravenous feeding. I wrote a long note in the patient's chart and spoke briefly to the physician in charge of her intravenous feeding. I could see that the physician thought that I was crazy, and I was not surprised that my advice was ignored.

The reader might well be surprised to know that doctors mistrust a physician who comes up with something that is not currently acceptable in usual and customary terms. At that time, absolutely no one was thinking of serious disease in nutritional terms. It matters little whether the suggested treatment is completely harmless and might be "worth a shot." Another deeply rooted concept is that a specialist knows all about his specialty and that a doctor for adults has little or nothing to do with pediatrics. Since I was a pediatrician and he was a super-specialist, I had two strikes against me.

Because of this atmosphere of mistrust, it was totally impossible for me to suggest the use of vitamins in any one of the patients that had abnormal chromatograms. In fact, it became a slow erosion of trust in virtually all of the dealings that I had with my colleagues. With my own patients, I was more or less free to prescribe the treatment that I believed to be an honest attempt to help them. I say "more or less" because I later began to learn that my use of nutrients was considered to be disreputable and earning my department a "bad name." New knowledge comes very hard to anyone. To put it into action is often even harder. Physicians are people and, like everyone, they resist any form of change, even if it is a change that is capable of helping their patients in a harmless way.

If the patient was under my care as a clinician, I would begin to try to influence the illness by the use of vitamin B_1 in the large dose to which I had become accustomed and which was completely harmless even if it did not work on a given patient. I was astonished! In so many cases, I found that the patient's well-being was improved, even when I had absolutely no idea what name to give to the disease. One of my fundamental discoveries was that symptoms which were considered to be unrelated to the primary disease cleared up. Let me describe an example.

One day, a mother brought in her son. He had suffered from a tremor of the hands since childhood, and she wondered whether a vitamin might help since she had heard that I was using vitamins on my patients. Since vitamin B_1 does have a modifying effect on the nervous system, I suggested it. They could easily obtain it from any health food store.

Several months later, I had a postcard from the mother. She said that the tremor was unaffected by the use of the vitamin, but I was amazed to see her statement that "the diarrhea that he has had throughout his life ceased." Now, in the first place I did not know that he had diarrhea. This was not mentioned to me; the complaint was tremor. How on earth did diarrhea relate to the use of vitamin B_1? In a later chapter, we shall see how I was able to use this simple fact in constructing a new model for disease.

Another discovery was that drugs, even common drugs like antibiotics, generally accepted as harmless, could cause harm without anyone suspecting that they were the potential culprits. Here is the story. I had become aware of the fact that the part of the brain known as the limbic system (which I have long since called "the computer") was frequently involved in what appeared to be purely physical disease. One day, an infant was admitted for study and the urine chromatogram showed a couple of spots which I had never seen before. The infant died subsequently, and the autopsy showed that there were many cysts in the brain which were the cause of death. My thinking has always been directed toward looking for the *reason* for the development of cysts like this, or any other structural change, using the analogy of the hurricane again. Therefore, I wondered whether the spots on the chromatogram were major clues to the underlying cause. I did not know that the infant had been treated with anything prior to his arrival in our clinic.

Some months later, the technician, who was as interested and excited as I about this research, brought me a chromatogram made from the urine of an adult patient who had undergone surgery for a kidney transplant. The same two spots were seen on this chromatogram; we both remembered the first one and wondered whether it was this "new disease." After surgery, he had suddenly stopped breathing and had to be resuscitated. Again, I thought in terms of the limbic system of the brain, the computer, where breathing is controlled. Could this be a biochemical disorder, perhaps triggered by the stress of surgery?

Over the next year or so, we saw this chromatogram about sixteen times. If the patient was in the hospital I would go and visit the ward and read the chart, and in every case I found evidence that the brainstem, the computer, was in some way involved in the disease process. It was never clear whether the patient had entered the

WHY I LEFT ORTHODOX MEDICINE

hospital with this as an important part of the problem, or whether it was a complication.

Then one day I became aware, from another physician, that the spots on these chromatograms were produced when the patient had been receiving a semi-synthetic penicillin which is used extremely commonly. Researching the charts of the patients from whom these urine chromatograms had been obtained, I found that all of them had received this antibiotic.

I turned the question over to a biochemist colleague, who researched it and found that this semi-synthetic penicillin actually goes through a gradual state of degeneration in the vial before it is given as an injection to the patient. Two substances are formed, penicillinoic and penicillinamic acids. I found that these substances were considered to be nontoxic when they had been injected into rats, and no further consideration given to this effect.

Now, of course, the question was whether the antibiotic was the *cause* of the brainstem disease or whether the brainstem complication of the primary disease was the reason for *giving* the antibiotic to the patient. (Aside from this issue, of course, another question that arises is whether the antibiotic is therapeutically effective if it is degenerating in the vial as it stands on the shelf.)

I could not answer these questions, and to implicate a drug of this considered importance without sufficient evidence could easily have made me a laughing stock. Several years later, the Atlanta Disease Center sent a physician to investigate a series of deaths in infants in several cities. Each one had received this antibiotic and each had suffered some devastating effect to brainstem function. The conclusion of this physician was published; she stated that her research had not revealed any relationship between the drug and brainstem disease in these patients. I wrote to her to describe my personal experience and willingness to collaborate if she wished to pursue this further. I was ignored.

Why do scientists not follow up clues like this? Surely the public has become well aware that powerful, money-driven forces prevent disclosures of this nature because of selfish vested interest. Everyone, in fact, has his price! I have always been sorry that I did not pursue this matter further, but it certainly taught me not to use this antibiotic in any of my own patients. It is important to describe my cause-and-effect conclusions drawn from slender evidence to help the reader understand the medical jungle and why patients are sometimes not the most important consideration in medical practice.

But, to return to my story, I had become an expert in the science of vitamin B_1 through my own experience and as a result of my library research. So I want to describe several cases which led me to an appreciation of the importance of the computer and which led later to an understanding of crib death and many conditions which could be explained only in biochemical terms. Many physicians, both inside and outside the clinic, had become aware of my research interest because of the fact that I was using so much vitamin B_1. The chief of service had even approached my wife at a party and asked her to plead with me to discontinue my "disreputable" research.

What they did not know, and which I seemed to be powerless to tell them, was that this particular vitamin stands at the very center of energy metabolism which enables every cell in the body to function. In fact, in a highly scientific symposium, a paper published in the prestigious *Annals of the New York Academy of Sciences* in 1962 reported on the use of vitamin B_1 in more than 230 different conditions. In many of these cases, the patients had experienced some beneficial effect. It has long been believed that a biochemical reaction which is dependent upon a given vitamin cannot be pushed beyond its maximum ability by increasing the amount of the vitamin above the usual concentration. This is the main argument against the use of so-called megavitamins in the treatment of illness. Many detractors say that it is "merely enriching the sewer system" since it results in massive overflow of the vitamins in the urine. In fact, there is some evidence that an enzyme system can be accelerated beyond its usual rate by an increased amount of the cofactor. I know of at least one experiment that showed that vitamin B_1 could act as a "super-cofactor." My own experience has certainly suggested time and time again that the patient who responds to large doses of vitamins is not "vitamin deficient" in the usual and customary sense. The vitamin, under those circumstances, is behaving as a drug which stimulates a metabolic response.

Of course, it must be clearly understood that vitamin B_1 is a vitally important member of a vitally important team of non-caloric nutrients which, collectively, enable fuel in the cell to be burned to provide energy. The subject will be discussed in more detail in a later chapter. In the meantime, I had become very much aware from early research studies on vitamin B_1 that it had an incredibly important part to play in running the brain computer, the brainstem. Thus, I was particularly on the lookout for patients who had obviously defective "computers."

So it was, then, that I sat down to lunch with a physician who knew of my interest in brainstem dysfunction. He was a specialist in ear, nose, and throat surgery. He had been called to the Intensive Care Unit to see a middle-aged woman who had simply stopped breathing. He had performed an emergency tracheostomy, an operation which inserts a breathing tube into the windpipe through the neck. He suggested that I see her because of her inexplicable cessation of breathing. It turned out that her condition was a complete mystery to her attending physicians. She had a history of beer-drinking and smoking and had developed a disease of the brain and nervous system involving periods of unconsciousness of twenty minutes at a time. She had paralysis of the wrists and ankles and crossed eyes and was absolutely huge in body because she was literally full of water, or edema fluid, in the tissues.

To cut the story short, we were able to prove, by laboratory methods, that she had classic beriberi, the nutritional disease caused predominantly by deficiency of vitamin B_1. Absolutely no one believed it! It was considered to be an incongruous and bizarre notion in the mind of a crackpot pediatrician who had no business seeing an adult patient in the first place.

Anyway, I managed to get the primary physician to give her large doses of vitamin B_1. She began to pour out urine as she pumped her body dry. Her wrists and ankles recovered from paralysis, her eyes uncrossed, and she proved to be a witty and highly intelligent lady. It is probably hard for the reader to understand that the physicians who had her primary care were mystified by her recovery. One thing that they were certain of was that it had nothing to do with the vitamin!

During her recovery she began to develop a rapidly progressive anemia. Nobody asked me about it, and the primary physicians were performing x-rays of the bowel to see if she was bleeding internally. In the meantime I took some of her urine and found a spot on the chromatogram due to a substance known as ethanolamine, a byproduct of metabolism. I took it to a biochemist friend in the research division and said, "Bob, why would I find ethanolamine in this lady's urine?"

I told him the story of her response to vitamin B_1, and he suggested that this substance was due to deficiency of another B vitamin known as folic acid.

This made complete sense, since I was aware of the biochemistry involved, so I started to give her folic acid. Again, she made a spectacular recovery from the anemia and, again, her physicians were unable to grasp the relationship with the vitamin. Although these physicians were as aware as I was that the blood is affected by deficiency of this vitamin, the anemia had not behaved like that seen with this deficiency. Therefore, they refused to believe that it was the answer.

The long history of abuse of the nervous system had left her partly paralyzed, and the patient became a wheelchair case. I had no participation in her care although she continued to take folic acid and vitamin B_1. The next time that I saw her, she had been readmitted to the hospital to study complications in her "obscure" disease. When I was talking to her, I noticed that she had some peculiar pigmentation on her arms and happened to remember a relatively recent paper in which this kind of pigmentation had been found to be related to vitamin B_{12} deficiency.

It was as though I had just found the latest piece in a complex jigsaw puzzle. It has long been known that folic acid should not be given without vitamin B_{12} in the treatment of pernicious anemia, the blood disease that is considered to be the classic expression of deficiency of one or other of these two vitamins. It was, of course, true that this patient should have received vitamin B_{12} all along, but I had not helped to take care of her and I had forgotten this relationship when I first gave her folic acid. It was also important for me to realize also that in spite of a deficiency in folic acid and vitamin B_{12}, she had not developed the particular form of anemia known as "pernicious."

Unfortunately, folic acid given without B_{12} produces an effect on the spinal cord known as subacute combined degeneration. Put into simple language, the nervous messages are not getting through from the brain to the body. This patient's paralysis had become worse. She received an injection of vitamin B_{12} on a Friday, and I did not see her again until the following Monday. Over the weekend she had experienced fever and aches and pains in the limbs which "felt like flu" but quickly resolved.

This case taught me about the "healing crisis" which we will be discussing in greater detail later. What I now know is that if the nutritional prescription is right, the symptoms often become immediately worse before the patient begins to get better. It has been referred to as the "healing crisis," although I personally call it paradox since it is the opposite of what the patient expects. It is easily seen that this development might create a distinct barrier between the physician and his patient if this is not understood. The usual explanation by the patient is that he believes that he is allergic to the vitamins. It is, however, an almost unequivocal sign of ultimate success in treating the patient with that particular nutrient or group of nutrients.

What did I learn from this fascinating case? I deduced that her primary deficiency had been that of vitamin B_1. When she received large doses of it, she began a process of recovery which unmasked a latent deficiency of folic acid and B_{12}. I believe that it works like this: vitamin B_1 deficiency produces a severe drop in the rate of metabolism, equivalent to constricting the gasoline line in a car. Under these circumstances, she had enough folic acid and B_{12} to preserve the state of the blood, but as her metabolic rate accelerated under the influence of B_1, the folic acid deficiency was unmasked and produced anemia. Without B_{12}, the folic acid produced further damage in the spinal cord, thus assuring that she would continue to be a wheelchair-bound individual.

One aspect of her care was highly significant, in my view. She was an addicted cigarette smoker and the nicotine had a poisoning effect on the nervous system that made her plight worse. I never was able to get her to quit smoking; doing so may have enabled her to obtain further recovery.

Perhaps the next highly significant case in my learning process was that of a sixteen-year-old boy whose history was so dramatic that I still wonder at it. He had some trouble with breathing at birth and was a chronically irritable infant. Early development was delayed and he had become hyperactive, with a short attention span. He was extremely sensitive to noise and had experienced periodic asthmatic wheezing. He was mildly retarded mentally. Over the years, he had repeated episodes of bloody diarrhea and vomiting of blood. Later, I learned that this symptom is a significant marker of abnormal energy metabolism. This may seem to be incongruous, but I hope that it will become clearer later.

At age sixteen, he developed an acute attack of gastric flu, as it is so often called, consisting of abdominal pain and fast beating of his heart. When he was in the process of recovering, his parents took him for a picnic in the mountains. It was a hot day, and while sitting in the sun he suddenly developed partial paralysis in the right arm and leg, like a stroke. He was immediately put into an air-conditioned car and recovered from the paralysis on his way to a hospital.

At the hospital he was found to have an enlargement of the heart and was transferred to our clinic for further study. When I first saw him he was obviously acutely ill; he had an irritating cough and rapid respirations and a pulse of 140 beats a minute, very fast for a resting pulse.

My unusual knowledge of beriberi immediately suggested that he had the extremely acute and fulminating variety of the disease that had been called *shoshin* by the Chinese. Because of this I gave him a very large dose of vitamin B_1 by injection. He was considerably better on the following day and improved steadily. However, he began to experience unusual sweating, breathlessness, palpitations of the heart, and an acute sense of anxiety. His condition rapidly worsened, and I started to give him a form of vitamin B_1 that was discovered in Japan and is much more powerful than the usual. There was a remarkable and striking improvement. A chest x-ray showed that his enlarged heart had reduced in size. A little while later he began to get worse again, and the dose of the vitamin had to be increased. Further relapses were helped by increasing the dose each time, but he gradually became resistant to the vitamin and died.

What had I learned? This child had a disease which exactly imitated a very acute form of beriberi but responded only partially to huge doses of vitamin B_1. Today, with increased knowledge, I would give him a whole array of vitamin and nutritional supplements in the belief that he had a complex breakdown of an ability to derive energy from food. There is little doubt that he had an obscure inherited disease and we certainly never obtained information which led us to an accurate determination of the biochemical cause. He represented one of the conditions discussed under the heading of vitamin dependency.

My knowledge of beriberi proved to be extraordinarily helpful. Although this is generally considered to be due to a deficiency of vitamin B_1, it clearly is not. In reality it is a nutritional excess of high-calorie carbohydrate foods, with vitamin B_1 needs accelerated. Let me illustrate this.

Back in the early years of the century, beriberi was found to be related to an anti-beriberi factor found in rice polishings. Rice consists of a central core of pure starch which is white in color, so it is called white rice. Around it is the husk, a fibrous covering which contains the vitamin B complex, of which vitamin B_1 is the most important in the process of metabolizing carbohydrate foods such as starch. If the rice is polished, the husk is removed and only the white rice is consumed.

It was observed in the East that outbreaks of beriberi occurred more often when there was greater affluence, and this is how it worked. Peasants considered white rice, placed on the table to impress guests, to be a mark of having risen in the world. So when they made more money, they would take their brown rice to the mill to be polished, not knowing that they were discarding the vital elements that made the rice nourishing. Looks became more important than nutrition. Is that not a warning for us today?

Anyway, I came to realize that beriberi was the prototype of dysautonomia. The prefix *dys-* means abnormal, and *autonomia* refers to the autonomic nervous system. This is an automatic system that is directed by the brain computer and, as we shall see later, is a vital part of our ability as organisms to adapt to changes in our environment. So we can say that the nuts and bolts of beriberi is that the function of adaptation is compromised because of an imbalance in the reflex responses that the brain makes in response to stress.

With this knowledge, I became aware that many of the children whom I saw were dysautonomic in the sense that autonomic reflexes were compromised. Thus they had a condition which, if not classic beriberi, was certainly very similar.

I was asked to see a ten-year-old girl who had headaches and blacking-out spells. Her school work was substandard and she was hyperactive and disruptive, both at home and at school. Her headaches began to be associated with paroxysms of abdominal pain, and the left pupil of the eye would be observed to be more dilated than that of the right eye. She improved for a time with medication but then began to have peculiar additional symptoms. When she became upset, the left pupil dilated and excessive sweating would be noted on the left half of her body, which also became flushed while the right half remained pale. Then she would develop a headache in one half of her head, usually the left side, which was accompanied by nausea and abdominal pain. Repeated attacks of abdominal distension had been a problem, and occasionally she had brief periods of cessation of breathing during sleep. Exercise caused undue breathlessness and precipitated a headache.

Menstrual periods were frequent and heavy, lasting nine to ten days, and she had severe cramps. Frequently she experienced rapid heartbeat and she was easily upset or irritated. In the hospital we performed studies on her that demonstrated that she had asymmetric reflexes of her autonomic nervous system in the two halves of the body. Blood pressure was completely different in the two arms, and this asymmetry was markedly increased when she was injected with a substance that is known to stimulate a rise in blood pressure. An unusual finding was that brain waves produced by one half of the brain in an electroencephalogram were different from those in the other half.

Her diet was appalling, as so often the case with American

children, and I directed her mother to make drastic changes, encouraging the proper intake of natural organic food. She also received a supplement of a multivitamin and some vitamin B_1. She was studied again in a similar way a year later, and the asymmetry had gone.

I learned about asymmetry from this case and at least one other with a similar story. All human beings are asymmetric. One foot, or hand, is a little bit bigger than the other, facts that are not important of themselves and of which we may be totally unaware. However, under certain conditions, when the brain computer goes awry, this built-in asymmetry may become grotesquely exaggerated. In recent years I have become well aware that the exaggeration of asymmetry means exaggerated activity in the computer, thus increasing the imbalance. Many women with premenstrual syndrome (PMS) have one breast bigger than the other, usually the left. It does not seem to correlate with right-handedness versus left-handedness.

What does this information mean? Although no basic knowledge exists to explain it, there is a great deal of evidence that tissue growth is controlled by extremely low-amperage electric currents. Perhaps, as soon as the brain computer is formed in the developing embryo, it becomes a battery as part of its many functions. Even more fanciful, it may actually create two batteries, one to guide growth in the left half of the body and one for the right side.

It is suggested that this "battery-like state" is the function of biochemical reactions, just the same as the electricity from a car battery emanates from a chemical reaction. In my patient, her malnutrition had excited the computer so that the two halves of her body were controlled differently. This is not too surprising when we remember that the higher brain controls the opposite side of the body for its motor function. A stroke on the right side of this part of the brain produces paralysis in the left half of the body.

The reason that I believe this asymmetry to be an early function is that growth from the very beginning of life in an individual is still a mysterious process. Why does an early human embryo form tiny buds which become the limbs? Something guides the process, obviously. It would make some sense to conclude that this process is electrical in nature.

In the 1930s, a doctor named Adie described a number of patients who had asymmetric pupil size in the two eyes. They also had differences in their right-sided and left-sided reflexes. I have also seen a case, similar to that which has been described in medical literature, where a young boy had one half of his body bigger than the other. It was difficult to tell whether the small side or the big side was abnormal.

I have become very much aware that, although asymmetry is something seen in most people, asymmetric function is exaggerated by bad diet. I believe nutrition and the therapeutic use of nutrient elements to be *the* most important thing that we can do for ourselves, no matter what the disease is. But it should also be obvious that one does not make a diagnosis of a disease and then apply "the appropriate vitamin for that disease." The problem to be solved is the biochemical changes in the body that have caused the tissue and organ reactions that may loosely be called—the "hurricane"!

My increasing interest in thiamin led me into many strange situations. For example, there was one little boy about three years of age who was repeatedly admitted to our hospital through the emergency room. He would develop croup, and any mother that has had a small child with croup knows how frightening it is. An irritating cough is accompanied by gradually increasing difficulty in breathing and a loud noise known as stridor. If severe enough, it can produce so much swelling in the mucous membrane lining of the windpipe or larynx that it cuts off respirations and death ensues from suffocation. It is, of course, intensely frightening to the child also, and his panic leads to more swelling in the tissues.

One day, after this child had one of his admissions, the mother came to see me in my office. She sat down heavily, with obvious despair in her face, and said, "Doctor, why do I have four children, all of whom have had repeated, life-threatening croup in the first four years of their lives?"

Each of her children had been repeatedly admitted to the hospital with this problem, producing severe acute stress on the family each time. Certainly, I had no answer for her, but I gave it some thought.

I was aware of a condition in horses called "Roaring Disease." The affected animal eats some foliage from a yew tree, which is known to contain a substance which destroys vitamin B_1 in the intestine. As the animal becomes more deficient in the vitamin, a nerve called the recurrent laryngeal becomes partially paralyzed. This nerve controls a vocal cord, and paralysis of one of the cords results in a roaring noise when the animal tries to neigh. I reasoned that croup was as much of a "nervous" mechanism as anything else and did a test on the child that showed that his system was indeed short of this vitamin. With nothing to lose, I sent him home on large doses of thiamin.

A year later, his mother called me to ask whether she should continue giving him the supplement. I confessed that I had forgotten all about him and asked what the medical history had been. She said that the child had not suffered any more croup, so I suggested that possibly the thiamin had been unnecessary, or perhaps he had outgrown its need. I directed her to stop it. Three weeks later he was readmitted to the hospital with another attack of croup. It is traditional to think of croup as being caused by a viral infection. From that time, however, I have thought of it as an abnormal response to stress as we shall define that word later. The point is that a virus may well be the stressor and is really the trigger to the mechanism of the croup. However, the metabolic machinery has to be marginal for the reaction to occur. Essentially, croup is a metabolic condition, a statement that may be extremely controversial. It is extremely hard to get people to understand the unusual logic of this approach. Scientific medicine in the twentieth century says that you must make the diagnosis, name the disease, and then consider means of killing the disease enemy. Hence the conventional treatment for croup is by means of antibiotics (which have no effect on viruses) and supportive treatment, which may include tracheostomy.

The unconventional approach is to detect what is called, in scientific language, the biochemical lesion. This explains why so many different diseases, classified by custom in medical nomenclature, can actually be treated by means of the same nutrients. It also explains why several people who have the *same* disease may well be treated differently. The illness expresses itself through symptoms, but the same symptoms can be caused by different biochemical lesions. The center of action is the abnormal biochemistry.

Allithiamine

My interest in thiamin (the terminal *e* in *thiamine* has now been dropped for the same reason as *vitamine* became *vitamin*) led me to a form of the vitamin that was discovered in Japan.

It was a curious discovery, as indeed many such discoveries are. As many people are aware, garlic has some profound therapeutic benefits. As in all plants which have biologic effect for either good or ill, there are active principles. For example, the active principle of foxglove leaves is digitalis, an alkaloid which has powerful effects on the heart. It turns out that garlic has a large number of substances in it known as disulfides. Sulfur metabolism in the body is of enormous importance, and disulfides play a significant part in this process. They are used by body cells for regulating certain functions of the cell.

Consider that each cell (there are as many as 100 trillion in the body) is a power unit or factory in its own right. It has to be able to take in nutrients and oxygen, from which it derives its energy. It then has to export its product back into the bloodstream for transport to other parts of the body.

Well, disulfides make it easier for a molecule which contains it to enter a cell. When garlic bulbs are cut with a knife or crushed, an enzyme within the bulb is activated. It causes vitamin B_1, which is present also, to be converted into a disulfide derivative of the vitamin. This natural phenomenon creates a form of thiamin which passes very easily into body cells, where it is vital in enabling the cell to produce its needed energy. Thus it becomes an exquisitely simple way to get vitamin B_1 into the cells which need it.

It has long been a source of interest to me that a much-used folklore treatment for many different ailments was to hang a necklace of cut garlic around the neck or apply a crushed garlic poultice to the feet. Disulfide derivatives in garlic are now known to pass through the skin into the body, so this ancient procedure now makes sense in the light of our modern knowledge of this interesting plant.

Thiamin that we obtain from our food is in a form which makes it soluble in water. It has to be actively transported into body cells by means of an enzyme in the cell membrane. Its absorption into the body is therefore somewhat limited. A very large dose is required if it is used therapeutically. It was mentioned earlier that hundreds of milligrams of it are required daily for months to treat beriberi victims.

The vitamin B_1 that occurs when garlic is cut is known as allithiamine (the terminal *e* was never removed), named after the allium species in which it is formed. Garlic is a member of this species of plants. Its big advantage is that a relatively small dose goes a long way because it is so much more easily absorbed into the body. Because of its ability to pass through the fatty substances that create a kind of waterproofing of each cell, it is also known as fat-soluble thiamin. A Japanese manufacturer synthesized this substance; it has a long and difficult name, so it is known by the initials TTFD.

A very comprehensive series of studies of TTFD by Japanese scientists proved that it is efficacious in a large number of disease conditions and that it is completely safe, even in large doses. Because of complex rules made by the Food and Drug Administration (FDA) this very valuable agent has never been imported into the U.S.A.

I had an idea that I could do some clinical studies with TTFD in order to explore its merits as published by the Japanese. I applied for and obtained an Independent Investigator License (IND), so for many years I have studied this remarkable agent. With it, I have been successful in helping large numbers of people. There is no magic to it. It simply boosts energy chemistry and that energy is used by cells within the deprived tissue to repair themselves and to create a greater degree of energy efficiency. It is the disulfide that enables the molecule to be easily absorbed into cells. It has been suggested by Japanese investigators that this also gives it some additional therapeutic properties other than those of vitamin B_1, but this has not been completely settled.

Medical tradition has established the rule that any drug to be tested clinically is given to the experimental human subjects under what is called double-blind, controlled conditions. This means that both the patient and the physician are "blind" to whether the subject is receiving the authentic compound or an imitation of it known as a placebo. A placebo has no active principle in it and is therefore designed to fool the patient as to whether he is receiving the real thing or not. He may believe that the placebo is giving him benefit, and in all drug trials a certain number of people do better on the placebo than on the authentic drug. This is, of course, an exposure of the power of the mind and is a supremely important factor in the doctor/patient relationship. We do better if we believe in the treatment.

I attempted to carry out double-blind studies and found that they did not work, for several reasons. First, TTFD makes the urine turn a tell-tale bright yellow, for completely harmless reasons. Secondly, if TTFD were given first, the nutritional effect would last over into and affect the placebo period. That meant that I would have to give the placebo first to all the study patients; thus I would no longer be "blind." Lastly, nutrient substances work very slowly because they are addressing the cause of the problem and not just treating symptoms. Neither do they work singly, for each vitamin is a member of a large nutrient team.

I had to find new ways of testing the efficacy of TTFD, or any other nutrient approach. The best way of proving it is to find a blood test that is abnormal, give the nutrient or nutrients, and correlate its improvement with the way that the patient feels clinically.

Over the years I have been impressed by several facts. The patient slowly but surely feels better over a relatively long period. The proof of efficacy can be detected only by biochemical testing. If clinical improvement is correlated with biochemical improvement, there is a pretty good chance that a physician is fooling neither the patient nor himself.

I have seen some remarkable improvements in many different diseases. These have often been conditions for which medicine has no answers. It will be remembered that we used to have epidemics of a disease called Reye's syndrome. This disease is lethal in almost every case and it was, for a long time, believed to be associated with outbreaks of flu. It sometimes occurred after other viral diseases such as chicken pox or mononucleosis. Eventually it was recognized that it was caused by aspirin that was frequently used to treat various aspects of the viral disease such as fever.

We would expect an outbreak of Reye's syndrome in the flu season, usually in the early spring or late winter season. The history of the disease in an individual child is much the same from case to case. The child suddenly starts vomiting in the later stages of his viral illness, rapidly becomes increasingly lethargic, and goes into a coma. The mechanisms for controlling automatic functions such as breathing usually becomes compromised and death occurs, sometimes within hours. The disease was considered to be a neurological one since it affected the brain, and the treatment was invariably under the care of a pediatric neurologist.

My interest in this scourge was that there were always signs of some crisis in energy metabolism. Urine from affected children had extremely abnormal amino acid patterns. I recall that another pediatrician who was interested in metabolic disease had told us that these patterns were similar to those seen in urine from children with aspirin poisoning. Unfortunately, at the time, which was years before there was an official recognition of its association with aspirin, we did not take too much notice.

Even so, it was clear to me that this was a metabolic disease and that there must be some kind of association with nutritional factors. The disease is always so critical that it was very hard for anyone to sit down with the parents and discuss the child's diet. In several cases where I was able to do so I had learned that the child was indeed a "junk food junkie," but it was not sufficient evidence to be able to relate diet as a risk factor for the disease in general.

Because I was convinced that energy played a very great part in this horrible situation, I had the opportunity to treat one child with TTFD. The patient was an eighteen-month-old girl who was admitted to the hospital in a coma because of Reye's syndrome. She received conventional emergency treatment under the care of a pediatric neurologist. As in most cases, this treatment did not have any effect, and within a few days she was in a state of coma which required a machine to breathe for her. I remember the neurologist bringing in a visiting colleague and demonstrating the neurologic findings on this child. He mentioned that her chances of recovery were virtually zero.

I was the general pediatrician on the case, number two on the team, and my function was to stand by and help the experts. Here she was with death as the expected outcome and no treatment available. TTFD was available, and I knew it to be harmless and nontoxic; I could not do her any harm. What was there to lose?

I began giving her enormous doses of the vitamin. Since she was in a coma, some of it was given as tablets that were crushed and then flushed down a tube into the stomach. Other equally large doses were given intravenously. The first thing that was visible was that the lip vermilion became bright red and there were "roses" in her cheeks. This meant that oxygen was being more appropriately used in the tissues and I hoped, of course, that this would be happening in her brain. In fact, this was exactly what seemed to be happening, because over the next week or so she slowly recovered and eventually walked out of the hospital.

During the recovery phase she passed through a stage known as *coma vigilum*. She was unconscious but would fix her eyes on an observer's face and track him as he moved in front of her. She could swallow food and would respond to stimulus such as tickling. I began to understand that this condition represented the recovery of that part of the brain which we are calling the computer. When this child eventually reached school age she behaved in very bizarre fashion; she would suddenly get up from her desk and hit another child, or she would wander around the class and was unable to learn properly. She had sustained permanent damage to the involuntary brain.

I have described this case in some detail to illustrate what I believe to be a fundamental principle. Health can be defined as an intact brain/body machine (the human organism) in which the *utilization* of oxygen for the delivery of energy is in the normal range of efficiency. Notice the critical word, *utilization*. If oxygen is delivered to the tissues by the blood, but individual cells are unable to use it, the situation is equivalent to there being no oxygen present. This use of the oxygen is called *oxidation* and is a vital phenomenon to be discussed later.

What I am trying to illustrate here is the essential learning process that I have had to go through in order to have confidence in nutritional therapy as a practical approach to virtually any disease to which the human being is prone. Most of our diseases are brought upon ourselves by widespread cultural activities such as smoking, bad diet, and over-use of alcohol, caffeine, and soft drinks. Although we will deal with this concept in more detail in association with oxidation, it is a principle that should be emphasized repeatedly as I try to show the reader a different way of thinking about health and why and how we lose it by default.

Another patient was a ten-year-old boy who had experienced more than thirty episodes of a disease which behaved like Reye's syndrome. From each of these he had made a spontaneous recovery. A brother had died from a disease that behaved like this, and a sibling had experienced something which has been called rheumatoid arthritis, which had remitted spontaneously.

I was involved with two of these mysterious attacks, and I remember the situation vividly. In the first of these he had been admitted to the hospital in a coma. Since nobody had the slightest idea what this disease was, and since he usually recovered spontaneously, I merely collected his urine continuously. When it was analyzed, it became obvious that there was a progressive improvement in his body chemistry and he did recover without being provided with any treatment.

The second episode was more dramatic. His situation was considered to be so critical that his parents had him brought to our hospital by helicopter. He was comatose again, and on this occasion I used the information that I had obtained from his former admission. I collected urine throughout the episode while administering TTFD. There was a dramatic response, and he recovered completely. It is immediately obvious that TTFD could not be proved to have been "responsible" in the traditional analysis of a "cure." However, when the pattern of the urine tests was examined, it was clear that there had been a rapid improvement as soon as the TTFD was started. I think that it was legitimate to conclude that the illness had been influenced and recovery hastened.

These repeated spontaneously-occurring episodes had been previously reported as "recurrent Reye's syndrome" but, to my knowledge, nothing like this had been written about. We were truly dealing with the unknown. My metabolic tests had said that the metabolic engine was running badly, but they did not tell me precisely why. However, since I had demonstrated the fact that

TTFD had apparently helped the recovery of one of these frightening illnesses, I suggested to the parents that the boy should continue to take a preventive dose of the vitamin.

It is incredibly hard to educate a parent into an understanding of the principles involved. They saw their child as having a disease which doctors could not understand or name. They gave him the tablets for a while but apparently discontinued them for unknown reasons. The next episode of his illness was lethal. He was rushed to the nearest hospital, where he died. An autopsy was carried out but was quite inadequate to obtain the valuable information that might have been acquired if it had been done properly. This was so even though I had called the pathologist at the hospital to explain his bizarre history.

Tradition puts us into a straight-jacket and medicine is just as much guided by tradition as anything else. Unfortunately, the rigidity imposed by that tradition makes it very difficult for us to accept innovation. It prevents us from learning from our own mistakes. When the experience is new, we try to fit it into the mold. When it does not fit, we try to fit it in by rationalizing its misfit so that it does conform. It is difficult for us to see that the mold, not the experience, may be the problem.

Chapter 6

Adaptive Mechanisms

The word *adapt* usually conjures up the concept of evolution. Darwin, in his *Origin of Species*, provided evidence that animals evolve over millions of years by means of gene mutations. They change in order to meet environmental pressures, and this kind of mutation occurs once every million years or so.

It is not my intention to discuss the argument that still rages between the evolutionists and the creationists. However, one thing is absolutely certain: the human body is made up of individual units called cells. Everyone today knows this fact, but in my discussions with patients, I have found that there is only the vaguest notion of what this really means. What, indeed, is a cell?

The human is a member of the animal kingdom, and our nearest relatives are the great apes. Biologically, we are classified as multicellular organisms. Contemplation of this concept has given me many hours of thought about the *why* of our existence, something with which many philosophers have struggled throughout the ages. The seventeenth-century philosopher Descartes thought of the human body as a machine; indeed, it most certainly is when you get down to the pragmatic issues of health and disease.

I have a somewhat fanciful vision of what evolution is. Anyone with even the most superficial thoughts must be forcefully impressed by the beauty of the intricate patterns which are found in nature, literally everywhere you look. Nothing seems to clash, and there is always a delicate balance that is struck—that is, if man does not come along and superimpose his selfish whims and prejudices.

The colors are right for our eyes, and the indescribable beauty seems to have been made specifically for our pleasure. Anyone who has been scuba diving or snorkeling must have been overwhelmed by the colorful beauty which lies under the surface of the ocean, normally completely hidden from us. The question that I ask myself is this: do the fish, that are themselves exquisitely colorful, "enjoy" the beauty of their surroundings? When we study their environment, we find that it is a very dangerous place for all of them. To eat, to be eaten, and to procreate are the only things that really matter down there. Why is it so beautiful to our eyes when we were never intended to see it?

This exquisite pattern, of which we are a part, either was designed or happened purely by chance. Since it is so complex and the natural jigsaw puzzle fits always so neatly, I have preferred to think of it as having been designed. This immediately brings me into contact with the concept of God. Of course, it is this mystery which pervades the whole picture which originally gave rise to worship when man had developed a brain which was complex enough to be able to appreciate the wonder of it all. My personal concept of God is one that I have struggled with a great deal, as have many others. I believe that our finite minds cannot really grasp the infinite. With our very limited and primitive vision, we have to substitute symbols to represent what ends.

Ancient people had a very rational approach in their worship of the sun, "the giver of life." In medieval times, God was often pictured as an elderly gentleman with a long grey beard, a symbol for both wisdom and antiquity. I have a personal picture of an inveterate experimenter, Mother Nature, seeking some kind of perfection for her creation. I have devoted some words to this idea because it creates a picture in the mind. Mother Nature is working in her laboratory; I will call her MN from this point on.

When she invented the first live cell, one can imagine that MN was pleased. This kind of cell, known in biology as a one-celled organism, has as its only responsibility to nourish itself and procreate. Such a cell still exists; it is known as an amoeba and it lives in natural collections of water such as ponds. It is completely dependent upon water, just as our bodies are. These cells collect together if the pond dries up, creating a kind of gelatin which gives each of the cells a chance to survive. When the water returns, they separate and go their own way.

This, in the fanciful experiment envisaged, is MN's first effort at helping her invention to survive. She had said that if these one-celled organisms got together in a crisis situation, they had a better chance. It was, in fact, perhaps the earliest experiment with a multi-celled organism.

Perhaps MN then looked at this situation and said," Well, perhaps if we get some of these one-celled organisms to specialize, maybe each one could take on a different function and all could work together." Various additional experiments were then undertaken in order to invent specialization.

A very early success was the development of a tiny animal called a hydra. Here, specialization is in a relatively primitive state. The hydra consists of a little tube, with an opening, called a stoma, at one end. The inside of the tube, called the celom, is lined with cells which are capable of carrying out digestion of particles as they come into the celom. Around the stoma are several arms which wave in such a way that a minute current of fluid wafts particles of food through the stoma into the celom. This is a primitive multi-celled organism in which some cells have specialized in digestion and some in providing the arms with the capacity for movement.

It is relatively easy to follow this line of reasoning, seeing each organism as the achievement of another experiment. Now let us look at an earthworm, which is much more complex. It is built with the ability to crawl or slither by means of muscular contractions. It has a straight bowel which takes in soil at the mouth, or stoma, and ejects it at the anus at the other end. Special cells in the bowel undertake the process of digestion, extracting nutrients from the soil as it passes through.

The earthworm has a nervous system. A cord of nervous tissue runs from one end to the other, starting at the front end with two little knobs of tissue that represent the brain. These are the coordination centers which receive incoming messages from the body and send out executive signals that result in function. The worm is built in compartments or segments and, within each segment, a nerve branch goes out from the main cord to distribute tiny nerves to the entire segment. It has a communication system which is directed and coordinated by a primitive brain.

Does this worm "know" that it is alive? Does it feel the pain when we tread on it? Yes, it squirms and wriggles intensely and intuitively we feel sorry that we have trodden on it (that is, if we think about it at all) because we can observe its reaction to pain. But of course we do not know. We cannot communicate with it in any way, so we have absolutely no idea how much conscious awareness it has. Now that we know so much about brain function, it would be very surprising indeed to find consciousness in the earthworm because the brain is not big enough and it has not obtained the degree of specialization that is required. This kind of reasoning suggests that each advance made in developing a new animal was an original experiment in design. We believe that man is the most intelligent creature on earth, but we do not know for sure. The brain of an elephant, for example, is very complex, as it is in whales and dolphins. But unless we can find ways and means of communication, we cannot know with certainty how intelligent or how aware these animals are.

As we climb the evolutionary tree, the complexity and diversity becomes ever more spectacular. What is MN striving for? Again, we have not the faintest idea. However, if we accept that we are guinea pigs in the laboratory of MN, we begin to formulate some of the basic principles of our place within the animal kingdom. Have we, in fact, been selected as the major guinea pig, to go on to a greater and greater potential of achievement?

My own thoughts suggest to me that, since we are ruining our world, that we have reached a relatively primitive state of evolution—a state of transition between no conscious awareness and a super-conscious awareness. If that is so, at what developmental level in the animal kingdom can consciousness be found? When, in the evolutionary tree, does an animal become aware of itself? Are our brains not yet big enough for us to do something about our increasingly dangerous environment? Are we destined to destroy ourselves and disappear from the face of the earth? The dinosaurs, with their relatively small brains, lasted 200 million years. We have done more harm to the earth in several thousand years than they did in their 200 million. Is this because we have been clever enough to preserve our species by artificial means but have not enough brain capacity to use wisdom? In other words, has the development of the human brain been a handicap to us, in the long run?

I believe that we are selected for greater things if we are able to survive as a species long enough. I do not think that the brain is a handicap. It has made homo sapiens a very successful experiment, but this stage of transition may be too dangerous for our ultimate survival.

Let us continue the experimental theme of MN. I like to think of "her" in finite terms and the only way I can do that in my own mind is to see her as a kind of glorified "person." In that case, she may want her top guinea pig to develop to a state where he, amongst all the species of the earth, can at least perceive the intricate beauty of her designs. That would explain why we can see beauty under the surface of the ocean, even though it was not designed for our benefit. In strictly human terms, an experimenter likes to have his inventions admired.

I also see MN as a very strict disciplinarian. Her experiments have given rise to the latest model, homo sapiens, and she is trying to coax us through this transitional phase without us wrecking the course of the experiment—at least on this planet! As a mechanic, she is fantastic; she invented the computer long before her guinea pig did.

The Computer

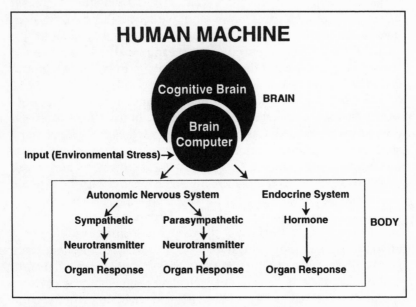

Figure 1.

It seems very logical to me that the human body, being as complex as it is, must be equipped with a computer to keep it all together. Remember that we have evolved into a most sophisticated machine, consisting of up to 100 trillion highly specialized one-celled organisms. Each cell in the human body might be seen as having been derived from the amoeba or its ancestor. These cells have "agreed" to stick together in groups as they become more and more highly specialized, thus forming organs.

Could we see the human body as a kind of city with 100 trillion inhabitants? If each of the citizens went his own way without a central government, there would be chaos and anarchy. So the brain is made up of those citizens that, collectively, became the governing body of the whole organism. That means, of course, that absolutely nothing can happen to the body citizens without the government being notified. In order to do this, MN developed an extremely complex communications system.

Let us start with the brain. Exquisitely complex as it is, we can easily see that even if it is not one big computer, certainly part of it is. The part that I shall call the computer from here on is known as the limbic system, which is the first factor that we must grasp.

Every mammal known has a brain plan which is similar, though certain parts of it have become more highly developed in various species to direct specific activities peculiar to the habitat of that species. The evidence for a process of evolution is enormous. For functional purposes, I try to indicate that the computer is the "primitive man." Freud called this part of the brain the subconscious, but then computers had not been invented in his lifetime.

Let us think a little while what is meant by *primitive man*. This is the part of the brain that we had before we evolved into humans. It continues to direct a colossal amount of our activity. It is responsible for the sensations that we call hunger, thirst, sex-drive, and, in fact, all the instincts that we possess. It is sometimes referred to as the reptilian system, because that is all the brain that a reptile possesses.

It is extremely important, in my view, to give this part of the human brain its proper place. For example, we do not wake up on a Monday morning and say, "I wonder what kind of emotion I will produce today—should it be anger, depression, hostility, happiness—or what?" No, an emotion is a sensation that is produced as a result of chemical reactions that occur in the computer when a given stimulus is perceived. Because we have been taught by common experience, we recognize the sensation as the result of a certain kind of stimulus. An insult produces a reaction perceived as a sensation called anger. A kind word results in another chemical reaction called happiness or pleasure—and so forth.

It is very important that we understand that messages from this part of the brain will also go to the body so that an appropriate physical reaction will accompany the emotion. For example, an insulted male may strike an aggressive pose or may even punch the person who issued the insult. A female may react differently, but all of us react in the ways dictated by our training, personality, and sex. The reaction may be so overwhelming that the conscious or cognitive brain is barely aware of the action being dictated by the computer.

The Cognitive Brain

Although I have introduced a considerable amount of over-simplification, the computer is the lower brain and the cognitive is the higher brain. Cognitive comes from the Latin *cogno*, meaning *I know.* It is the brain that gives us conscious awareness, can decipher beauty from ugliness, deals with abstract phenomena such as mathematics, and is the evolutionary addition that has given us the incredible gift of intelligence.

The question that I ask myself frequently is whether this part of the brain is a computer as well. Is the whole brain, consisting of these two functional components, really a computer? If that is so, then intelligence is little more than a vast build-up of complex reflexes which are conditioned by our experience and training. Is there such a thing as free will? Are our choices delusionary, in the sense that they are merely massive reflexes? As my theme is developed, I believe that many people will certainly think about it, even if they completely reject the concept.

For the purposes of this book, which makes no pretense to address philosophy, let us leave out the cognitive brain and call it something that we still do not understand. From a functional point of view, this part of the brain acts as an advisor to the computer. It is the rational brain, the part that retains the memory of experience, the creator of the civilized person that owns it. Shortly, we must consider how these two brains talk to each other and why. When they are properly integrated, they represent intelligence.

If the two parts of the brain are functionally separated, we have a "mad" person whose irrational acts are driven by the primitive computer. Hence, violent or senseless crime, or even vandalism, is possible in a person whose cognitive brain "goes blind" and leaves the computer to its own devices. We have every reason to believe that the computer can become so trigger-happy that it can overwhelm the rational cognitive brain and the person may be described in colloquial language as "seeing red."

I remember an extremely brutal rape-murder that took place many years ago. The victim, a ten-year-old girl, was stabbed with a pen knife several hundred times. The coroner said that the degree of brutality was beyond his previous experience. The murderer was a twenty-four-year-old man who left such a trail of blood that the police merely followed it to his apartment and arrested him. When they took him to the morgue to face him with what he had done, he categorically denied that he had committed the crime. I remember that the report in the paper mentioned that a great many pop bottles had been found in his car, a reference to his dissolute life.

Nobody would possibly believe that the man may well have been telling the truth—that he did not know that he had committed this crime. We may use it as an example of what I believe to be not nearly as rare as we care to think. Let me construct a scenario which might give a rational explanation in terms of the two-part brain. Suppose that this man hated his mother, not a terribly uncommon human trait, unfortunate as it may seem. He takes the child into the bushes to rape her, a computer urge which is "permitted" by the cognitive brain. During the sexual act the sensory stimuli that go into his pleasure centers in the computer eventually overwhelm him, shutting off advice and consent from cognitive function. He "sees red" as the saying goes, and he commits murder with his mother's image as the target. As I see it, it is only a little different from sleepwalking. However, the essential difference is that the computer can be made to be trigger-happy by malnutrition, involving high-calorie junk food and drink, including soft drinks and alcohol. This dreadful murder that I have described may have been directly related to the murderer's nutrition. That is why I was so interested in the newspaper report about the soft drink bottles found in his car.

What has all this to do with adaptation? We started this chapter with a reference to Darwinian or genetic adaptation. But we must consider the mechanisms of adaptation on an everyday basis. How does a human being adapt to the cold, to heat, to darkness, to the rigorous and forceful changes of an essentially hostile environment? His body is really an instrument upon which his computer plays, in much the same way as a conductor plays an orchestra. Each instrument in the orchestra is controlled by a player, but the total result of the orchestral effort is a symphony only because each player follows the overall direction of the conductor. In the case of the human body, the conductor is the computer and the organs in the body represent the instrumentalists. The behavior of the person is the symphony.

Circadian Rhythm

Most people today know that a person who flies to Europe in a jet is prone to jet lag. What *is* jet lag? Our computers regulate the functions of the body by a shifting day/night rhythm. Circadian means "about twenty-four hours" and body activity is relatively increased by day compared with night. Imagine a car which is put away in the garage overnight. The engine is stopped since fuel consumption is saved. We obviously cannot stop the engines of the body so the computer just cuts down their activity, also to conserve unnecessary energy waste. At about 4AM, the computer starts awakening the body orchestra to meet the new day's activities, and fuel consumption is increased. This is circadian rhythm. When we travel quickly to a new time zone, our brain-controlled rhythm must adapt to a different day/night rhythm. Until this happens, the computer is out of synch with the environment. It will adapt the body to nighttime during the day and vice versa at night. Hence, during waking hours the jet lag victim will be totally maladapted to normal daytime responsibilities and decisions. Jet lag is a little like the sensation that is felt by anyone, such as a physician, who is awakened in the small hours of the morning from a deep sleep in order to carry out some definitive action.

What is it that resets the computer, putting it back in synch? The answer is light from the sun, contrasted with the darkness of night. Light rays, entering the eye, stimulate the retina, which sends messages back to a gland known as the pineal which then adapts the computer to a light/dark schedule. As winter approaches in both the northern and southern hemispheres, the nights become longer and the days shorter, so the computer makes the necessary gradual adjustments which constitute an extremely important adaptive mechanism. Although the symptoms of jet lag last only a day or so for most people, it actually takes about three weeks for circadian rhythm to readapt completely to a new time zone. As part of a preventive health regimen, the Incas would deliberately look at the sun in the morning to get a charge from its rays. It is hardly surprising that sun worship was practiced by many of our ancestors.

Later, I hope to show why circadian rhythm is so important to our overall health patterns. It is quite easy to see that a work place involving swing shifts might be detrimental to some people since the day/night stimulus is constantly changing. What is to be stressed is that this kind of adaptive response is much smoother when our body chemistry is in good shape through good nutrition. Healthy body chemistry is the reason some people can travel and not develop much jet lag.

I must mention one last thing about circadian rhythm which illustrates to me the wonderful pattern that exists in our relationship with our environment. Experiments have been conducted with a volunteer living in an underground room, so that he was separated from the natural alternating rhythm of darkness by night and sunlight by day. These experiments revealed the curious fact that the unstimulated rhythm of the brain under these circumstances revolves through twenty-five hours instead of the expected twenty-four hours.

Although the reason for this is unknown, it is possible to formulate a theoretical explanation. Since we live in a twenty-four-hour day, the alternating stimulus of darkness and light forces the natural, but unstimulated, twenty-five-hour rhythm to adapt to that of our world. It is as though MN has deliberately equipped us each with brain rhythm that is always being challenged by our very existence. I see it as a discipline imposed on us which says, in essence, "Adapt and keep on adapting or reap the consequences!" Since failure to carry out this adaptive process affects the function of the brain computer, it inevitably causes health changes. It is another stress imposed upon us that forces us to obey. Perhaps on another planet, where life may exist in another part of our galaxy, the day is longer or shorter than that of our world. The creatures may then have a circadian rhythm that conforms to that of this different world.

Returning our attention to life on this planet, it is to be noted that this rhythm does not change much at the equator. The shifting relationship between day and night is greater and greater as we travel further north or south. The pineal gland, which controls this adaptation, is therefore more stressed as one moves further south or north.

Now that we have considered the master computer, we have to consider how the "body citizens" must be told what to do and when to do it—how they are instructed to carry out the process of adaptation on a day-by-day basis.

The Endocrine System

I must begin by making a blunt statement that the body is nothing more than a complex dumb instrument upon which the computer plays its ever-shifting role. To return to the analogy of the orchestra, each instrumentalist is a living creature. He plays an instrument with all the skill that it demands. We could say, then, that any instrumentalist has a discrete and ordered ability in his own right. The quality of the music produced by each instrumentalist is a personal characteristic, but in order to create the ultimate symphony each must obey the directions from the conductor.

This is an obvious analogy to illustrate that any organ within the body also has autonomous and self-regulatory mechanisms built in. The organ responds to the signal that is sent from the computer, and it will operate in the way that it is instructed until another signal turns it off.

The endocrine system is a fancy term for a whole group of glands in the body—the thyroid, the adrenal, the pituitary, and so forth. Each of these glands is equipped to produce a chemical substance known as a *hormone.* It is secreted from the gland and travels in the bloodstream. When it gets to other organs within the body, it locks in like a spaceship docking to a satellite, and it gives the receiving organ a signal which makes the organ go to work. One can say that the hormone is merely a messenger sent by the computer to carry out its desired aim, which is essentially adaptive in nature.

The action of the computer can be illustrated with reference to the endocrine system by turning our attention to the menstrual cycle in a healthy woman. We have mentioned the daily rhythm of the computer, but it also has a twenty-eight-day rhythm, at least in the female. It is not known whether the twenty-eight-day cycle is coincident with the lunar cycle or whether the gravitational force of the moon does have an effect upon the menstrual cycle. It is fairly well-known that emergency rooms are filled with patients when the moon is full, so this gravitational force does affect the human computer. We will examine later whether or not this effect on a person is normal.

When the computer gets to the point in time to begin the cycle, a message goes to the glands involved and appropriate hormones, particularly estrogen, are released. Here we come to an important point, because the computer is also signalled by the circulating hormone. This constitutes a biofeedback system that enables the computer to control the concentration of circulating hormone. At mid-cycle, estrogen is replaced by progesterone, which is controlled in the same way.

In this way, the various events in the cycle, including ovulation and menstruation, are controlled by the computer, which is able to regulate hormonal concentration through the biofeedback loop system. If we measure concentrations of hormones in the blood at different times within the cycle, we find that they are complexly increased and decreased by the regulatory action of the computer. Of course, the menstrual periods can be manipulated by pills given by mouth, but it is obvious that, if the hormones are provided in this way, the functions of this biofeedback loop system are jeopardized. The tail of the dog is wagging the dog. In the next chapter, we will examine how this therapeutic (or social) interference may have far-reaching detrimental effects.

It is important to draw attention to this example of the endocrine system at work. The menstrual cycle is of enormous complexity, but it is the computer that must be in charge of it. Consider that the biology of this cycle is related closely to the act of procreation, the most important event in any organism from the standpoint of evolution. However, it is clear that every other gland in the endocrine system is under the basic control of the computer and each can be seen as part of an adaptive reaction by which we make proper adjustments in our physiology in order to survive and run the whole machine properly.

The Autonomic System

The hormone messengers make gross adjustments to the adaptive machinery. The autonomic system may be seen as carrying out the fine adjustments. Because this system is controlled by the computer, it is entirely automatic under usual conditions. Some people, by using advanced mental techniques, can learn to control it voluntarily and there are some people who can actually stop and restart the beating action of the heart. But under usual conditions it is entirely automatic.

It consists of two parts, known as the sympathetic and the parasympathetic components, although there is no need to be concerned about the names. They can be thought of as a double telephone line which goes from the computer to all tissues in the body. One telephone line causes an organ to perform in a manner exactly opposite to that ordered by the other one.

The easiest organ response to understand is that of the heart because we know when it is beating unusually fast, that this is an effect produced by activity of the sympathetic component which dominates the physical situation. When sympathetic and parasympathetic stimulation is withdrawn, the heart will beat at a speed intermediate between slow and fast. This stability is maintained when a person is at rest and the pulse is said to be a "resting pulse."

The moment that the computer senses a need for either mental of physical activity, it accelerates the heart accordingly. The computer is exceedingly sophisticated and it will calibrate the speed of the heart to the oxygen needs of the now-activated organism. Under normal conditions, the speed of the heart exactly matches the amount of oxygenated blood required to meet the degree of mental or physical activity that is required. When the action is completed, the computer decreases sympathetic activity and the physiology of the person goes into homeostasis, the name that is sometimes used to indicate the resting state.

The Fight-or-Flight Reflex

Let us imagine a hypothetical cave man, one of our ancestors. He is living in a natural state which preceded civilization. One morning, he leaves his cave and sees a saber-toothed tiger. Light rays from the tiger enter the man's eye and stimulate his retina. This, in turn, sends a signal to the brain, which interprets it as indicating the immediate presence of a tiger. Experience has taught his brain to remember that tigers are dangerous. The computer is then signalled to instigate a survival mechanism that is known as the fight-or-flight reflex.

This reflex is designed to put the man into a state of maximal activity so that he can either kill the tiger or get away and perhaps climb a tree. His brain becomes ultra-clear and extremely perceptive. The pupils of his eyes dilate for greater visual perception, and his field of vision is expanded. He has a sensation of fear or excitement, and his heart begins to beat faster to pump oxygenated blood to all parts of the body. Muscles are put into state of tone and his digestive mechanisms are paralyzed, for there is no need of digestion in a time of crisis. If we were to look closely at his skin, we would see that it is covered in goose bumps, achieved by tiny muscles that operate on skin follicles which contain only minute hairs that stand up, or become erect. His physical capacity is enhanced far above his usual and he can become "superhuman."

This reflex is designed only for short-term response to enable the man to perform his victorious kill or to escape. It is enormously energy-consuming, and after the necessary action has resulted in survival he will be fatigued but satisfied with himself and elated. Now the computer turns on the parasympathetic component. His appetite and bowel action return, and he can relax. Sleep will result in restoration of his store of energy.

Modern man is equipped with exactly the same system as his ancestor the cave man. But civilization has put us into a very different environment. The telephone, traffic, deadlines, business confrontations—all the trappings of civilization—have replaced the tiger. This is part of the stress that modern man has to deal with. His fight-or-flight reflex is not as suitable for dealing with it. He cannot run away from the tiger. Neither can he kill it.

It is important to note that the fight-or-flight reflex is a *preparation* for supreme activity. The resolution of the reflex comes from the action which follows. The athlete is one of the few modern examples of the reflex being used for its original purpose as a physical outlet. Note that the entire reflex is controlled and coordinated by the action of the computer, even though the action is purely physical. Roger Bannister declared that the four-minute mile was a mental barrier, not so much a physical one, though obviously physical perfection was a necessity also.

Other Messenger Systems

I have indicated that the process of adaptation is a coordinated brain/body relationship accomplished by messengers. The endocrine messengers are hormones. The messengers of the autonomic nervous system are chemical substances known as neurotransmitters. There is, as we well know, a nervous system that is controlled by the cognitive brain. This is known as the voluntary nervous system; it enables us to move the trunk and limbs of the body at will by using those muscles which are termed *voluntary*. Both the autonomic and voluntary systems depend upon a chemical messenger called acetyl choline, though there are other neurotransmitters.I have already indicated that the willed mental process still remains mysterious; this is not the nervous system that we are dealing with in our discussion here. Rather, it is the autonomic system which is controlled by the computer with which we are concerned. Again, this is automatic and is not normally operated at will.

The subject of neurotransmitters is very complex indeed, if we examine its mechanisms in chemical detail, but it can be described relatively simply. An input message comes to the computer from outside the body and is referred to as an environmental stressor. The information—either physical or mental—is "data processed" in the computer, which has to make a decision whether adjustments in the body or brain are a necessary response. Input information comes into the computer also from the various organs in the body. The computer has to be notified of everything and anything that happens, inside or outside, since it has to cause the adaptive responses.

Let us refer to examples already mentioned. Sweating may occur if the stressor is an upward temperature change in the environment, shivering if it is a downward change. Either one is an adaptive change in body function which is automated by the computer. The executive signal that is sent out from the computer goes through the appropriate branch of the autonomic nervous system to the organ which carries out the response to the command. When a message of this nature arrives at the end of the nerve where it connects with the responsive body organ, a chemical substance called a neurotransmitter is released. This substance actually works by converting chemical energy to electrical energy and is therefore really an *energy transducer*. The electrical energy gives rise to an extremely complex process which activates the organ, such as a gland, which begins to respond. Hence, it is really a slave to the orders of the computer.

The input signal may come, as we mentioned above, from within the body. When food goes into the stomach, for example, messages go into the computer to notify it of the arrival of the food. This signal is intensified as the stomach fills with food, and the computer eventually reaches a threshold when it indicates that the stomach is full. The person has a sensation of fullness or satiety, a sensation with which all of us are familiar. Note, however, that it is the brain computer that gives rise to the sensation, not the stomach. In some mentally retarded people, this signal is not properly functioning, and they have a compulsion to eat and eat. Since the satiety mechanism does not operate, the individual may then vomit and, having emptied the stomach, goes back to eating again. I remember a severely retarded adult who was housed in an institution. She lay perpetually in a crib, naked and with no bedclothes. This unfortunate person had a totally abnormal reflex computer mechanism. If her attendants gave her bedclothes, she would try to eat them. The same thing would happen with a nightdress. The only way to deal with her was to keep her naked, even though that seemed cruel to the casual observer.

Another complex mechanism is known as the gastro-colic reflex. The input signal from the stomach goes to the computer. An executive signal goes to the part of the bowel known as the colon, where fecal material is stored prior to periodic disposal in the form of bowel movements. This signal causes the bowel to start its slow wave pattern of propulsion known as peristalsis. The contents of the colon are thus propelled toward the rectum, where input signals to the computer are sensed as a need for a visit to the bathroom. This process explains why many people have a bowel movement following a meal and the gastro-colic reflex can be trained by habit, so that the reaction may take place on a time schedule such as 8:30AM after breakfast, for example.

These hormones and neurotransmitters were named as "the first messenger" by Sutherland in his Nobel-Prize-winning work. He discovered that activity within cells was turned on by an additional messenger which occurs within each cell. He called this "the second messenger." The functions of adaptation depend completely upon these mechanisms working appropriately to produce a coordinated brain/body response. If they are working properly, the adaptive responses are smooth, harmonious, and efficient and occur, of course, completely unconsciously. We automatically adjust to hot, cold, barometric pressure, humidity, gravity, and all the other forces of the environment, hardly giving them a thought. The cognitive brain is free to preside over other purposes which are the sophisticated thoughts and actions that take care of the business of the day.

We will see later how such reactions give rise to sensations called *symptoms* when they become exaggerated or defective.

We have seen that environmental changes give rise to input signals to the computer. The computer talks to the cognitive brain and automatically adjusts the body and mind to suit the ever-changing scene. In effect, the computer talks to the body and the body talks to the brain. The language is a chemical language; it is very similar to the principle of communication used by insects. When ants meet, their antennae may touch and a chemical substance is passed from one to the other. The chemical signal is interpreted, hence giving rise to an extremely sophisticated form of language.

These totally unconscious reactions, involving hosts of chemical messengers, are responsible for much of human behavior that sometimes seems to be peculiar, even to ourselves. How often do we say, "I wonder why I did that?" Each person is surrounded by an invisible energy field which can cause reactions to other people that may give rise to an instant feeling of liking or disliking when two fields come into contact. There is also evidence for an unconscious mechanism of dominance, or a pecking order, as illustrated by the following experiment.

One dozen people were asked to participate in the experiment. Each subject was seated in front of a window which was obscured by a blind. All he knew was that another person, on the other side of the window, would confront him as the blind was suddenly removed. Cameras were trained on the eyes of each of the two individuals, and a photograph was taken immediately upon the initial impact of confrontation. One of the individuals always averted the eyes, while those of the other remained steady. It was discovered that a pecking order could be distinguished in relation to this quite primitive reflex pattern. Number 1, the head of the pecking order, always caused aversion of the eyes in Number 2, who caused aversion in Number 3, and so on down the line to Number 12. The experiment could be repeated, and the numerical order of dominance was always the same.

Finally, we must discuss how body cells talk to body cells. There is a three-way discourse going on in the body at all times; silent, sophisticated, and enormously complex. The brain talks to the body, the body talks to itself, and the body talks back to the brain. This is a chemical language and, in spite of its awesome complexity, it can be reduced to basic principles. The only point of discussing these physiologic and biochemical details, as far as this book is concerned, is to prepare the reader for what happens when they go wrong. We will be able to see how disease patterns are caused and why our present medical model is so inadequate. Therefore, although the messengers that give information from body cell to body cell are very numerous, for the sake of later discussion of disease, we must specifically discuss the prostaglandins briefly.

Prostaglandins

We have already mentioned that prostaglandins are messengers. The reactions of cells to their messages constitute an important part of internal body language. A simplified diagram is helpful in understanding that these substances are manufactured in the body from fatty acids that we take in with our food. Also, it will enable the reader to understand the use of certain nutrients that are used by physicians and nutritionists to influence this vitally important mechanism.

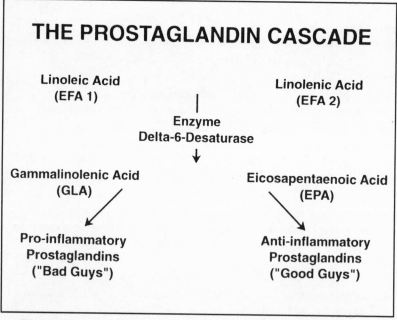

THE PROSTAGLANDIN CASCADE

Linoleic Acid
(EFA 1)

Linolenic Acid
(EFA 2)

Enzyme
Delta-6-Desaturase

Gammalinolenic Acid
(GLA)

Eicosapentaenoic Acid
(EPA)

Pro-inflammatory
Prostaglandins
("Bad Guys")

Anti-inflammatory
Prostaglandins
("Good Guys")

Figure 2.

At the top of Figure 2 we see two nutrient substances which we have called EFA 1 and EFA 2. The initials *EFA* stand for *essential fatty acid*; there are only two of these that are vital to life. Though we take in many different polyunsaturated fatty acids in our food, only two of them are essential. This means that they are *essential to life*, and they cannot be synthesized by the body. Hence the two are sometimes referred to collectively as vitamin F. The name for EFA 1 is alpha-linoleic acid; the name for EFA 2 is alpha-linolenic acid. The first is known as an omega-6 polyunsaturated fatty acid (PUFA). EFA 2 is an omega-3 PUFA. Both are obtained from nuts and seeds; their source will be discussed later.

The next step in processing these two nutrients is that they are each converted to a more complex PUFA by means of an enzyme such as those that we discussed in Chapter 2. The reader will remember that each enzyme is constructed in the body from an inherited mechanism. So this enzyme, which is called delta-6-desaturase, is present in the system when EFA 1 and EFA 2 arrive. This enzyme converts EFA 1 to another PUFA with the initials of GLA, while EFA 2 is converted to one with the initials EPA. These conversions are vital steps in the synthesis of prostaglandins.

A combination of activities, starting with formation of GLA and EPA, gives rise to a whole series of PUFAs which make up a vast family of key substances which create the sophisticated language of the prostaglandin messengers. We do not need to discuss any of the details, only to indicate that there are two families of these compounds produced. One family is called pro-inflammatory; it activates the process of inflammation. The other is anti-inflammatory; it deactivates the process. It is for this reason that the ones which encourage inflammation are sometimes known casually as "the bad guys," whereas the others are termed the "good guys."

The obvious question is: Why should the body ever require inflammation? The answer is, of course, that it is an exquisitely designed mechanism of defense. All of us know that an inflamed area in the body is painful and that it generally means that this reaction is developed to wall off a foe such as a germ that has attacked part of the body. Let us examine it in reference to something that we can all understand. If we see the body as a fortress city of 100 trillion inhabitants, there are microorganisms that attack the fortress. Suppose, in someone's shoe, there is a nail that injures the foot. The "government" in the brain is notified in the form of a message that is interpreted as pain. The first thing that this message does is to alert the person so that he can take off his shoe and ascertain the cause of the pain. Suppose that the wound becomes infected. A staphylococcus gets into the foot and it sets up a local attack in the same way as an invading army might set up a beach-head. The brain is notified of the event through more pain, and a defense reaction is set up. White cell soldiers are rushed to the beach-head to kill the invading army and are themselves killed in action, thus forming the material that we call pus. The beach-head is walled off by the prostaglandin-mediated process of inflammation, thus preventing further invasion by the infecting organisms.

The local war may thus be contained, and the only evidence of it is that the foot remains painful and swollen until the war is over and the invading germs vanquished. There may be a small mound of inflammation, usually called a boil, which comes to a head and exudes pus. A carbuncle is similar but is much bigger and leaks pus from multiple heads. Suppose, however, as sometimes happens, the invading germs are stronger than the defensive militia can contain. Analogous to the Normandy invasion, the germs move on into the bloodstream and cause septicemia. Now the whole organism is endangered, and a generalized reaction is conducted by the computer. White blood cells are produced in the thousands by the bone marrow and the white cell count is found to be increased if it is examined in the laboratory. The patient's temperature goes up, also part of the defensive response, because the efficiency of the invading germs is damaged if they are forced to operate in a higher temperature within the body that they are attacking. Septicemia was a much more dangerous illness before antibiotics. However, it is still a war and there is only one winner. The brain is as much involved in the action as the body, and it is sometimes *more* involved.

Yin and Yang

The ancient Chinese formulated a philosophy which recognized that nothing was absolute in itself. Everything in the universe is relative to something else. To simplify the philosophy, Yin represents one extreme and Yang the opposite. Cold is the opposite to hot, wet to dry, dark to light, long to short and so forth.

This philosophy can be used in a scientific sense to apply to the human body, and the ancient Chinese physicians used it in formulating their medical approach with acupuncture. They knew that a sick person could receive acupuncture which brought him from a Yin state toward a Yang state. They also were able to recognize a point of balance, which was the state of wellness. If the procedure were to continue, the patient would move physiologically into the Yang state and would become worse. What an incredible observation to make.

The body does indeed work on the basis of balance in virtually everything. We now know that low blood cholesterol portends risk of certain diseases, whereas a high level portends other risks. The low cholesterol might be viewed as a Yin state, the high cholesterol as a Yang state. Please recognize that this is an oversimplification to illustrate a *principle* that I am attempting to illustrate. The Chinese philosophers pointed out that one extreme was not automatically bad and the other one good. Their philosophy incorporated Yin as an essential part of Yang, and vice versa.

This principle can now be applied to prostaglandins, which cannot be described as good or bad. The body does not normally produce substances which are noxious to itself, and both families of the prostaglandins are essential components in a complex defensive process. Inflammation, engineered appropriately, is a proper act of defense. We shall see later what happens if the Yin/Yang balance in these important hormone-like fatty acids becomes distorted.

Now, at last, we are in a position to see the brain/body relationship in a proper perspective. If we focus on prostaglandins in health and disease, without taking into account the action of the computer in their complex, message-dependent relationship, we cannot see the big picture. We are like the blind men attempting to describe the elephant in Chapter 1. If we focus only on the autonomic system, we do the same thing. I would like to think that the model that is being described here glimpses the totality of the elephant.

Diagram of the Elephant

Note that the vital factors illustrated in this chapter and incorporated into the diagram of the elephant depend completely on adequate communication. The language of the body is a chemical one, and its tremendous diversity represents syllables and words which make sense only to the cell units that are capable of reading them.

There is a separate language in the interior of each cell, each of which is an incredibly complex piece of machinery. Physicians have been busy identifying this language for many years with the goal of learning how to influence the machinery when it goes wrong and causes disease. It turns out that the safest and most efficient way of having such an influence is through the use of non-caloric nutrients. These are, as most people now are aware, the vitamins and minerals that are the nuts and bolts of the messenger system, as well as the spark plugs that enable the metabolic engines to run properly.

Imagine the complexity of orchestrating 100 trillion units and maintaining a state of law and order which enables the whole organism to function in an efficient manner. In my quiet moments, as I contemplate the fantastic wonder of the human body, I am truly amazed that it works at all. We have covered only the principles. It would be superfluous for every reader to be aware of the total vocabulary in this amazing language, which involves many different substances other than those described here. In the next chapter, we shall see how this model works both in the interpretation of disease and the methods by which the machine can be influenced *only* by increasing the efficiency of its metabolic processes—the *engines."* After that we need to discuss what makes the engines tick.

Chapter 7

What Happens When
the Adaptive Mechanisms Fail?

In the previous chapter, we explored the basic principles of anatomy and physiology which constitute the brain/body relationship. It is quite extraordinary that we have concluded, in orthodox medical thought, that mental disease is distinct from physical disease. In trying to explain this to patients, I say that "medicine has cut off the head of the patient and everything above the neck is mental. Everything below the neck is physical." Even more extraordinary is the fact that the condition of psychosomatic disease has come to be interpreted in the same bracket as malingering. Patients become angry when the subject is addressed. They say that "the doctor said that it was all in my head."

Let us make clear the difference between psychosomatic disease and malingering. I have gone to great pains to describe the lower brain as a computer. When the computer is disturbed in a biochemical sense, it will cause automatic signals to the body which are not necessary for an adaptive change. They are essentially maladaptive in nature. Malingering refers to the patient *consciously* inventing symptoms that enable him to escape some action that he wishes to avoid. It is agreed that the difference may be occasionally difficult to perceive, but there are ways and means of ascertaining it in doubtful cases.

I believe that it was Freud, the father of modern psychology, who led us toward the concept that it is the subconscious mind that gives rise to somatic symptoms as well as emotional overflow. He was dead right, of course, because the subconscious is a computer when analyzed in terms of our present knowledge. It is our refusal to believe that the brain is capable of automatic function which is at the seat of the problem. As a species, our clever brains have developed a concept of ourselves in unrealistic terms, and we use words like *spirit* and *soul* to suggest that we have risen, in some mysterious way, above the biologic laws that govern the animal kingdom.

I have already acknowledged that we do not fully understand the cognitive or "upper" brain. It is perfectly true that a deep psychologic trauma such as child abuse will remain in memory *in perpetuum*. This memory becomes an internal stress factor which is a trigger to abnormal retaliatory behavior. But in my view, it is essential to segregate the *stress factor* from the result that it triggers. I believe this to be such an important difference that I have dedicated a chapter to it, which I refer to as "The Three Circles of Health."

So, let us see what is meant by *maladaptation*. First, I will remind the reader that each of us exists in an essentially hostile environment, a point to which I shall keep returning. So the life of a human being, like that of any other animal, consists of a perpetual attack/defense struggle. We discussed earlier how modern medicine has developed, almost exclusively, along the lines of killing the enemy. Most medical disciplines, on the other hand, that have been in existence for several thousand years, have been devoted to assisting the defensive mechanisms. It should be emphasized that the modern concept was formulated because of the discovery of one type of enemy, disease-causing microorganisms. Before that, we did not know what this enemy was and so we were unable to think about killing it. I have also emphasized the fact that this dramatic discovery caused us to place it in much too narrow a focus and that we became preoccupied with it as the most important advance in centuries.

How does the brain become involved in an attack? I have tried to show that it literally computes the defense. This chapter is devoted to a discussion of what happens when the defensive mechanisms break down. Perhaps we can start with an example which I draw from my own experience. As in every other occupation, a physician learns the finer points of his trade by doing it.

In my first job as a medical resident in my university teaching hospital in England, I was under the direction of an extraordinarily knowledgeable consultant physician. As a resident, I was responsible for the day-to-day care of the patients whom he admitted to his wards. The wards were huge, multi-bedded rooms presided over by a head nurse known as a sister.

To digress for a moment, I should explain that English hospitals were originally monasteries, and the nurses in them were known as lay sisters. Thus, these remarkable women are still known as sisters and wear a cap which is derived from the original habits worn by nuns. I say remarkable because sisters in an English hospital were, in my day, women to be feared by medical students and young residents. They were fiercely loyal to the chief and their medical knowledge was profound. They always knew everything about each of the patients in their wards without consulting the patient's personal chart. A resident could not get away with anything that he may have overlooked or skimped on. I was eternally grateful to the sisters of my acquaintance in those days, since they gave me enormous gifts of profound wisdom which cannot be obtained from books.

This digression may provide a picture of the scenario. One could stand at the main door opening into the ward and see every patient in the ward. I was also responsible for admitting emergency cases to the ward at night, and so it happened one night that I was called to see a middle-aged man who had come into the emergency room. His history was known to the hospital because he had been treated for chronic tuberculosis for some years. However, on this occasion he had pneumonia, and I admitted him to the ward. It is amazing to note that this was before the days of antibiotics, a fact that emphasizes their very recent introduction. Sulfonamides were just beginning to come in, and I started the patient on a sulfonamide that was still known by its code name, M&B 693.

In the morning, I didn't notice that my chief had come into the ward, as I was standing by the sister's desk, until I heard him say, "Lonsdale, I see that you have a dying patient."

Somewhat shaken, I turned around to him and said, "How do you know that, sir?"

He pointed to my patient with pneumonia and said, "Do you see how he is picking at the edge of the bedclothes? Notice also that he occasionally reaches out with his hand and picks at something that is not there."

I could see that the man was indeed holding on to the edge of the bedclothes and his fingers were working in a sort of picking action. Occasionally, one hand would advance in front of him and he would use a similar picking action at thin air. Although his eyes were open, they did not register any sight, for he was unconscious.

My chief explained that this was a "toxic brain" typical of overwhelming infection and that it spelled death for the patient. Naturally, I never forgot this scene, but in addition to this profound lesson, I became deeply interested in the mechanisms. I noted that this man never had fever, did not have an elevated white cell count in the blood as is usually seen in infections, and did not, in fact, have any abnormal laboratory tests.

When he died, his body was subjected to autopsy and every organ in it contained abscesses that contained staphylococcal pus. He did not stand the faintest chance of surviving. With the modern insistence on abnormal laboratory studies indicating the diagnosis, he would represent a paradox to any student of today. Perhaps, if I showed the laboratory data to such a student and asked him what disease the patient had, he might say that he was not seriously ill with such normal studies. He might be surprised if I told him that the patient was dead from the effects of overwhelming infection.

I put this case together, in my present state of knowledge, in the following manner. Tuberculosis is really caused by a bacillus which is opportunist in nature. *Opportunist* means that such an organism does not cause infection unless the immune mechanisms of the patient are compromised. We shall be looking at the opportunist organisms in more detail later, for there are many. Of course, since infection represents a war between the attacker and the defender, it can be said that virtually *any* microorganism that causes disease is opportunist. However, the term *opportunist* is usually reserved for those microorganisms that are considered to cause infectious disease only when the defensive mechanisms of the host are compromised.

Tuberculosis was eradicated by public health measures, including better housing, nutrition, and hygiene. It was not eradicated by the wonder drugs of modern medicine. Indeed, it is very instructive that we have seen a resurgence of this scourge recently in association with the appearance of the modern disease, AIDS. AIDS is a disease in which the immune mechanism is the target of the HIV virus, and it is not at all surprising to find that it is associated with tuberculosis, among other opportunists.

Appropriate nutrition is a vital necessity to the functional efficiency of every organ in the body, including the immune system. So it is possible to think about the patient that I have just described as being malnourished. This state provided the opportunity for the tubercle bacillus to attack him. In his already weakened state, he developed a super-added pneumonia. The patient, including his brain, was completely overwhelmed by the toxemia of infection. His computer never recognized the imminent danger and so it did not organize the defensive responses to meet the foe. As if it were attacking an ill-prepared fortress, the invading army just swamped his system. Since body temperature is ordered by the computer, this never changed from normal to high and he did not develop fever, the usual response to any kind of infection. No message went to his various stores of white blood cells in order to mobilize them and ncrease their numbers in the bloodstream. The defending army remained in barracks because the commanding officer did not order it out.

I have seen this kind of "toxic brain" only once since then. I was called one evening to see a middle-aged man in his home. (Doctors still make house calls in Britain.) I was shown upstairs to the patient's room. It contained no furniture, other than a double bed, and was lit by an eerie blue light from a single bulb hanging from the ceiling. As I entered the room, the patient was staring at me from the center of the bed. He was kneeling in the all-fours position, and he reached toward me with the same kind of picking action that I described above in the tuberculosis patient. He had experienced a cold which became pneumonia, and the infection then spread to the spinal cord, causing an overwhelming meningitis, from which he subsequently died.

I cause a little surprise when I tell my patients that flu is a psychosomatic disease. At first, this notion appears to be completely absurd. It certainly does not fit the modern classification of disease as most of us have been taught. But consider the fact that it is *only* the brain which can sense danger to the body as a whole. Oh sure, there are many local defense mechanisms that can and do work independently of the brain. But the big picture requires central mobilization of physical resources and that must be coordinated by the computer, like a general in the field mobilizing his troops.

The term *psychosomatic* is quite in conflict with the model that I am introducing. It always conjures up the vision of fraud in almost anyone's mind. It has become ingrained in our culture in this sense, and if I use the word at all I always try to turn the patient toward seeing it within the framework of a computerized machine.

Assuming that the computer is structurally intact, there are only two possibilities for its overseeing action in organizing our defenses. Either it does not respond at all or it over-responds. The under-response is what we have described above. It is relatively uncommon, and both of the patients that I discussed represent examples of a distorted and dramatically defective response. This is what we might call the Yin extreme, whereas the opposite, the much more common over-responsiveness, can be called the Yang extreme. Another name for the former state might be *anergy,* whereas the latter state is called *allergy.* I want to emphasize the old adage that "a rose by any other name smells just as sweet." We tend to become preoccupied with the name of any disease that we are supposed to have, a direct result of medical development and the way that we have been taught to think. I always try to bring my patient back to the idea that he is a machine that has to be in balance with the environment which will always be his enemy. Allergy is so common today that it is rare not to see a patient who talks about "my allergies" in a tone that has come to accept the symptoms as a normal event to be tolerated. Such a patient is likely to say "doesn't everyone have allergies?"

I am going to turn to the condition known as beriberi to illustrate the point that I want to make. This would surprise a few people, particularly any physicians who might read this. Beriberi is generally classified as a specific disease caused by deficiency of vitamin B_1. This classification is not strictly true, even though vitamin B_1 is an important nutrient deficiency in the disease. It is actually caused by high-calorie nutrition with an inadequate presence of the non-caloric nutrients, particularly vitamin B_1, as discussed earlier. This disease causes autonomic imbalance in its early stages and paralysis of this system in its later stages. The imbalance may be dominance of either the sympathetic or the parasympathetic branch of the system, so the symptoms can be extremely variable, depending upon which branch is in a state of dominance.

I see this as a kind of early warning system. The brain senses an inefficient process of combustion, known in biochemistry as oxidation. The brain concludes that the environment is potentially dangerous and it sounds the alarm, thus providing the person with a means of escape. Remember, this is a perception in machine terms. The brain does not "know" that the environment is dangerous. It *perceives* it as such. The system that is used to alert the individual to danger is the sympathetic branch, by triggering the fight-or-flight reflex. Modern malnutrition is producing a state of affairs which is very like this condition. I do not see people with classic beriberi. I see them with snippets of it. I also see vestiges of scurvy and pellagra, also not in their classic states.

So, the opposite of a hypoactive Yin response is a hyperactive Yang response, and we will now see how this is responsible for a massive amount of disease in the modern world. These conditions are due to a computer that has become what I call *trigger-happy*. It over-responds to a trivial stimulus. So the first condition that I want to describe is one that is known to be affecting as many as 30 million women in the U.S.

Premenstrual Syndrome

If I use this condition to illustrate the opposite of anergy, the reader will conclude that I am fitting this syndrome into a general classification under the heading of allergy. It only illustrates the futility of our present concepts. I would prefer to consider one extreme—the hypoactive—to be represented by Yin and the other extreme—the hyperactive—by Yang. This approach uses the philosophical idea of the ancient Chinese and transposes it to represent *extremes.*

Premenstrual syndrome, a very common condition, is an excellent example of the refusal of modern medicine to recognize the intimate functional relationship that exists between the brain and body. It is usually relegated to that category of diagnosis known as "neurosis." It is a condition which, treated in a conventional manner, illustrates the way in which disease conditions are pigeon-holed.

Perhaps it is best to describe a typical history of premenstrual syndrome (PMS), also, though not as commonly, known as premenstrual tension syndrome (PMTS). I usually begin a consultation, in the way of all physicians, by asking the patient why she has come to see me. What is of extreme importance is the *prevailing* symptom which is of most concern to the patient. I say prevailing because PMS has as many symptoms as you can think of, so I am going to describe a hypothetical case which typifies the usual presentation. Let us imagine such a patient, named Mrs. John Doe. She is 35, is married, and has two children.

"How do you do, Mrs. Doe. I am pleased to meet you. What can I do for you?"

"Well, Doctor, I'm not sure because I have so many problems. But I have had constant, chronic fatigue now ever since my last child three years ago."

"Do you have any other symptoms that concern you?"

"I have had many bouts of diarrhea, alternating with periods of constipation, and I often have palpitations of the heart for no reason. Oh, by the way, my menstrual periods are horrible. They are irregular and I have awful cramps, for which I have to take medicine."

I provide my patients with a questionnaire which they fill in before they come to the office. This patient answered all the questions in the positive, meaning that she had all the symptoms mentioned in this detailed questionnaire. After I go through these imaginary answers, I will explain the mechanism or give my interpretation of their meaning. As you read this, bear in mind the model of the brain/body relationship as depicted in the last chapter. Remember that the brain talks continuously to the body and that body cells talk to each other and also back to the brain.

The questionnaire is framed to cover what is called system review in assessment of a patient. All physicians are taught to go through this with every patient. But because time is money, the main complaint voiced by the patient often categorizes the nature of the condition from the start and becomes the focal point of the physician's attention. Thus, in the hypothetical patient above, she might well be categorized as having a gastrointestinal problem because of the leading symptoms of diarrhea/constipation. We will see that this patient had a much wider spectrum of symptoms than that. However, she will tend to volunteer the symptoms that are of most concern to her. To volunteer everything that she experiences would be considered by her to project to the physician that she is a hypochondriac or is neurotic. Unfortunately, with the present conceptual climate in medicine, she often *is* classed in this bracket. Traditional medical approach is then to refer to a psychiatrist because her complaints are either "imaginary" or "exaggerated."

The first category that I examine in the questionnaire refers to the brain and nervous system. I find that this patient has a number of symptoms which she has indicated by her answers. She has insomnia and awakens frequently during the night, often with a panic attack, meaning that she has an acute sense of fear, a racing heart, and sweating. She experiences nightmares and is excessively emotional. She becomes easily irritated and "flies off the handle" with her husband and children.

She always feels cold, even when the weather is warm, but will suddenly experience a hot flash. When she stands up out of a chair or gets out of bed, she becomes dizzy or light-headed for a second or two and has blacked out on several occasions. Her hands and feet are usually cold, and she wears socks in bed in the winter. Also, for no apparent reason, she notices "pins and needles" in hands and feet and often will experience muscle cramps in the night which awaken her from sleep. For three years now, ever since the birth of her last child, she is only very occasionally aware of having dreams and never remembers them. She awakens in the morning feeling unrefreshed and exhausted. She notices that many of her symptoms are worse when the weather changes from wet to dry, cold to hot, or vice versa, and even notices a difference when there is a full moon.

The next category is in relation to the heart and vascular system. She experiences frequent palpitations of the heart at irregular intervals. This is often associated with a pain which is felt under the left breast or behind the breastbone in the middle of the chest. She recognizes that this pain appears when she feels that she is under emotional stress but is also concerned that she might have a heart problem. Another associated symptom that she has with the pain is a feeling of suffocation or "running out of air," which causes her to sigh or take a deep breath.

The next category has to do with breathing and lung function. She has nasal congestion which comes and goes and which is worse in the morning and with both spring and fall seasons. She refers to this as "my allergies," or "my sinuses," because this is what she has been told is the cause of her congestion. This common associated symptom is usually treated with repeated courses of antibiotics, unless an allergist is consulted and then it is often treated with allergy desensitization. Occasionally this symptom is treated by reconstruction of the nasal septum.

Our hypothetical patient has bouts of coughing and sneezing, particularly at night, and the cough may keep her husband, as well as her, awake at night. It is an irritating, useless cough which is a response to a perpetual tickle at the back of the throat. Sneezing comes in runs of ten or twelve at a time and is not related to any obvious phenomenon.

In this woman, the urogenital system is peppered with problems. Her period cycle is a scourge. Menstrual periods are irregular, very heavy in nature, and associated with severe abdominal cramps, for which she takes a medication for pain relief. She experiences bloating of the abdomen and water retention in her hands and feet, which become swollen before the period begins. She frequently has to treat vaginal yeast infections which tend to come on before the period begins.

The week before the period is a veritable nightmare. All her symptoms are at their height. She frequently sits down and bursts into tears, feels depressed and has violent mood swings. Her family keeps well away from her during this unpleasant and critical week, saying, "Oh well! Mom has her period!"

She has pain in the right lower part of the abdomen fourteen days before the period begins, but this pain is on the left side with alternate periods and is called by the German name of *mittelschmerz* meaning *middle pain*. This pain occurs at the time of ovulation and is abnormal, of course. Her breasts become painful and tender, and she notices lumps in both breasts which become bigger and more tender with each period. She has seen her gynecologist and has been told that this is fibrocystic disease and that she should avoid taking coffee. Lastly, she often notices frequency of urination, sometimes with a powerful desire to urinate urgently. On one or two occasions this has been so powerful that she has wet herself on the way to a bathroom.

Now we turn to those functions considered to be related to the alimentary, or gastrointestinal system. The patient's appetite is poor, particularly in the morning, but in the week before the period she develops an insane craving for sweets, particularly chocolate, and a voracious and insatiable appetite for all kinds of food. As we have mentioned, she has diarrhea alternating with constipation and this is particularly marked in the week before the period. With diarrhea, she develops abdominal cramps and notes loud growling noises arising from her abdomen, often heralding a required visit to a bathroom.

Her diet is fairly typical of an average American. For breakfast she has cereal and toast, a sandwich for lunch, and the usual kind of meat-and-potatoes meal for dinner. She drinks three cups of coffee, two cups of tea, sixteen ounces of fruit juice, twelve ounces of diet cola, and two glasses of milk in the course of the day. She has an occasional shot of gin or whisky for social occasions. Her craving for sweets is fairly controlled except for the premenstrual week, when it increases dramatically and she binges. This is also accompanied by a craving for salt, and she satisfies this, together with her voracious appetite, by consuming potato chips and pretzels between meals.

Another notable complaint, when the patient's attention is drawn to it, is that her skin is excessively dry, particularly in winter, and she has to lubricate it with skin creams. This complaint is seldom volunteered, since it is regarded as a phenomenon for the attention of either the beautician or the dermatologist. This dryness is accompanied by an inordinate thirst which is hard to quench at times.

In my examination, I look for certain things which are often ignored by physicians or considered to be trivial. The patient's feet are cold to the touch, and there is a kind of mottled appearance of the skin in the lower legs which make them look as though they are made of pink marble. Knee reflexes are exaggerated, more so in the left side than the right. There is a small patch of rough skin just below each knee which looks as though she has been kneeling a lot. When I stroke the legs gently with the tip of my finger there is a brief blanching in the line of the stroke. This is followed by a brief flush, and three seconds later there is a slow appearance of profound blanching. This phenomenon is known as dermographia, or "skin writing."

I find that the main artery to each leg is audible when I place my stethoscope over the groin area, where this vessel emerges from the torso on its way to supplying the leg with arterial blood. The passage of the pulse in this artery, therefore, is so turbulent that it can actually be heard as well as felt.

I find that the left breast is smaller than the right. Heart activity, like the pulse just described, is turbulent and beating at the rate of ninety beats a minute, a rather fast pulse. However, I also hear a tiny click in the heart valve, which indicates that she has a commonly detected anomaly known as mitral valve prolapse. This is known to affect 6 to 10 percent of the American population. The blood pressure is 130/40, indicating a wide gap between the two pressure readings. This is known as the pulse pressure, a figure which is obtained by subtracting the lower reading from the upper one.

When I put the tip of my finger into each ear and ask the patient to open her mouth, I feel a little click, diagnostic of early temporo-mandibular joint changes. This condition is often found by dentists and is frequently associated with many symptoms. These include vicious headaches or pain radiating up into the side of the head. I ask her to stick out her tongue, and I observe that there are indentations on the edge of her tongue. These are caused by unconscious pressing of the tongue against the back of the teeth. She does this during sleep but may also do it when concentrating on a task such as writing a letter. She also is known to grind her teeth during sleep.

Let us try to assess the meaning of these many different symptoms. Conventionally, symptoms are complaints made by the patient and are supposed to guide the physician to the particular type of disease from which that patient is suffering. For example, if the patient has joint symptoms such as pain and stiffness, she may be referred to a rheumatologist. During the consultation, she asks the rheumatologist about her diarrhea. He replies that this is not within his specialty and she must see a gastroenterologist. If she mentions palpitations of the heart, that is to be dealt with by a cardiologist, and her emotional state, of course, is considered to be the realm of a psychiatrist. This represents an artificial, man-made classification of disease. The whole aim is to make a diagnosis, which is then given a name, often in Latin. For example, Lupus Erythematosus literally means "red wolf," a term which is merely descriptive because it describes the appearance of the patient. It is otherwise meaningless.

After hearing about the symptoms, the physician does his examination to identify things that he can observe which are abnormal. These are called "signs," meaning that they are signs which point to the diagnosis. Each disease is supposed to have its own constellation of symptoms and signs, pointing inexorably to the correct diagnosis, which is then named. This becomes the *expected* diagnosis, to be confirmed by laboratory studies. In some instances, a physician may have observed a number of patients with a similar constellation of symptoms and signs. If he is unable to recognize the constellation as fitting the rules for making the diagnosis of a known disease, the constellation is named after him. It is then known as John Doe's syndrome. This gives a veneer of erudition when a physician tells a patient that he or she has So-and-so's syndrome. It is otherwise quite meaningless.

The third stage of the process is to perform laboratory tests, which either tend to confirm this diagnosis or refute it. For example, a patient with joint symptoms may be given the provisional diagnosis of arthritis. If the laboratory does not reveal a plethora of abnormalities known as "acute phase reactants," the physician may be confused. He may say that the patient has arthritis but that it is "too early for the tests to have become positive." Or he may indicate that the symptoms are "all in the patient's head" because there is nothing to confirm that these symptoms are genuine.

I totally disagree with this approach. First of all, symptoms are always indications of distress. Nobody invents them. Often, because the complaint is bizarre in the eyes of the physician and because he himself does not understand its true meaning, the symptom will tend to confirm that the patient is neurotic—*in the physician's eyes.*

A modern automobile is equipped with a panel of lights on the dashboard. These lights go on only when the engine is under stress and might be compared with symptoms expressed by a human being. They are literally warning phenomena that announce that the engine is running badly, whether it be an automobile engine or a human engine.

If a car is taken to a gas station because a light on the dashboard has come on, would the owner expect the mechanic to remove the bulb? That would be the equivalent of controlling a symptom with a medication such as a pain pill. Surely, a good mechanic would ask *why* the light came on and begin to examine the engine to identify the cause. Thus, in the analysis of my patient's problems, symptoms are merely indicators of distress in the electro-chemical mechanism of the brain/body functional relationship.

We know much about the projections of autonomic and endocrine dysfunction by the nature of the symptom, and I will give only a few as a general indicator of what I mean. Palpitations of the heart, particularly if associated with a sense of anxiety and sweating, are typical of a sympathetic reflex activity. Abdominal pain, associated with audible growling noises from the abdomen, is typical of a parasympathetic reflex. The major question is *why* such unnecessary reflexes are occurring without any need. Observe that they represent *normal* physiological activities that are controlled from the computer. The point is really very simple. The computer is trigger-happy and is over-responding to an input signal as though that signal were arising from some threat to the person as a whole. That input, which I categorize under the heading of "environmental stress" is just as normal. The whole thrust of this idea is that it is not the *stress* which is the important factor, for that is something that we ordinarily adapt to smoothly and appropriately, without fuss, under the automatic orders of the computer. It is the abnormally trigger-happy computer that is the problem!

Now, let us return to my patient, Mrs. Doe. First of all, having gained the information described above, I can sit down with her and tell her that I know exactly what is wrong with her. I do *not* need tests to make a diagnosis. I need tests to delineate her abnormal biochemistry, *if* that abnormality exists within the framework of the tests that I choose.

Laboratory tests are really a fishing expedition. We are hanging out a line to see what kind of fish we catch. If there are no fish caught, conventional medicine says that the complaints of the patient are "functional" and she may be offered a medication called a tranquilizer which is supposed to modify the activity of her overwrought nervous system. If I find that the tests do not tell me anything, I conclude that I have not thrown out the right kind of bait for the fish, or that the fish are not there.

Look at it this way. If the computer is bombarding the body with orders night and day, day-in, day-out, month by month, sometimes for years, will there not be extraordinary wear and tear on the "slave organs" that are responding to the largely unnecessary orders? But if the genetically-determined constitution of the individual is strong, such wear and tear may go on for years without causing any cracks in the structure. The laboratory actually gives us indications that the wear and tear is taking its toll. Thus it can be used to *forecast* the possibilities of serious disease in the indeterminate future of the individual.

What I believe happens is this. Suppose that Mrs. Doe goes to the various physicians who examine her within their individual specialty. Each one does a series of tests, and every single one of them is negative. The x-rays are normal, and the CAT scan shows no abnormality. The blood tests show no evidence of anemia or disease. Each physician comes to the same conclusion, that Mrs. Doe has a functional problem equated with her "inadequate personality." Her husband becomes increasingly estranged because she has experienced a complete disappearance of libido. He naturally interprets her refusal of sex as the fact that she does not love him any more and may well seek other sources of natural release.

She finally settles for the conclusion that she is indeed neurotic and may have the frightening thought that she may be going mad. The fact that each day is a veritable hell passes observers by because they do not experience what she feels, and she does her best to "keep up appearances." To neighbors and friends, all is apparently well within the family structure. This perception is magnified by the fact that Mrs. Doe does not *look* ill, although she might look very fatigued if she does not cover it with make-up.

It may well be true that she finds a sympathetic family doctor or a gynecologist, neither of whom ever asks her what she is eating or drinking. She may like the doctor very much and he helps her by providing her with various medications which, like alcohol or coffee, become crutches. Perhaps she goes to this doctor for years. Every time that she enters his office, he sighs and says to himself, "Here comes that neurotic Mrs. Doe. I wonder what new symptom she has this time?"

After many years of indifferent or appallingly bad health, during which she has a non-disease, she walks into the doctor's office with a lump in her breast which turns out to be cancer.

"Ah," says the doctor, " Mrs. Doe now has a real disease. At last we can help her because this was what I was trained for." Unfortunately, as many women have found out, this is much like shutting the door after the horse has bolted. It is too late. The cancer should never have occurred, but treating it now is less than ideal to say the least. Mrs. Doe is, however, intelligent. She has had a lot of time to think about this, so she asks the doctor a simple question.

"Doctor, I have been coming to you with my non-disease for many years. Now that I have a real disease, is there any connection?"

The doctor answers her, "No, Mrs. Doe, I am afraid that there is absolutely no connection. Your new and real disease could not have been foreseen or prevented."

The new modern preventive development in medicine answers this question quite differently. The patient's non-disease was the original evidence of severe and unnecessary stress *response*. It should have been attended to by the physician and treated as such.

The delinquency was the fact that the physician never asked her what she was eating, drinking, or smoking. Neither did he ask her about her lifestyle. He prescribed drugs to control symptoms and (often) unnecessary antibiotics and hormones. If you really want an answer for poor Mrs. Doe, the nice physician was the innocent cause of her ultimately developing cancer. This may seem like an unfair indictment, but medicine has already come far enough to be able to see that this is correct. It is incumbent upon the medical profession to awaken to the facts. The vast majority of the public think that American medicine is fantastic space-age, miracle-making stuff. A rapid revision of that perception is timely and a vital necessity. Why is it that the mortality has always gone down in localities where physician strikes have occurred?

In PMS, the computer is victimized in only two ways. The nature of the diet, or nutrition, is the more important. The genetically-determined quality of the computer is the other. Although the computer comes under very considerable input stress, particularly during the premenstrual week, it is a normal part of the cycle. Because the computer is trigger-happy and has a low threshold of response, it fires off a whole plethora of signals that constitute both mental (emotional) and physical (somatic) activity. It is easy to see how the concept of psychosomatic disease came into being.

Because of our ingrained belief that our behavior is totally under voluntary control, we conclude that Mrs. Doe's sudden weeping attacks are "psychological" and that she is out of control. Note that her marriage may well be endangered because of this concept. Her husband and children do not see her as ill; they see her in the same light as the rest of the world does.

Essentially then, we can explain virtually all the functional reactions of the body and mind by this computer model, where the organs of the body are slaves to the commands resulting from environmental stress. Can we explain the abnormal organ responses such as fibrocystic disease of the breasts? Why, for instance, is this condition associated with consumption of coffee? Well, we know exactly how caffeine works. It is a pharmacological action that has been known for years. It enhances activity of certain nervous functions. Then, how does it impose an organic change in the breasts?

The answer is simple in principle, though devastatingly complex in detail. The reader will remember that we discussed the substances called prostaglandins that are produced in the body. Some of these cause inflammation, and some of them inhibit it. It will also be remembered that they are part of the chemical language of the body.

During the menstrual cycle, these are hormonal messengers that affect the breasts. They are orchestrated by the computer. The problem is that the chemical language is distorted and the breast tissue releases inflammatory prostaglandins instead of a proper balance of both. Not only is there a flood of commands from the computer, but the "slave" mechanisms respond in an abnormal way also.

It will be remembered that Mrs. Doe's right breast was significantly larger than the left. In talking about this to a woman whose job was to fit brassieres, I learned that asymmetry was extremely common in women. She had noted that the right breast was usually the larger, a phenomenon that I have noted myself. It does not seem to be associated with right- or left-handedness. Perhaps its common appearance in women in general explains why I have noted it so commonly in my patients with PMS. However, it does remind us that asymmetry between the left and right halves of the body is common, as we discussed earlier. My explanation for it is that one half of the computer guides the growth and development of one half of the body and vice versa. Asymmetry is normal in minor degree, but if it becomes exaggerated as in the cases described by Adie (see Chapter 5), it is abnormal and represents chemical/electrical hyperfunction in the larger side or hypofunction in the smaller. It may be true, therefore, that women with PMS may have a proneness to asymmetric breasts because their computers have exaggerated functional responses to input stimuli.

To wrap up the case of Mrs. Doe, let us see why she has nasal congestion which is worse in the morning, responds to seasonal and weather changes, and is a symptom that most people call "my sinuses" or "my allergies." Because the entire nervous system is much too sensitive, an input signal comes from the nose, maybe caused by a tiny grain of dust. A response is triggered in the computer, giving rise to a message that goes back to the nose, activating the mucus-secreting glands.

The usual and customary explanation for this situation is that the patient is allergic to dust. Under normal, physiological conditions, local action at the site of dust contact would take care of the problem. Or perhaps it might give rise to a reflex sneeze, also a perfectly normal reflex. What we are dealing with is that Mrs. Doe's nervous system is much too responsive and sets off an exaggeration of what is normal "with the volume turned up." We can now see why she has attacks of unnecessary coughing and sneezing. They are nervous in origin.

I remember a patient whose auditory input was so sensitive that she could detect, from the other side of the room, a slight fizzing in a light bulb before it blew. Naturally, she also had PMS.

Dysperceptions

I have emphasized that we know that the world exists only because of interpretation of information that enters the brain. Just the miracle of standing up is a complex intertwining of automatic adjustments in muscles. The only reason that we recognize a table, or anything else, is because light rays from the table stimulate nerve endings in the retina which then transmit a picture to the brain where it is interpreted as such. Suppose, however, that the signals were *mis*interpreted by the brain, as in the patient in Chapter 2 who was under the impression that she was standing at an angle of forty-five degrees to the vertical. Interestingly, her cognitive brain recognized the dysperception by the computer because she knew that if it were true, that she would fall over. By correcting dietary indiscretion and by providing her with a few nutrient supplements, the dysperception cleared up. The cause of the problem had been a biochemical change which upset the decoding mechanism in the brain.

There are thousands, perhaps millions, of people in America who have dysperceptions of this nature, although few are as bizarre as that. Many, often adolescent, complain of feeling cold when the weather is warm, or feel hot in bed when it is a cold night, sometimes even throwing off the bedclothes. Pain, a universal symptom known to us all, is occurring because the brain is falsely perceiving it. It refers the origin of the pain to a distant part of the body, giving the impression that it is that part which hurts. It is sometimes called "psychologic pain," though it is really a biochemical mechanism affecting the brain's ability to decode perception of the real world.

I was asked to lecture to a group that was called The Self-Help Phobia Group. Phobias are quite common today. The word means "fear," and it is directed to very ordinary, everyday activities such as just leaving the house to go to work or any other form of stress. The audience filled the room and overflowed into the corridor. I turned to my host and told him that I had no idea that there were so many people with phobias. He replied that these were "just the people that were able to leave their houses." One of their members had been unable to leave his apartment for fourteen years!

There is a relatively common condition in children that is called school phobia. As soon as a child with this problem gets to school,

141

he develops abdominal pain and may vomit. Sometimes there is an associated headache. The teacher calls his mother to take him home and all symptoms disappear. It is only natural to believe that this is "psychological" if we follow Freudian leadership. Such children are usually referred to a psychologist. I love to see such children, because it is usually very easy to relieve by changing the child's diet and providing a few nutrient supplements.

I was always interested in the fact that they are almost invariably bright children who like the teacher, are popular with their friends, but are compulsive about their school work. The real mechanism is that the computer has become trigger-happy because of various nutritional abuses. Going to school is an ordinary, everyday stress, just the same as for all the other children. This *normal stress* causes the computer to fire off signals that are unnecessary, resulting in the somatic symptoms described. The bowel is signalled to action which is more powerful than usual, causing pain, and reversed peristalsis in the stomach results in vomiting. The headache is caused by changes in blood vessels supplying the scalp or brain and is much like a migraine. I find that resolution of this abnormal brain/body reaction is one of the most rewarding aspects of taking care of such children. They quickly find that the advice is correct and they learn to take care of themselves. They no longer require a physician to cure them of a psychological disease, and the mother's sense of guilt evaporates. After all, even if she has not been told directly that it is her upbringing that is at fault, it is implied.

Dysperceptions can occur as a result of disruption of electrical rhythms in the brain, as illustrated by the following story. An elderly lady had been struck by lightning. Afterwards she had some temporary balance problems, but she was left with severe, crippling, and intractable headaches. She had been to headache specialists, internists, and many different doctors, none of whom had helped her. I gave her nutritional supplements and intravenous chelation, which is often beneficial for many different disorders. This treatment did not help either.

I work closely with a very innovative and unusual man who was trained as an audiologist, a person who studies defects in hearing. He has taken it well beyond that and uses a series of electro-physiologic studies to test that part of the brain which we have named as the computer. This includes a study known as brainstem auditory evoked potential. Electrodes are attached to the patient's head and an earphone is placed over one ear at a time. Thus, auditory input can be tested in each ear separately. The machine makes clicking noises through the earphone which cause stimulation of the computer, which responds by electrical activity. This is then picked up by the electrodes and translated into wave patterns that are printed out on paper and can be analyzed.

In this lady, my colleague found the wave patterns to vary with the strength of the stimulus, suggesting that her computer was not processing information correctly. Because of his previous experience in another patient, he fashioned plastic tubes for her ears which fitted into the meatus, the canal that leads from the outside down to the ear drum. Now, as she talked and ate food, moving her jaw caused the tubes in the ears to stimulate her sensory nervous system, thus sending almost continuous messages into the brain computer. Within a month her headaches had ceased.

How do we put this together? Well, in the first place we have to conclude that brain electrical rhythms were distorted by the lightning strike, not a terribly difficult thing to imagine. We can go on to conclude from this that the computer had dysperceptions which were translated into headache, not too different from the case of the lady who thought that she was not standing vertically.

Our brains are obviously programmed by our life experiences. Memory dictates our behavior when we are exposed to similar experiences. Continually stimulating this patient's computer exercised it and apparently this revived its ability to perform. At least, that is the theory. It is never possible to *prove* something of this nature. The fact is that she obtained relief from an intolerable burden, and we are attempting to explain it from the data. However, it is at least clear that the headache was a brain/body relationship or, if you will, a maladaptation which was associated with, or caused by, a lightning strike.

Opportunist Organisms

I have already indicated that all microorganisms that are capable of causing human disease are really opportunist in nature. This means, of course, that they have to overcome the defensive mechanisms of the body in order to cause disease. *Opportunist*, however, is the term reserved for microorganisms that do not normally cause disease at all. They are "smart" enough to recognize the unusually weakened state of an individual and literally take advantage of the situation.

Within the model that I presented earlier, such organisms are the watch dogs of MN. She has indicated to them that they should

143

eliminate the weakened animal as part of the cruel state of survival of the fittest.

Perhaps the best known opportunist is candida albicans. Candida is the commonest yeast in the human body; when a human being is in a state of healthy balance, candida is symbiotic. That means that it is provided with "room and board" in return for certain services associated with recycling of organic matter. It normally lives in the bowel in all of us. It is only when the defensive balance is compromised that it becomes an enemy instead of a friend, hence it recognizes its opportunity.

One of the commonest ways to get a yeast infection, meaning that candida has turned ugly, is to get a broad-spectrum antibiotic. This wipes out the friendly germs that live in the bowel and which have an enormously important bearing on digestion of food. When these become wiped out, yeast overgrows and turns from its benign to its malignant form. As anyone knows, various forms of mould are found in damp places. They develop slender, hair-like extensions called mycelia which grow in a crisscross fashion, thus giving the whitish peach-fuzz appearance that is characteristic of mouldy fruit, or any other infected article. It is a sign, *par excellence*, of death and decay in the natural world, the way in which MN tidies up rotten material and recycles it.

Well, this process happens in the human bowel if its normal chemical balance is damaged. The mycelia may grow through the bowel wall and then break off, seeding other parts of the body via the bloodstream. This is evidence that the victim's immune system is weakened, and it is the obvious reason that yeast infections are so common in AIDS patients. A patient with PMS does not have anything as dangerous as AIDS, but she frequently has a compromised immune system, as we have discussed. Therefore, it is not too surprising that yeast is a relatively common problem in PMS, particularly if the patient has had repeated antibiotics given to her in the mistaken approach to her symptoms. I always place massive emphasis on nutrition in rehabilitating PMS victims. This will sometimes enable the body to throw off its opportunist predators without making the slightest attempt to kill the yeast. Killing the yeast represents a traditional approach, and we certainly have weapons for that. However, supporting the defensive mechanisms in the process of day-to-day adaptation is achieved by nutrient therapy which will be discussed further later on.

Chapter 8

Crib Death and Hyperactivity

The title of this chapter will confuse many. How can the common problem of hyperactivity in children possibly be linked with the relatively uncommon problem of crib death? I hope to show that, although these two phenomena are regarded as distinct and separate diseases, they are really much closer than it would seem. Both are due to immature reactions within the computer.

First of all, what *is* crib death? In modern medical terminology, it is called Sudden Infant Death Syndrome, usually known as SIDS. It has been recognized throughout the ages. When I was taking my final medical examinations, there was a section on Public Health. I remember that one of the questions that I was asked was "What is overlaying?" This term referred to the fact that small infants were known to be found dead sometimes in the bed of the mother. It was considered to be due to the mother rolling over onto the infant in her sleep, thus causing suffocation of the infant. Nobody had ever been able to prove that this was the mechanism because the mother, of course, was invariably asleep herself and therefore unaware of what she was doing. The fact that this question was asked in a Public Health examination indicated that the phenomenon occurred often enough to have become considered as a public health hazard. That means that it was not just a rare accident in one individual situation. The public health angle was to make budding physicians aware of it and to discourage mothers from having their infants sleep in the same bed.

We now know, of course, that SIDS occurs in infants sleeping in their own cribs, hence the alternative name of crib death. In England it is known as cot death. Actual overlaying deaths were probably rare or may have been nonexistent; these deaths were probable examples of SIDS.

The typical history of SIDS is shocking. A young mother notices that her three-month-old infant has a "little bit of a cold." Perhaps he is a little "snuffly" in his breathing, but he does not have any fever and she is not alarmed at all. She has recognized that this infant has tended to be rather irritable as compared with other infants of a similar age, but since that has been an ongoing problem, perhaps since shortly after birth, she is not alarmed. She places the infant in his crib, tucks him up and departs from the nursery.

During the night, the mother and father hear nothing at all in the way of a cry or an alarm. Even if she has one of the modern radio systems that are commonly used, no action of the infant is heard or is sufficient to awaken her. She goes into the nursery in the morning and finds the infant dead in his crib. The trauma to the parents, particularly the mother, is overwhelming as anyone can imagine. She may have an excessive sense of guilt that she did not take the infant to a pediatrician the day before. Another, even more ghastly scenario can be conjured up. Suppose that she had, in fact, taken the infant to a pediatrician and had been told that the infant only had a cold. Perhaps no treatment was offered because there really is none that is effective for a cold, or, worse yet, a cold remedy *was* prescribed. Who is the mother going to blame? I say "worse yet" because anger generated from a concept of incompetence by another person is perhaps even harder to bear than self-incrimination, however vague.

The family physician or pediatrician is called and the infant has to be subjected to autopsy. Autopsy examination of an infant is exceedingly traumatic to many mothers who see it as a mutilation, often refusing to give permission, saying that "he has suffered enough." In this case, the death comes under the jurisdiction of the coroner and she has no choice, since the autopsy is a legal necessity. The result of the autopsy is that no cause of death can be found.

For many years, coroners were the only physicians that had any interest in SIDS cases. They collected the statistics and were often asked to rule out homicidal causes such as suffocation. It was hard for them sometimes to be sure that a given death was or was not homicidal. One can imagine the additional trauma to a mother who is being subliminally accused of killing her infant deliberately.

Gradually, over many years of documentation, the epidemiology of SIDS became known and it became a recognizable entity in its own right, without having to introduce endless, additional trauma to the family. During my years at the big clinic, I became intensely interested in the whole subject of SIDS because it was obvious that the cause was abnormal chemistry in the computer. Perhaps this gives a hint of why I have bracketed SIDS and hyperactivity together in the same chapter. Both are due to immaturity in the control mechanisms of the lower brain, the computer.

The recognizable epidemiologic facts in SIDS are now well-known and published. They are curious if the underlying mechanisms are not understood. The event almost always occurs at night between midnight and 6AM, although it has happened during daytime naps. Sleep is the primary association. It is more common in boys, and the seasonal peak is late winter/early spring. It is more common in babies who are bottle-fed rather than breast-fed, and there is often a trivial cold noted on the evening before the death. It is rare under one month of age, and becomes increasingly uncommon after the age of six months, although occasional deaths attributed to SIDS have occurred as late as two years of age; the peak incidence is between three and four months.

Infants who eventually succumb to SIDS have been noted to be more irritable in their short life on earth. They seem to cry a lot and their mothers have some difficulty in consoling the infants. Perhaps, of greatest importance, is the epidemiology associated with pregnancy. The disaster has some association with smoking of tobacco during pregnancy, and the diet, in my experience, is of critical importance. An excess of so-called junk food is another risk factor. I believe that consumption of soft drinks, particularly colas, is an especially important risk factor, and I do not think that the so-called diet colas diminish the risk. The cards may well be stacked against the infant on the day of his birth. By the way, the reference to the infant in the male sex is legitimate in this case, because male infants are at a little greater risk than females.

In order to show how my interest in SIDS developed, I must return to some of the experience described in earlier chapters in reference to my increasing interest in thiamin, vitamin B_1. The reader will remember that I had embarked on a "voyage of discovery" in the medical library. This work was an attempt to glean all the information that I could acquire on the subject of thiamin and the disease with which it was most closely associated, beriberi.

As I have mentioned, beriberi is a fascinating disease. It will occur in several different forms, depending upon the basic mechanisms of its induction. Its clinical expression is dependent upon how acute or chronic the deficiency and is particularly associated with the intake of "naked" or "empty" calories. Food, like gasoline in an engine, must be burned, giving rise to calories as units of energy. High-calorie-producing foods which do not have a sufficient density of vitamins and minerals that enable the food to be properly burned, are referred to as "empty" or "naked."

Beriberi is also extremely closely related to the age of the patient and is broadly divided into infantile, childhood, and adult, which represent the major classifications of the disease. The infantile variety is extremely acute; less so is the childhood type, and the adult expression is much more drawn-out, or chronic. These differences are clearly related to the metabolic rate, the rate being much more dynamic in an infant and slowing down through childhood to the adult rate.

It was when I was reading about the infantile variety of the disease that I was completely amazed by its similarity to modern SIDS. The most acute form of the disease causes sudden death. In epidemiologic studies in the Philippines and other eastern countries, it was reported years ago that this sudden death was rare in babies under one month of age; it unusually occurred after six months and had a peak incidence between three and four months—an incidence strikingly similar to modern SIDS. Furthermore, it was more likely in male infants, occurred more commonly in the spring, and was sometimes associated with a slight cold. The growth of the brain in an infant accelerates rapidly after birth, requiring nutrients to power the acceleration. One can easily see, therefore, that the nutritional deficiency will not necessarily occur at one month and may reach a peak at three to four months, as growth accelerates. After six months, this acceleration slows down. Thus the epidemiology can be explained.

I discovered a paper in the prestigious *British Medical Journal* written by a physician by the name of Fehily. Before World War II, it will be remembered that the Japanese invaded Hong Kong. During the Japanese occupation, which was quite a short period of time, the Chinese population was subjected to privation as seems inevitable with all conquering armies. This included malnutrition, of course. Hong Kong was under direct British rule and Fehily was an English Officer of public health. She was sent to the colony to study the state of health of the infants of the Chinese mothers after the Japanese had withdrawn.

Fehily reported a disastrous situation. The infancy death rate was 350 per 1000 live births, and this included all the diseases that occur secondarily to malnutrition. However, what struck her, and what was the main text of her paper in the *British Medical Journal*, was a condition that was quite startling in its epidemiology. There was a form of sudden death that occurred in many of the Chinese infants. They occurred in three- to four-month-old infants, and the mothers had invented a number of explanations. They reported that such deaths occurred during the night and often struck the male infant who was considered to be the healthiest and chubbiest member of the family. They believed that evil spirits were jealous of the fine appearance of the infant and "blew a noxious wind into the mouth," thus killing him. This belief led them to fit fake ears onto the top of the infant's head in many cases, and artificial whiskers were painted on their faces, in an attempt to make the infant "look like a fox" in order to frighten away the evil spirit.

This description was quite dramatic and nobody had the slightest idea what was the cause until Fehily demonstrated that it was infantile beriberi. But she also found some other important facts. No formula foods were available and the Chinese mothers were breast-feeding their infants. Since they themselves had various states of beriberi, they were passing the disease to their babies through their breast milk. In fact, the condition came to be known as breast-milk toxicity until it was identified as beriberi by Fehily's studies.

Perhaps the most dramatic discovery that Fehily made was the fact that the occurrence of sudden death in infants virtually disappeared during the Japanese occupation and instantly reappeared when they withdrew. The explanation may be a little surprising. During the occupation of Hong Kong, the Japanese invaders reduced the intake of rice by the Chinese population to near-starvation levels. Although the mothers were severely malnourished, sudden death ceased in their three- and four-month-old infants, even though they also suffered the effects of malnourishment in other ways. After the Japanese withdrew from the colony, rice was again plentiful, but the sudden death in the breast-fed infants reappeared.

The major lesson to be learned from this story is that the excess of empty calories in the form of plentiful supplies of vitamin-depleted rice consumed by the mothers was even more dangerous to their infants than semi-starvation amounts of the same vitamin-depleted rice. It is, in principle, exactly the same as choking an internal combustion engine in a car. In no way is this to be taken as an implication that starvation of mothers is a cure for sudden death in their infants. It merely illustrates the fact that high-calorie malnutrition has effects which differ considerably from those of starvation.

I will explain this concept further in the next chapter when I discuss the fundamentals of how the body burns fuel to create energy. What I learned is that the effect of naked calories is equivalent to a choked automobile engine. If there is too much gasoline and insufficient *burning capacity*, gasoline is burned incompletely and hydrocarbons are produced which appear as black smoke from the exhaust pipe. The body produces similar compounds under similar circumstances, and they can be found in the urine if the loss of efficiency is great enough. The principle is simple. What we call fuel consumption in an engine refers to an ignition which gives rise to energy. This is known as oxidative metabolism in body chemistry. Inefficient combustion gives rise to changes in the performance of an engine; in the human body, energy production is just as important. In fact, it is the means by which we are able to survive. Loss of efficiency causes illness, and in the immature infant it may give rise to death.

The discovery of this important paper was very dramatic for me. Fehily herself asked in her paper, "Is modern cot death in England really beriberi?" So did I. But the next problem was a difficult one to grapple with. If infant death of this nature occurred suddenly and without warning, how on earth could it be prevented? Because of the interest that was being developed, it was discovered that some of these infants would get certain symptom characteristics which caused them to be called "threatened" or "aborted" SIDS.

I began to see families with a terrifying story. The parents would bring their three-month-old infant. They would claim that they had observed that the baby stopped breathing on numerous occasions. They described the fact that "a little noise" had attracted their attention when he was in the crib. Going to the crib at once, they had found him blue in color and not breathing. They would pick the infant up and slap his buttocks. After a gasp, he would start breathing again and normal color would return to his features.

Such parents would take this infant to the nearest emergency room of a hospital. By the time they arrived, he would be quite normal, and the examining physician would tell the parents that he could find nothing wrong. On returning home, the infant would be placed in the crib, only for the same reaction to recur.

This was a repetitive story and it was impossible not to be moved by the state of alarm exhibited by the parents. They had the double trauma of seeing the phenomenon and having the physician in the emergency room obviously indicate that he thought them to be neurotic alarmists. If studies were done on these babies, nothing showed up, thus "proving" that there was nothing wrong.

I applied my new-found knowledge of infantile beriberi and "put two and two together." I knew, by this time, that the infantile variety of the disease had an effect on the brainstem computer and that this was where the vital controls of automatic breathing were. Perhaps these infants were deficient in thiamin and their brain computers were jeopardized; so why not give them thiamin on clinical trial?

I discovered, by trial and error, that I could give an infant like this as much as 50 milligrams of the vitamin three times a day. The recommended daily allowance is about 1 to 1.5 milligrams a day. These peculiar stoppages in breathing gradually ceased and I would send the baby home while I held my breath! I remember two distraught parents, each of whom had slept in shifts through the night while the other parent observed the child. They had visited several emergency rooms, all of which gave them the cold shoulder, as it were. I admitted the patient and had his breathing monitored while giving him thiamin. The episodes ceased.

At this time, the pediatric medical community had barely accepted SIDS and had absolutely no consideration for the possibility of what later became known as "threatened" SIDS. I worked in isolation because my colleagues thought that I had taken leave of my senses. This attitude was illustrated very forcefully by the following story.

Our department was responsible for giving complete pediatric training to aspiring physicians who were doing their residency. We sent them in rotation to a big community hospital where there was a very large number of infants born, to give them newborn nursery training. There was one young physician who was unusually bright and who had the added advantage of not being arrogant as so many of them were. He was also open-minded to new facts. It may seem a little odd to say, but such open-mindedness is relatively rare in physicians and many of those in training still have the natural arrogance of youth as well.

This physician was doing this particular part of his training when he called me one day. He had an infant who kept having stoppages of respiration. The technical term for this is *apnea*. By this time, I had seen enough of these infants to be reasonably sure that thiamin almost invariably cured the infant of his apnea and *never did any harm*. I suggested a clinical trial, using 50 milligrams of thiamin by injection. He called me again to tell me that this infant had developed an extremely fast heart rate after the injection, so I advised reducing the next dose to 25 milligrams, with the same result. We found that 10 milligrams given for each injection did not do this, but incidents of apnea disappeared completely.

From this case, I thought that I had been giving some of these infants too big a dose of thiamin. However, the next threatened SIDS that I saw needed 50 milligrams three times a day in order to treat him successfully. Each infant apparently required an individualized dose to be maximally efficient.

As a result of this experiment, the resident felt that it was high time that the pediatric staff of the big hospital heard my story and arranged for me to go over and give them a lecture. Absolutely nobody believed me and they made it clear that they thought me to be deluding myself. I became known as "the thiamin man" and it was widely believed by those that thought they knew me that I was "giving *all* my patients thiamin, no matter what was wrong with them."

I will tell one more story of this type to illustrate how advances can be stifled. We had a six-month-old infant in the hospital who had suffered repeated life-threatening episodes of apnea which had required emergency resuscitation. Because of choking on food, and other symptoms, the working diagnosis by the chief of the service was that the child had been born with a congenital abnormality known as a tracheoesophageal fistula. This is a hole in both the windpipe and the esophagus, with a connecting tunnel between them. This defect causes the baby to choke when he is fed. Repeated radiologic studies had failed to show the presence of such an anatomical defect. I considered that he had a metabolic disease and proved it by performing a laboratory test which showed that he had abnormal thiamin metabolism.

While the studies were in process, I had to be absent for a day or two. The chief of service arranged for the infant to go to surgery in my absence to "mend a TE fistula that had not been seen on x-ray studies." It was not there and the surgery was basically unnecessary, although it did prove that that was not the mechanism. After I started him on thiamin, the episodes ceased within a week or so. In spite of this success, not one of my colleagues, to my surprise, ever tried to discuss the mechanism or why I treated him this way. It was considered to be coincidental and therefore unrelated to thiamin administration.

Both parents of this child had tests which yielded similar results, although much less strong. I was not too surprised, therefore, when the mother called me a few months later to say that she was in the hospital and had been told that she had multiple sclerosis. Her son is now twenty years of age and I still see him for health problems. If he allows his diet to deteriorate, he develops symptoms which arise in the nervous system. His mother also gives ample demonstration that she has metabolic handicaps, whether it is called multiple sclerosis or not. Here we see another example of how useless disease classification has become. When we place a patient in a diagnostic pigeon-hole such as multiple sclerosis, it turns off our thought processes. We are apt to say that there is no treatment available for this incurable disease. In actual fact, nutrient therapy has been very helpful for both mother and son in this case, whatever official diagnosis is appended.

It must be understood, of course, that vitamin therapy is often considered a brand of quack therapy and it has always been a surprise to me that physicians are so frequently antagonistic to things that do not fit with their preconceived ideas. How quickly an innovator can be relegated to the ranks of the fraudulent has been shown repeatedly throughout the history of medicine.

Gradually, the pediatric community came to realize that sudden death was not always the first evidence of potential SIDS. Some studies performed by Dr. Steinschneider, a pediatrician at the Upstate Medical Center in Syracuse, clearly showed that many of these infants would have symptoms which indicated that they were indeed at risk. Threatened SIDS at last became a "respectable" diagnosis.

At this point I was happy to be able to team up with a physician whose specialty was in the pediatric intensive care unit. He was only too well aware that threatened SIDS was an important entity that required definition. We asked another doctor to help us. This doctor had a machine that was capable of testing the brain computer, even in a small infant. The machine is called Brainstem Auditory Evoked Potential (BAEP). It embraces the same basic principles that govern the use of the electroencephalogram (EEG) which is used in the diagnosis of epilepsy.

As we have discussed, chemistry in the brain generates electricity, so during an EEG the electrodes placed on the head of a patient pick up these electrical rhythms. The machine magnifies the rhythms and wave patterns are printed out and then read by a specialist. With the BAEP machine, an earphone is placed over the infant's ear; this makes little clicking noises, the intensity of which can be controlled by the operator. Electrodes on the head pick up only the electrical rhythms that are generated in the brainstem, the computer. The clicking noises in the ear stimulate the auditory nerve which passes a signal into the brainstem, generating wave patterns that can be printed out and analyzed like those of the EEG.

We found that the patterns generated by some of these infants with threatened SIDS were abnormal. Other research, from detailed microscopic studies of brains from infants that had died, showed that that part of the brain had suffered numerous biochemical insults. What these researchers found was that minute areas had been deprived of oxygen long enough to cause a visible change that could be seen under the microscope.

The conclusion that has been reached so far by the majority of workers in this field is that the episodes of apnea lead to loss of oxygen which is responsible for the damaged areas. It is the classic chicken-and-the-egg argument. Which comes first? Is the damage that is seen evidence of the cause? Or the effect?

I believe that there is a quite natural explanation which actually provides a reason for my discovery of thiamin response in these infants. It is an explanation that will become much clearer in the next chapter when we discuss how the body *uses* oxygen. A great research scientist by the name of Sir Rudolph Peters performed some of the early research work with thiamin. It had been known for years that a condition called polyneuritis could easily be induced in pigeons by giving them a thiamin-deficient diet. It was used as a model in the studies of beriberi and its relationship with this vitamin.

Peters was trying to find out how thiamin deficiency caused its effects in the brain and nervous system. He used thiamin-deficient pigeon brain in his experiments, and he discovered something which was, I believe, of the utmost importance in understanding the basis of SIDS. It is so fundamental that I must describe it in some detail.

It is possible to make a test-tube preparation of pigeon brain cells while the cells are still alive. If the brain is quickly removed from the bird, some of the cells to be studied can be made, by using a blunt bone spatula, into a sort of tissue mulch called brei. By measuring carbon dioxide emitted from the cells, a researcher can evaluate respiration in the cells. By *respiration* we mean that the cells take up oxygen and burn sugar, thus forming the oxide of carbon, or carbon dioxide gas. Peters measured respiration of cells taken from brainstems of thiamin-deficient pigeons and compared it with that seen in normal, thiamin-replete pigeons. To his surprise, there was no difference at all—until he added glucose to the preparation! It was immediately obvious that the thiamin-deficient cells did not produce any more carbon dioxide than they had before glucose was added. The cells from normal thiamin-replete pigeons, however, produced a greatly increased amount of carbon dioxide. They were burning the glucose as fuel, a process known in cellular biology as *oxidation.*

From this experiment, Peters went on to study the oxidation process in more detail, providing us with highly significant information about the role of thiamin in this vital, life-sustaining process. He made another discovery whose importance has probably not been sufficiently emphasized. The lower part of a pigeon's brain was much more active in the oxidation process than the upper brain. If this finding can be extrapolated to the human brain, we are talking about the brainstem, the computer.

There is circumstantial evidence to support this notion that the brainstem computer requires more oxygen than the upper brain to carry on its diverse activities. One of the specific effects of thiamin deficiency in man, sometimes seen in alcoholics, is a brain condition described by a doctor named Wernicke. In this disease, the computer is badly affected, and autonomic nervous system control is seriously jeopardized. In infants, an inherited disease is seen that is also known to be associated with abnormal thiamin metabolism. These infants die from prolonged apnea which results in suffocation. At autopsy, they are found to have in the brainstem microscopic changes very similar to those seen in adults with the condition described by Wernicke.

Now, the obvious question is whether thiamin deficiency is *the* specific cause of SIDS. To that we can safely answer—no, it is not! We know from the work of several researchers that magnesium deficiency will cause sudden death if the deficiency affects the brain computer. A relatively recent paper from Norwegian investigators has shown that SIDS deaths are associated with the biochemical fingerprints of a dysfunction in the process of oxidation. Thus it is possible to suggest that death in these infants is associated with inefficient use of oxygen in the brain cells. Oxygen is obviously ineffective unless it is *used* by the tissues.

It is not the oxygen that is lacking. Neither is it lack of fuel. We can be fairly safe in stating that it is respiration of cells that is affected. The catalysts that are needed for this complex process are lacking. Again we turn to the analogy of an automobile engine: gasoline cannot be burned without a spark plug to ignite the reaction. Oxidation cannot take place in human tissues unless vitamin and mineral catalysts are present. Thus, it is possible that any one or more of these deficiencies can result in inefficient oxidation. Thiamin and magnesium have been found to be important therapeutic tools, but you can be sure that they are not the only ones and will not save all the infants affected by the mechanism of SIDS. We know, for example, that deficiency of selenium, another "spark plug" or non-caloric nutrient, causes sudden death in calves.

Well, what *is* the mechanism? To explain this, we have to return to what happens in moderately thiamin-depleted individuals. They become irritable and quarrelsome and develop what I call a trigger-happy autonomic nervous system. They develop fragments of the fight-or-flight reflex that was described in detail in the last chapter. Why does the computer become more highly reactive under these conditions? Although I do not know the answer, I can postulate a reason. Let's go back to considering how MN would handle the situation. What could present a greater danger to her experimental animal than being in an environment that has insufficient oxygen? So the computer tries to activate the whole organism by executive signals that go out to the various organs of the body in a fight-or-flight mechanism. The computer, being a machine in its own right, cannot distinguish between lack of oxygen and lack of the catalysts that enable cells to use it. Disorganized autonomic and endocrine resources are mobilized and, by awakening the whole organism, alert it to its environmental danger.

However, in the case of the infant, the system is immature and the disorganized reflexes either stop the infant's breathing or stop the heart from beating. We have ample information that tells us that these infants stop breathing or die from cardiac arrest. In threatened SIDS cases, it is now possible to affix to the infant's body electrodes which are connected to an electronic alarm system. If apnea lasts longer than a certain preset period, or if heart rate drops below preset speed, an alarm sounds. This awakens the parents and, on some occasions the infant has been found blue and limp. Picking him up and/or slapping his buttocks will signal the computer, and the heart or breathing mechanism resumes its normal activity. On other occasions, the alarm gives an auditory stimulus to the infant, causing resumption of normal heart or respiratory activity. When the frightened parents reach their infant, he has already resumed this automatic activity. It may not be possible to differentiate between a false alarm, because of poor electrode contact with skin, from a true incident which corrects the situation by auditory input to the infant.

My own experience with infant alarms of this type was very rich. I found repeatedly that when I gave the infant large doses of thiamin, the alarms ceased and I was rewarded by seeing normal, healthy infants emerge into well children of happy and relieved parents. I remember a pediatric neurologist who had seen many such cases of threatened SIDS. He would place them on the alarm systems, and when he started giving them thiamin he said to me one day, "I cannot tell you what a relief it is to me to find that those alarms on my patients stop ringing."

Why have specialists in this field not picked up this simple measure? The subject of SIDS has financed many a research grant, and it is wrapped up in mystery and complex technology. If an answer as simple as this were to become known, there would be a loss of research grant money. Indeed, there is *no* money in the use of nutrients which can be readily obtained at a health food store. Also, I believe that we have so encouraged the mystique of medicine through advanced technology that we are largely incapable of developing a relatively simple therapeutic approach to *any* medical problem. We need to heed the words of Dr. Johan Bjorksten, former president of the American Institute of Chemists and now president of his own research foundation: "The way of evolution and of nature is to favor simple solutions over the complex."

In the professional climate that I was in, it was virtually impossible to get anything published on this approach. Physicians who send papers to prestigious medical journals, or who give erudite reports to research meetings, must perform clinical experiments in a method known as a double-blind controlled approach. This means that the patients must become human guinea pigs, and the studies have to be financed by research money. It is obviously unethical to ask a patient to finance his treatment when he is actually only receiving a sugar pill. The sugar pill, called a placebo, looks like the real thing. The genuine treatment is expected to be better than the placebo if it is effective.

In the case of threatened SIDS infants, I considered it unethical to give *any* of them a placebo when I knew that thiamin had helped a number of them and was so completely safe. The fundamental and deeply incarcerated antagonism to any form of vitamin therapy expressed by the vast body of orthodox medical philosophy made it certain that no research grant money would be obtainable from those who hold the purse strings.

During this exciting and rewarding period, I had a call from a professor at an Australian university. He had read a letter that I had written to the editor of *Lancet,* a prestigious English medical journal. This letter, which was published a few years before, had documented the case of an infant that had responded to large doses of thiamin. It had caused him to search the medical literature for further evidence of thiamin-responsive disease. He also had concluded that SIDS was related to brainstem deficiency of this vitamin.

He invited me to go to Australia to cooperate with him. Unfortunately, he must have been surprised that I accepted his invitation, for when I got there he had no plans at all for me to work with him and in fact actually became quite paranoid that I might steal the results of his own work. However, it had some very definite dividends. I learned that at the reference laboratory for the whole continent scientists were studying the concentration of specific vitamins in the blood of Australians. I learned also that a number of SIDS infants had been found to have extremely high concentrations of thiamin in their blood and other body fluids. Some of them had high concentrations of folic acid and B_{12}, both B vitamins.

This finding was, of course, completely the opposite of what we had expected. It was hard to claim deficiency of a vitamin when it was found to be markedly increased in the blood. The doctor in the laboratory knew the professor who had given me the invitation, and they had reasoned an explanation. It is an axiom that a vitamin is *not* the pill that the patient takes. The pill actually contains a stable precursor, meaning that it has to be converted by the body into the metabolically active substance. The biochemical conversions that have to take place in the body are called activations. To activate thiamin, it has to go through several complex reactions before it becomes biologically effective. It was suggested that thiamin, and the other B vitamins that had been found to be increased, were collecting in the body in a biologically inactive form. This reasoning makes sense because there was a *biologic* deficiency, even though thiamin was present in an excessive—but *inert*—amount. It is possible, if this were true, that some of my large doses of thiamin given to my threatened SIDS infants had, in some way, "barged through" to an active form simply by their huge concentration. That possibility, however, has never been investigated further, to my knowledge.

When I returned to America, I received a letter from a previous resident who was in practice in New Zealand and knew of my interest in SIDS. He wrote to ask whether there was anything new in the field, because he had experienced a relatively large number of SIDS deaths in his locality. I wrote back and told him about my experience in Australia.

He then did something very constructive and imaginative. He took twenty samples of blood and sent them to the Australian vitamin laboratory. Each sample was from a different person who was either sick or well and each was codified with a number. No reference was made to whether the sample came from a sick or a well person, and no ages were provided. What the laboratory did not know was that three of these samples came from infants who had died from SIDS. Two of the three infants were easily identified by the quite extraordinary increase in thiamin that was found. The third infant did not have the elevation in thiamin, indicating that the condition has a number of different causes.

This finding was quite extraordinary and would be statistically very significant. It was never followed up properly, however. I did not have the research facilities, and what little research money I had previously been able to glean was no longer forthcoming. Vitamin therapy was still considered fraudulent. I maintain that this particular finding was a tremendously important one and might have led to a major understanding of the mechanisms involved in SIDS deaths.

By this time I had become interested in the fat-soluble form of thiamin, discussed in earlier chapters, called TTFD. I saw a number of infants who were having obvious brainstem computer-related problems. Their Brainstem Auditory Evoked Potentials (BAEP) would be wildly abnormal and they would respond clinically to TTFD. One was a little girl of about nine months when I first saw her. She had experienced so many episodes of prolonged apnea and repeated hospital admissions that the parents were beside themselves. I ascertained that the mother had consumed massive amounts of cola during pregnancy and was a junk-food junkie.

The BAEP produced a wave pattern that was so grossly abnormal that one of the leading experts in BAEP technology did not believe it when he saw it much later. He accused my BAEP operating colleague of ineptitude and even fraud. I gave this child an injection of TTFD intravenously. During the procedure, she had a brief apnea, indicating that the brainstem was biologically affected by the infusion. Much later, I learned that nutrients, when given to very sick people, make things symptomatically worse before they get better. I have called this phenomenon a paradox, meaning the opposite of what is expected by the patient. It is a very important event which obviously will strain the patient/doctor relationship unless it is understood by both physician and patient, since any treatment is naturally supposed to make the patient feel better rather than worse. The patient must always be warned of this possibility in any form of nutritional therapy.

The child was still hooked up to the BAEP machine as my colleague and I were discussing our next move. After about fifteen minutes, I said to him, "Rich, why don't you turn the machine on again and get another tracing?"

"Oh, that is absurd," he replied. "It is much too soon for anything to work that fast!"

"What have you got to lose?" I asked. "After all, the child is asleep and you will not disturb her."

All he had to do was to press a switch in order to obtain a new tracing from the child. He did so, and we were amazed to find that the tracing had indeed improved greatly—within fifteen minutes!

This response obviously meant that the problem in the child's brain was electrical in character and clearly related to chemistry in the brain cells. It was a very exciting moment for me because nobody believed that we were doing anything at all for this kind of child. Indeed, we received nothing but angry criticism.

We started this child on TTFD in the form of pills and kept retesting her BAEP every day or so. We were able to trace a gradual day-by-day improvement in the tracings which clearly correlated with her clinical improvement. They never became normal because too much damage had been done already, but her clinical well-being increased strikingly and she stopped having emergency admissions to hospital for sudden alarming symptoms such as apnea or slowing of the heart rate. We published her case and that of two other infants that we treated in this manner. We were so convinced that we had an effective new method of helping infants with threatened SIDS that we issued a press release—something that is "forbidden" in science unless you have absolute proof. We found ourselves surrounded by extreme hostility from every corner, and everything was done to prevent us continuing with the work.

Now, fourteen years later, I still see the child in this case. She has learning disabilities and is certainly not completely normal, but she would have died without our help. One of the most important complications that she has had is a twisted spine, a defect known as scoliosis. What few people know is that this defect is related to abnormal activity in the brain computer, or brainstem, the part of the brain that we proved to be in electrical trouble when she was an infant. There is no better example of the vastly important relationship between the brain and the body.

Ondine's Curse

Ondine: Live, Hans. You too will forget.
Hans: Live! It's easy to say. If at least I could work up a little interest in living, but I'm too tired to make the effort. Since you left me, Ondine, all the things my body once did by itself, it does now only by special order. . .It's an exhausting piece of management I've undertaken. I have to supervise five senses, two hundred bones, a thousand muscles. A single moment of inattention, and I forget to breathe. He died, they will say, because it was a nuisance to breathe.

Ondine, Act II by Jean Giraudaux

Strangely, there is a disease called Ondine's Curse. The name is derived from the mythological character depicted in the play. Ondine was a water nymph who fell in love with a mortal who jilted her. In her fury she cursed him with loss of automatic body functions.

A victim of Ondine's Curse is a person whose automatic breathing mechanism has been damaged or whose genetically-determined function in this respect has been compromised. The disease may not become clinically obvious for some years, and the respiratory paralysis may be triggered intermittently by a relatively simple stress factor. In a sense, SIDS is related to Ondine's Curse since most of the affected infants die from prolonged cessation of breathing. Some, however, die because the central mechanism in the computer stops the infant's heart. For that reason, SIDS alarm systems have to register both respiratory cessation and slowing of the heart.

There is absolutely no question in my mind that there is an hereditary element in SIDS, as indeed there is in every disease. The inheritance does not cause the disease to operate in the active sense. It represents a genetically-determined deficiency or inefficiency which operates under stress. The machinery is "weighed in the balance and found wanting." Therefore the stress factors in life are incredibly important. They are the triggers, not the cause.

I have seen many families in which there were several SIDS infants. In one large family, I discovered no less than thirteen instances where SIDS could be considered from the reported circumstances. In another, the child whom I saw had a compromised brain computer. There were two SIDS patients in the immediate family. When the mother investigated her family relationships, she found that she was related to her husband! We know, of course, that consanguinity of that nature increases the chance of a disadvantageous inheritance pattern.

Why should I spend virtually the best part of a chapter on the subject of SIDS? It is not something that would interest everybody, and many readers might assume that this was "merely one kind of special disease."

Ah! But that is just the point that I am trying to make. Disease is not what it seems and what we have been programmed to believe. The body is a complex machine that is organized and regulated by a computer in the brainstem—a reiteration which is designed to be remembered by those who read this book. The collapse of the automatic functions of the body must be a fairly well-known phenomenon throughout history, because Ondine had appeared and reappeared as a mythologic character. (She had also been called

Undine.) We can presume that the idea crept in because such a disaster was repeatedly observed.

I hope that this concept of the brain/body relationship in our ability to adapt to our environment is now perceived as one which makes some sense to the reader. Perhaps we are ready to see how hyperactivity in children can actually be seen as a phenomenon of the computer and how it is therefore distantly related to SIDS. Perhaps it will be easier to see why both of these disorders, so widely differing in our orthodox thinking, are really variations on a theme!

Hyperactivity

There is almost a classical and oft-repeated history in hyperactive children. The pregnancy is a poor guide because it is often classed as normal, in spite of the fact that mother often has nausea and vomiting throughout. This fact may, in itself, be a sign of poor nutrition, and it is worth remembering that it is the brain, not the abdominal organs, which is responsible for nausea and vomiting. The fetus is, of course, nourished by the mother, so her malnutrition can easily be reflected in the development of the fetus. It has been known for many years that vitamin intake *in sufficient quantity* in pregnancy is an efficient protection against developmental abnormalities in the fetus, but this relationship has not been explored properly until recently. It is now fairly well accepted, for example, that sufficient folic acid in the diet of the mother will prevent neural tube defects in her baby. In my own practice, I give pregnant mothers the megadoses of vitamins that they have when they are not pregnant. I find that the pregnancy is smoother, well-being increased, and the unusually peaceful personality of the baby is quite striking.

This digression is to state that nutrition in pregnancy is critical in the well-being and development of the baby. The next thing to be noted is that many hyperactive children have a history of jaundice at birth. Some of them are treated with blue-light therapy to reduce the jaundice, but it is seldom regarded as anything important. To me, it suggests that liver chemistry is inefficient in that infant. Persistence of inefficiency in other organs or tissues might later be the cause of clinical problems that are not directly related to liver function.

The next part of the history represents a phenomenon that has destroyed the sleep of many a mother—colic. The infant might cry almost constantly, day and night. He may be inconsolable. Many mothers walk the floor with the infant hoisted onto one shoulder while she pats the infant's back and jiggles herself up and down with a worried expression on her face. Or the colic may only occur between the hours of 6 and 10PM in milder cases. I have talked to mothers who have literally not had a complete night's sleep for two years! I do not know how they stand it. Phone calls to the pediatrician often result in change of formula. One day, when the colic ceases, as it always does sooner or later, the formula that the infant is then receiving will be hailed as the curative formula. If the infant is breast-fed, the mother will occasionally be told that her milk is insufficient or inadequate and she might be told to purchase a formula.

At about the end of the first or second year, the infant begins to get bouts of irritability, often associated with pulling at an ear. If there is associated fever, a pediatrician is consulted and a diagnosis of ear infection is made. An antibiotic is prescribed, and the supposed infection settles down, but the same process is gone through again a few weeks later. The child, now a toddler, has repeated courses of antibiotics. The episodes are frequently more common in winter, but may occur throughout the year. At about the age of four years, this mother is frequently told that the child needs to have ear tubes, small plastic tubes that are inserted through the eardrum by a specialist. Mothers often believe that such tubes are to drain the middle ear. In actual fact, however, the fluid behind the eardrum is more like Jell-o than fluid, and it does not run out. It is true that, in many instances, the infections cease, but let us get it clear why. The tubes let air into the middle ear and the oxygen is used for metabolic purposes which then causes the fluid to disappear.

The mother may have noted by this time that her child has temper tantrums, sometimes five or six times a day. He is often irritable, sleeps restlessly and sweats, grinds his teeth, and has nightmares. Sometimes there may be night terrors where he will sit up in bed with his heart pounding and scream. Or he may awaken and go into the parents' bedroom, complaining of a frightening dream. He may be overactive by this time, but over-activity is so common in American children that it may be judged as normal behavior. Such children have to be watched constantly, for they can wreck the average room or office within minutes. They fiddle with things, pull out drawers, and are constantly "looking for trouble."

The first intimation to the mother that the child is joining the ranks of the hyperactivity epidemic is the call from the kindergarten teacher, advising the mother that she is unable to cope with the child. The child may be referred to the school psychologist, depending on how bad the behavior is. From there, a child neurologist may be consulted and Ritalin prescribed. To see how common this process is, it is known that in one of the states in the Union as many as 5 percent of the grade-school children are receiving Ritalin. This drug is so widely used that a teacher may make the child's school attendance conditional on its use.

There is now a vast array of diagnostic tags or labels which are used to pigeon-hole these children. Hyperactivity and hyperkinesia are identical terms, but there is also Attention Deficit Syndrome (ADS), Minimal Brain Dysfunction (MBD) and, the *coup de grace*, Giles de la Tourette Syndrome.

When I examine such children, I am looking for simple physical evidence of hyperactivity generated in the computer. They often have an appearance of the tongue which superficially resembles a strawberry. Little red spots stick up on the surface and represent inflamed papillae, part of the structure of the surface of the tongue. A light coating completes the appearance. There is often a zone of pallor around the mouth which can be so obvious that the child looks as though he is made up as a clown. The heartbeat is often fast but may be slow, and there is often an excessively strong beat. Systolic blood pressure, the upper one that physicians record, may be high, and in some cases the lower one, called the diastolic, very low, in some cases zero. In fact, I have learned that the difference between these two pressures, known as the pulse pressure, is actually a very important way of examining the way in which the brain computer is functioning.

There are other changes which clearly delineate the fact that the autonomic nervous system is not carrying out its adaptive task with appropriate balance and efficiency. So we should try to analyze what is going on.

In order to understand the problem, let us go back to the brain/body mechanisms of a newborn infant. He has been defined as "a mass of unconditioned reflexes leaking at all orifices." The infant's brain is not finished off at birth, and, although all the parts are physically there, only the computer is really functioning. In other words, all body functions are automated. The bladder fills, sends an input signal to the computer that reflexes to the bladder, causing it to empty. The same thing happens with the bowel. Does such an infant have conscious awareness? I do not think so. Who amongst us remembers the day of his birth? The earliest memories vary from person to person and represent the first time that conscious awareness showed itself.

In physiologic terms, at this time the computer begins to talk to the upper, cognitive, brain. The cognitive brain, for example, becomes aware that the urinary bladder is full; however, it prevents the emptying reflex until the child can get to a place where the act may take place. We refer to this as "toilet training," but it is really an automatic development which comes under the heading of growing up or maturation. If this process is delayed, then the functional responses will remain infantile. (During the development, the cognitive brain may have less inhibiting power during sleep; hence, bed wetting, or enuresis, is fairly common in children but disappears as they mature.)

Since the computer produces emotional responses, it is responsible for much early childhood behavior. Temper tantrums are not *consciously* produced. They are involuntary, though the cognitive brain may well be aware that they are happening and be powerless to inhibit them. One of the earliest signs of a maturation process with respect to temper tantrums is that the child volunteers an apology. The conscious brain speaks after the heat of the event.

Now we can begin to see how the physical and the mental come together in understanding the hyperactive child whose history we have described. First of all, the computer is easily made trigger-happy by very ordinary circumstances related to the quality of diet. Many modern foods are difficult to burn in the body, and the manufacture of energy to drive the body as a whole is compromised. The initial evidence of an irritable brain is colic. It is not the bowel that is the problem. It is merely acting as a slave to whatever signal it gets from the computer.

The smooth interplay of the mental and physical is altered by poor metabolism in the brain. Curiously enough, it becomes more reactive to input stimulus and the adaptive traffic of executive messages is activated much too easily. Hence the colic is produced by reflex, and the ear infections are really evidence of inefficient metabolism in tissues that use oxygen heavily. Later on, the child develops hyperactivity and the related conditions which are named as though they were different diseases but are all really the same. They represent variations on a symphonic theme, with the more severe being due to the volume turned up. They are, in fact, different complex reflexes of the computer which affect the inappropriate naughty behavior of the child.

To understand the underlying mechanism of hyperactivity, it is necessary to know how energy for cellular function is generated. This process will be dealt with in a separate chapter when the whole process of oxidative metabolism will be reduced to everyday language. I believe that future generations of physicians will discard the present medical model more or less completely as an unrealistic concept of what disease really is. We have to see each human being as a live machine. Each of us is surrounded by a hostile environment to which we are forced to adapt, or we cannot survive. Disease represents a war between that environment and our ability to defend ourselves. Health means that we are in a state of equilibrium which is continuously monitored by the ever-watchful computer.

Chapter 9

Oxygen Drives the Adaptive Machinery

When a patient asks me why he is sick, I will often give an answer which is confusing if it is not thoroughly explained. I say "because cells in your body are using oxygen inefficiently." As one might expect, I will get a blank stare from the patient. So this chapter is written to explain how cells use oxygen and why.

Let us start by going back to some simple definitions:

Efficiency

Any machine uses fuel to generate energy which powers the machine. During the process, some of that energy is squandered in the form of heat, light, noise, and friction. Efficiency represents the percentage of energy produced from burning the fuel that is *consumed in useful work done by the machine*.

I am informed by a mechanical engineer that a modern automobile can have an efficiency as high as 50 percent, although when one considers the amount of friction in the working parts, the noise that it makes, and other mechanical factors, this seems surprisingly high. However, it means that only 50 percent is used in actually moving the vehicle. Cells within the human body also have engines which must burn fuel in order to power the activities of the cell. The efficiency is somewhere in the range of 75 percent, considerably better than the car engine. The energy expended is used in useful work performed by the cell, including heat production, which keeps our bodies warm. It is for that reason that we are called warm-blooded animals.

Of course, that body temperature is an important part of our adaptive mechanisms and is carefully controlled by the computer in the brain. When heat production is increased because of the imposition of a stress factor, body temperature goes up and we call it a fever.

I mention the word *stress* because I remember an incident when I was a student. It was a Saturday and while playing rugby I had received an injury to my knee. That evening I had been invited to a party and, during the course of the evening, I developed symptoms that made me believe that I was getting the flu. I was a guest at someone's house that night and returned there prematurely, leaving the party. I discovered that my temperature was somewhere around 101°F and was therefore convinced that it was indeed the flu. In the morning, I was completely well and had no fever. In trying to explain the situation, I gave the matter a great deal of thought. I decided that my brain computer had devised a response to the knee injury which was the equivalent of the kind of response that it might make to an infection. It was responding to stress in a general sense. I concluded that it represented an "overkill" and that it was the kind of reaction that might well occur in anybody, particularly if the computer is in an overactive state.

Oxidation

Fuel + Oxygen + Catalyst = Energy

High school physics and chemistry have taught us that combustion is a process by which an inflammable fuel is combined chemically with oxygen. We have many words to describe such a process—*explosion, burning, combustion,* and *fire* are a few of them. In every single instance, the phenomenon is related to the *speed* at which the reaction occurs. Obviously, an explosion is a very fast reaction, whereas smoldering is a slow and less dangerous state of combustion. As everyone knows, when oxygen combines with a fuel, energy is produced and an ash is formed. A more technical term for ash is *oxides,* clearly indicating that the ash is a byproduct of an oxygen-driven chemical reaction.

In the human body, we call the process of combustion *oxidation.* If there is too little oxidation, we call it hypo-oxidation and if there is too much, hyperoxidation. Maintaining the appropriate level of oxidation is much like the challenge of keeping a domestic fire under control. Obviously, if it is not burning very well, little heat energy will be produced. If it is too vigorous, however, the heat energy may cause ignition of nearby flammable fuel and spread the fire.

There is an extremely important principle that runs through this concept. *Energy is required to make energy.* Let me illustrate this truth by turning back to my favorite analogy, the internal combustion engine. Notice the simple equation above which we have used to indicate how oxidation yields energy.

Gasoline + Air + Spark Plug = Energy

Note that this equation is the same as the first one except for word substitutions. What *is* a spark plug? Well, as everyone knows, it is an electrical device that causes gasoline to ignite when it enters the cylinder. The explosion that occurs is carefully controlled, and the energy derived from it is used to move the vehicle. If such an explosion were to occur outside the engine, the energy from it would be dissipated in the form of heat, light, and sound and could not be used for useful work purposes. Therefore, an engine is really an energy transducer. It takes a form of energy and converts it to another form which can be used to perform useful work.

Notice that the spark plug requires a source of energy as well. That comes from a battery which is another energy transducer. It takes the energy that is locked up in the chemicals and transduces it to electrical energy. This is then used to create heat in the form of a spark. There is, as the saying goes, no "free lunch." Energy is created *only* by the consumption of energy. If all that energy were 100 percent converted into useful work, we would have something that engineers have sought for years, perpetual motion. Some of the energy that is produced from the transduction is lost in the process, and the percentage that is actually used in work is what is termed efficiency.

Why do I go into so much detail on this point? Very simply, I have found that my patients invariably enter my consulting room without the faintest notion of the major differences in my approach to their problems of health. When I tell them that their fibromyositis is due to lack of oxidative efficiency, they obviously do not understand what I am talking about. They have been taught that their painful muscles are inflamed and that the usual and customary approach is to prescribe an anti-inflammatory drug. What they fail to realize is the *basic reason* their muscles are inflamed. Indeed, I am less interested in the symptom than I am in the cause of it.

A catalyst is a substance that initiates a chemical reaction but does not, itself, participate in that reaction. Hence, a spark plug is a catalyst in the fusion of oxygen with gasoline. Vitamins and minerals that we ingest with our food are catalysts which act in the same way, at least in principle. They "ignite" the food in the process which we have described as oxidation.

Now, we can begin to focus on what happens. Food, consisting of the burnable components which we call calories, is mixed with the catalysts that enable the process to occur. That is why vitamins and minerals are called noncaloric nutrients. Meanwhile, we breathe into our lungs air, about 20 percent of which is oxygen, and the blood picks up the oxygen by a wonderful method. Red blood cells are coated with the pigment hemoglobin, which has an avidity to combine with oxygen. The blood thereby picks up oxygen from the lungs and transports it to the tissues throughout the body. Here a chemical reaction takes place, and the oxygen is donated to the cells, where it is combined with fuel to yield energy. Presently, we will see how this energy is formed and how it is stored.

The Engine

Each cell in the body has to be a self-contained unit. It has a function to perform, and groups of cells join together to form tissues, or organs. Cooperation of cells depends upon their ability to communicate. In a very complex chemical language, they talk to each other. Brain cells talk to body cells through the systems that we have already discussed. Body cells talk to each other and also back to the brain.

Each cell, in order to be self-contained, must have the ability to unlock chemical energy from nutrients and transduce it to another form of energy. Therefore, each cell has a group of subcellular components called mitochondria which, when working together, form the engine of the cell. How is this energy produced and how is it used?

Citric Acid Cycle

Biochemistry is massively complex and requires a great deal of knowledge to understand it. However, it can be reduced to basic principles. A mechanism known as the citric acid cycle is primarily responsible for the first part of the human engine. It can be likened to the crank case of an internal combustion engine. Imagine a wheel which rotates. Now think of a series of chemical reactions which occur on the circumference of the wheel in a chain. Starting with a substance A that is derived by a chemical reaction from glucose, the chain of reactions occurs around the circumference, returning to form substance A again. Each time this wheel rotates, it sucks in more glucose and energy is released in the form of charged electrons from the bottom of the wheel. The wheel can be slowed down or accelerated, so there is a built-in control mechanism that can be likened to a throttle or an accelerator.

The Electron Transfer Chain

Electrons delivered from the citric acid cycle are picked up by a chemical substance known as an electron carrier and delivered to the electron transfer chain. This chain is a remarkable device which uses the electrons in a power drive to create a substance known as adenosine triphosphate (ATP), the chemical form of energy stored in the cell.

In order to grasp this idea, let us take a much simpler engine in the form of a bow and arrow. Remember that we have always to be mindful that energy is derived only from the expenditure of energy. A man takes his bow, which is really an engine, and fits an arrow into place. As he draws back the bow string, he is expending energy, by the use of his arm, and converting it into energy stored in the taut bow string. All he has to do in order to fire the arrow is to let go of the string. The forces used are carefully controlled.

In order to use this analogy for our purpose, the archer's arm is the equivalent of the electron transfer chain. The taut bow string is the equivalent of the chemical energy stored as ATP in the cell. When a signal from the brain alerts a cell to action, the source of its energy is ATP, which is continuously formed as it is used. It is part of the supply economics of each cell and enables it to perform its function.

This magnified picture of a cellular engine, when translated into words, provides an impression of clanking pistons and grinding wheels. However, the reality is much more spectacular: these reactions are chemical in nature and are going on at the molecular level inside a cell unit that can be seen only with a microscope. Even more wonderful is the fact that this kind of engine provides the energy for every one of the hundred trillion cells that make up the body. As the engine runs, so fuel and oxygen are consumed. We can put together a fairly simple scenario to explain how oxidation is kept under control.

Bell-Shaped Curve

We have established the process through which the body extracts oxygen from air and transports it to tissues, where it participates in the complex process called oxidation. Oxygen is the primary nutrient for the body, vital to life. Nutrients are generally thought of as food, but a nutrient may be defined as a chemical substance that sustains life; and so oxygen is the primary nutrient. Herein lies a paradox. If we cannot obtain oxygen we die, or suffocate. On the other hand, too much oxygen is lethal too. We return to the ancient Chinese concept of Yin and Yang: too little oxygen causes death; too much also causes death. It is generally quite easy to understand that oxidation is impossible without oxygen. It is usually harder for people to understand why too much is damaging and, dependent upon the increasing concentration, eventually lethal. Every well-trained sports diver, for example, is trained to use only compressed air when diving because pure oxygen is highly toxic when breathed at greater than two atmospheres of pressure, which is achieved at thirty-three feet below the surface. And although oxygen is used medicinally, it must be controlled. To simplify this complex subject, we can simply say that oxygen is a lethal gas as well as the primary nutrient. The determining factor is the dose.

This Yin/Yang phenomenon applies to all nutrients, even water. A complete deficiency of a given vitamin will also be lethal. As the dose is increased beyond that which the body can handle, it gradually becomes toxic and ultimately lethal. A major difference between nutrients is that some are toxic with relatively small concentration increases, whereas others require an extremely large amount to be toxic or lethal. The wideness of this dose relationship is what I call *the dose window*. If the window is small, then only a small increase will cause toxicity. For example, selenium is now known to be a vital nutrient, but we require only a few micrograms a day. (A microgram is 1/1000 of a milligram, which is 1/1000 of a gram, so you can see why selenium is known as a trace element.) Selenium is so toxic in amounts greater than we need that in 1957 selenium was still classified as a poison.

Contrast that situation with vitamin C. We are learning that the recommended allowance of this vitamin in official circles is absurdly small. Yet doctors have given patients as much as 200 grams of this vitamin intravenously for therapeutic purposes; it can be said that the dose window is huge. It becomes clear, therefore, that introduction of a nutrient such as selenium as a therapeutic nutrient has to be done with much more care than, say, vitamin C, even though both are vital nutrients.

Now, let us turn to Figure 3, the bell-shaped curve. We have drawn a simple graphic chart in which the horizontal axis represents the volume of oxygen being used in a biochemical system within the body. The vertical axis is labeled *Efficiency*, and it will be remembered that normal efficiency in human chemistry is about 75 percent.

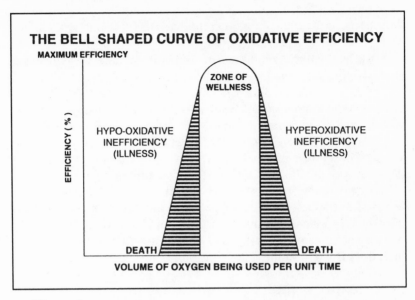

Figure 3.

We can see that as the volume of oxygen increases, the efficiency increases and then decreases, thus providing us with a curve that looks like a bell. Notice that efficiency is zero at both ends of the curve because that is what we call death. If a body is no longer using oxygen, life cannot be sustained. The moment we are born, we start to use oxygen and we rapidly gain efficiency of 75 percent—the prime of life. The body works to maintain that level of efficiency under all circumstances of activity.

Dietary indiscretion, together with the normal process of aging and coupled to the variable degree of stress imposed upon a given individual, will inevitably erode efficiency. As that efficiency declines to 74 percent, 70 percent, 65 percent—or whatever—sooner or later the body will begin to feel the difference and symptoms will begin. The brain, particularly the computer, is the organ that feels that loss first and reacts to it by sending out alarm signals to the body. The result is that the individual begins to suffer from functional changes in adaptive controls. Such a state of affairs might be loosely called maladaptation.

On the left side of the bell we have loss of efficiency because of lack of oxidation. On the right side we have loss of efficiency in spite of a high-oxygen consumption. Both these zones can be thought of as zones of sickness. Note that illness can therefore be construed in broadest terms as *loss of efficiency in metabolism.* I can hear a person say, "What utter nonsense—what about pneumonia? Isn't that due to an infection?"

I ask that person to think again. Why did the infecting organism successfully attack and cause the disease in the first place? Perhaps it was because the patient did not have the ability to mobilize an adequate defense. Why do some people walk into a room where there is a patient with flu and not succumb to the viral infection? Why do some people carry the HIV (AIDS) virus and not succumb to AIDS, sometimes for years? Simply because their own body defenses are good, in turn dependent upon efficiency which allows maximum protection.

To return to the graph, it is easy to understand inefficiency on the left side of the bell. Understanding it on the right is more difficult. If oxygen is not delivered to the tissues, or if it is not used properly because of inadequate catalysts, deprivation will be obvious. But— how does it work on the other side?

Free Oxygen Radicals

We are seeing more and more information in the health literature about a phenomenon called *free oxygen radicals*. What are they and how do they make people sick? It is best to use a simple analogy to explain this. In fact, the analogy will do much to educate the reader on the principles of oxidative metabolism as it applies to health and disease.

The Analogy of the Log Fire

Figure 4.

The simplest form of combustion is fire. Suppose that a camper decides to build a log fire in a clearing in the forest. The purpose is to use the heat energy to cook his dinner. He lights the fire and observes it as it increases in intensity. He may throw lighter fluid on it or blow into the fire to accelerate it. The heat is caused by the oxidation of wood, and the camper knows that he can set the forest on fire. He makes the fire in a fireplace to guard against this possibility but is worried when the fire is burning too vigorously because sparks are formed and these can jump onto the grass, set it on fire, and thus spread the fire to the forest. To prevent this process, the camper puts a wire grill over the fireplace to catch the sparks. He is protecting the forest by controlling the fire.

Each of our 100 trillion cells in the body has precisely the same challenge. It must be emphasized again that oxygen is a dangerous gas. It is capable of severe harm if its fundamental properties are not kept under control. The exquisite genius of MN is that these facts have been dealt with and the problems solved in the most efficient manner. It is indeed complex, but can be easily understood through the analogy.

The fuel that the cell burns is, of course, the calorigenic component of food: protein, fat, and carbohydrate. There are "fireplaces" in each cell, called mitochondria, minute organelles within the cell where the fuel-burning process takes place. Let us examine for a moment what happens when the body is put under any form of stress. The computer orders an increased rate of metabolism to supply the increased requirement of energy, causing oxidative metabolism in each mitochondrion to accelerate. It begins to throw out oxygen atoms, virtually like microscopic bullets, called free oxygen radicals. Just like sparks in the log fire, they cause oxidation to occur where they hit their target outside the mitochondrion. Like sparks, they are excited units of energy.

In her primeval wisdom, MN knew that the use of oxygen would have its dangers, and she therefore prepared a whole array of chemical substances which work together to quench the free oxygen radicals as they shoot out of the mitochondrion. This group of chemical substances works as a team and can be compare with the wire grating or grill in the fireplace analogy. Each one of the chemical substances is one wire in the grill. Some parts of the chemical grill are made in the body and therefore are not part of our nutrition. Many, however, must be consumed from external sources. They go by the names vitamin C, vitamin E, selenium, beta carotene, and many others. These non-calorigenic vitamins and minerals have to be taken into the body in our food; they are called antioxidants because they protect a cell from damage by its own oxygen. Just like a wire in the grill, they have to fit together in this process of protection.

The Cathedral Roof

Here is another analogy to consider. Imagine the nave of a cathedral. The struts in the roof form a skeleton, meeting at a point at the apex which makes the highest part of the roof. The struts can be compared with the array of vitamins and minerals that make up this nutritional team. The struts on one side are the oxidants; they preside over the process which enables oxygen to combine with fuel. This team takes care of the left side of the bell-shaped curve. The struts on the other side are the antioxidants, which take care of the right side of the curve.

Like the roof, they must form a balanced relationship. It is obvious that the roof will lean to one side or the other if the struts are weaker on that side. So it is with our nutrition. The oxidants must do their part and the antioxidants theirs, but they must balance against each other so as not to have the "roof" lean in either direction. Efficiency will be lost on the side where the nutritional deficiency occurs.

Like all analogies, the cathedral roof is imperfect, but it gives a mental picture which helps to explain in relatively simple terms a highly technical event. It is to be noted that the left side of the bell, the oxidative side, is governed by activity of the citric acid cycle. The catalysts that enable oxygen to be used in this process are primarily that group of vitamins known as the B group. Thiamin, the one that has been discussed in some detail, is one of the leaders in this mechanism and I have likened it to the accelerator or throttle in an internal combustion engine. It adjusts the speed of the citric acid cycle so that the delivery of charged electrons meets demand.

The right side of the curve is governed by the electron transfer chain that we have already mentioned. The catalysts that act here are the ones that we have described as antioxidants. It will be seen, therefore, that a sick person will lose efficiency on both sides of the curve if nutritional input involves deficiency of both types of catalyst. In fact, it could be said that nutritional deficiency rarely results in inadequate supplies of only one given catalyst or a specific group of them. Consequently, we have always to think about loss of efficiency due to weakness in the entire cathedral roof.

It is now possible to see that the oxidant nutrients are vital to the process of using oxygen in the synthesis of ATP, the energy store. Antioxidants are necessary to protect the structures of the cell outside the mitochondria from the damaging effect of free oxygen radicals.

We are now beginning to understand that the cause of many diseases lies in a failure to control free oxygen radicals. Note that they are perfectly normal components of oxidation reactions, just like sparks are normal in a brightly burning log fire. In fact, we would be in deep trouble without these "sparks," since it would indicate that the "fires" are not "burning" properly in the "fireplace."

Detection of Weaknesses

Since the human body is an electro-chemical, fuel-burning machine, the physician really has to imitate the function of the motor mechanic. He has to spot the causes of the trouble in the engine and must use ways and means of detecting those through tests. Such test procedures in medicine are carried out in the medical laboratory and will be discussed in a later chapter. So let us consider how the physician might imitate a motor mechanic.

Modern automobiles have a number of lights in the instrument panel which are designed to light up when something has gone wrong with the running characteristics of the engine. Imagine a scenario where you are driving your car and one of these lights comes on. You stop at the nearest gas station and tell the mechanic that this light has been noted. The mechanic has two options. He can remove the bulb from the light so that it no longer troubles you, or he can search for its cause. The first option is equivalent to the modern medical approach of relieving the symptom without ascertaining the underlying cause, which arises from a defective engine. Although symptom control is the primary goal of physicians in many situations, it is basically old-fashioned if one sees the logic of the new medicine.

Let us look at the second option which might be exercised by the most modern and up-to-date mechanic. The first thing, obviously, is to ascertain which light came on. Perhaps it indicated overheating. He makes sure that the radiator has adequate coolant and the oil sump is full. This step can be compared with laboratory tests performed by a physician who is versed in bio-oxidative medicine. Note that the first thing is something simple; the physician is basically looking for ways and means of *predicting* the possibilities of more serious disease.

Turning back to the analogy, it is obvious that the owner of a car may ignore the mechanic. Perhaps he does not believe the mechanic or it is too much trouble to wait for the required fluid to be put in. Who is the fool? Consider that the next problem will be that over-heating in the engine leads to a breakdown. This may seem much too simple in consideration of what is perceived by most people as the infinite complexity of disease. When doctors give long Latin names to diseases and we put patients through costly tests using high-tech machines, it is extremely confusing to be told that "you can really cure yourself through understanding the basics of your own body functions and exercising better knowledge of nutrition."

The Mitochondrion

Millions of years ago, a very primitive bacterium entered a very primitive cell. Imagine the scenario as though the cell were a room and the bacterium entered it basically for its own protection. It liked this nice cozy place and decided that it would like to stay. Since, as we've already mentioned, there is no "free lunch," the bacterium must "pay rent." How MN organized this is one of the great scientific mysteries. It was arranged that the bacterium would turn into a furnace that would manufacture the energy for its host cell. Over eons of time, this bacterium gradually became more and more specialized and eventually was transformed into the unit which is called a mitochondrion. Each cell has a number of these organelles, microscopic units where the business of energy production to power the cell is conducted.

Now, the original bacterium had its own genes and they dictated the way that it functioned. As it evolved, these genes also were responsible for its evolutionary development into this highly sophis-ticated "furnace" called a mitochondrion. In other words, mitochondrial function and its adaptation are presided over by its own genes. These are quite independent of the genes which are responsible for the direction of the cell which the mitochondrion serves.

The *cellular* genes are the ones that are responsible for our inherited characteristics and are derived from both parents. This genetic inheritance is sometimes referred to as Mendelian in-heritance, named after the monk who discovered some of the basics of how genes work in plants. However, the *mitochondrial* genes are passed only by the mother because the mitochondrial genes from the father are carried in the tail of the sperm, which is left outside the

178

egg when fertilization takes place. Thus, these genes are lost. Therefore, mitochondrial genes are inherited only from the mother, and that fact is relevant to our discussion here.

We have already pointed out that the cell is really a unit which operates on its own genetically-determined program and which is quite separate from the quality of its own mitochondria. Suppose that the function of the cell is extremely demanding of energy—oxygen utilization, if you will. This is a high-quality piece of machinery, and if all the cells in the body were of the same caliber, such an individual has the potential to be a high-quality person. Perhaps such a person might be well-coordinated and be a good athlete or have excellent academic ability. Indeed, both of these attributes may be present; we call people who have them especially "gifted."

Now, let us suppose that the mitochondria, which provide the energy for the cells, are genetically defective, so that energy supply does not automatically meet demand. We would expect the individual with this combination to fail under either physical or mental stress when energy requirement is necessarily increased. The expression of the functional failure may be either "mental" or "physical" or a combination of both. Since the genetic handicap is inherent in the mitochondria, it will be passed to the children only if the defect is present in the mother. Its presence in the father is irrelevant. However, both sexes in the children will be affected if they inherit the problem from their mother.

I have seen dozens of cases where the children have conditions which are more relevant to the mother's health history than the father's. I believe this inheritance pattern to be the result of a gap which develops in the supply economics of energy *production* versus its *utilization*. The mother has a condition which is due to inadequate energy metabolism and has passed her mitochondrial genes to all her children.

Let me make it as clear as possible. Assuming that we have correctly interpreted mitochondrial derivation from a primitive bacterium, can we use this understanding to explain disease patterns? Of course, we do not know for sure whether this explanation is applicable because it is not possible to prove that this is the mechanism in any given case; but it certainly makes sense, and I have been repeatedly amazed at family disease patterns. I know, for example, that a family history of alcoholism is often associated with diabetes, simply because I have seen it so often that I expect to find it when I ask the question of the patient. It has been my impression, over the years, that I can much more reliably predict problems in the children when the family history shows a problem to be in the mother's family. I have been deeply impressed that the only satisfactory explanation for this fact is in perceiving the variable disease patterns as related to energy metabolism.

The symptoms of disease may be totally different in each of the involved family members, even though all of them have the same biochemical handicap. Perhaps the mother has PMS because of inadequate energy metabolism affecting her brain computer. She has one child with a learning disability, another with allergy, and a third who has recurrent ear infections. All of them have their symptoms increase under stress. All of them do much worse on a poor diet. All of them respond to the same spectrum of nutrient supplements, no matter how their clinical condition has been labeled.

Furthermore, it will be obvious that a child who is well-endowed by Mendelian inheritance, who is consequently superior in ability, is likely to be in greater trouble than a child who is less well-endowed, if the mitochondrial function is inadequate for the demand. This knowledge is a very good foundation for understanding an inheritance pattern of disease that evolves from the maternal family and does not appear to be influenced at all from the paternal side. It is also relatively easy to see why each affected person will be more affected by stress.

It is true, of course, that a genetic trait could be passed from the mother to her boys, as in hemophilia. This sex-linked form of Mendelian inheritance is used as the conventional explanation of what I am describing. However, the ringer is that the pattern I am discussing is observed in both sons and daughters and not confined to the boys. This phenomenon requires explanation which does not fit with our present knowledge of classical cellular genetics. The inheritance pattern is better explained by visualizing an inadequate energy supply due to inefficiency in the mitochondria derived from the mother.

This explanation of disease patterns demonstrates why a given nutrient, thiamin for example, must be used to treat the biochemical *cause* of a disease and is not related to the clinical *projection* of the disease as we currently recognize in the form of what we call a "diagnosis." In the family that we discussed, therefore, in which a number of family members have different diagnoses in clinical terms, all of them must be treated with the same nutrient combination, which must be sought to make the underlying *biochemical* diagnosis.

This conclusion leads us to another type of scenario: imagine five different people from different families. They have no genetic relationship, but they all have the same disease as it has been diagnosed by modern disease classification. Suppose we call this disease rheumatoid arthritis. The *clinical* projection in all five patients is one where the joints are primarily involved, and therefore it is easy to treat all five ailments in the same manner. The underlying biochemical *cause* of the condition in each of the five patients, however, may be completely different. To treat those five patients on a nutritional basis, each would have to have a different approach, even though they all have the same clinical diagnosis. Thus, making a clinical diagnosis is useless and becomes irrelevant. The definitive diagnostic label must be based on the distorted biochemical events which have led to the maladaptive condition which we call disease.

Furthermore, it must be emphasized that rheumatoid arthritis is really not a disease of joints as an isolated entity. It is a general, biochemical change affecting the whole body; the joints have merely become a selective target. Similarly, glaucoma has long been recognized by eye doctors as not being a disease of the eye. It is a condition in which the eye has become a target of an imbalance in the nervous control of structures within the eye. Hence, glaucoma is really a biochemical event which is actually occurring in the computer. Not surprisingly, it is thus stress-related.

In this light, we see that there are two ways of classifying the condition of J.V., discussed in detail in Chapter 4. J.V.'s clinical condition was called cerebellar ataxia, a purely descriptive label which states that his loss of balance was due to a problem in that part of the brain called the cerebellum. The condition would have remained a complete mystery and could not have been successfully treated unless the biochemical cause had been found. We saw that this turned out to be a defective enzyme which is fundamentally vital in the citric acid cycle, the main engine of the cell. One of the cofactors upon which this enzyme depends is thiamin. It was found that J.V.'s biochemical machinery began to operate more efficiently when he received huge doses of thiamin. Hence, he was thiamin-dependent; that understanding was the secret of successful treatment.

In the approach of today, a physician would record on an insurance form the following diagnosis:

Cerebellar ataxia of unknown cause

Perhaps the physician of the 21st century would report the same disease to an insurance company as a diagnosis of:

Pyruvic dehydrogenase deficiency (thiamin-dependent)

181

Empty or Naked Calories

Empty or naked calories is a term applied to a high-calorie food with a deficiency in the density of non-caloric nutrients, the spark plugs of combustion. Why is a diet of such foods constitute a dangerous way to eat?

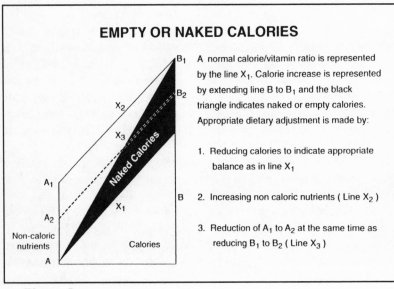

Figure 5.

Figure 5 shows us a theoretical view of the relationship between calorie-yielding nutrients and the non-caloric "spark plugs" that enable them to be oxidized. Line A in the figure represents a relatively tiny concentration of vitamins and minerals as compared with the element of the food that is to be oxidized, represented by line B. This graphic is not in scale, of course. The normal concentration of line A nutrients is in micrograms or milligrams, whereas those represented by line B are in grams.

If high-calorie food which does not contain an adequate density of non-caloric nutrients is eaten, line B will be lengthened if we represent the phenomenon mathematically. The line will be shifted to become A-B_1, representing a change in the ratio of calories to non-caloric nutrients. The black triangle has been used to represent *naked calories*. There are three ways in which this situation can be rectified:

1. Remove the naked calories from the diet, restoring the line to position X_1.

2. Increasing the non-caloric nutrients, thus extending line A until the line X_2 can be drawn parallel to X_1. Again, the correct ratio has been restored.

3. A mixture of both these approaches, with the result that the ratio is restored and represented by line X_3.

It will be readily seen why gluttony has been cast as one of the Seven Deadly Sins. In principle, it is exactly the same as choking an automobile engine. The concentration of naked calories represents an overload of gasoline relative to the ability to burn it. The result is that unburned hydrocarbons are lost in the exhaust pipe, giving rise to black smoke. Obviously, this situation is highly inefficient combustion, and engine efficiency will decrease sharply.

The human cell has the same problem. It must burn the fuel efficiently. If that happens, food will be oxidized finally to carbon dioxide and water as the lowest possible common denominators of oxidation. If there is an excess of naked calories, fuel consumption will be correspondingly less efficient. Oxidation will be incomplete, and a series of organic acids will be produced. Of course, we do not have an exhaust pipe to get rid of gases, as the automobile does.

There are two ways in which these substances can be excreted. The incomplete oxidation of sulfur-containing compounds gives rise to some volatile gases that can be excreted into the lung and exhaled. These gases are evil-smelling, as are most of the sulfur oxides, and become the cause of evil-smelling breath (halitosis). The most important excretory mechanism is, of course, the kidney. The organic acids are relatively easy to detect in urine. What they really represent is loss of oxidative efficiency. If a biochemist is able to recognize an organic acid, it is possible to identify the chemical reaction in the body where it is produced. If this reaction is known to require a given vitamin or mineral, its deficiency may be identified and restored by increasing the intake of that non-caloric nutrient in the diet.

Incidentally, I learned about halitosis through an interesting personal experience. Sometimes, when I came home from the office, my wife would greet me with the endearing comment, "Your breath smells." It gradually dawned on me that the condition was associated with fatigue arising from an unusually heavy work load on a particular day. It seemed to be quite realistic to draw the conclusion that it was related to inefficient oxidation of sulfur, accelerated by meeting an increased mental and physical demand which we usually refer to as stress.

Please understand that my deduction was based upon a simple personal experience. Recently, however, there has been some very supportive evidence for this conclusion. Because of advances in laboratory technology, it has been found that a gas called pentane is detectable in the breath when a person is in a metabolic state which gives rise to free oxygen radicals. Indeed, it is presently the best method that we have of detecting this phenomenon that is so inherently linked to disease as the underlying biochemical common denominator. We have established that free oxygen radicals are produced when the body is under stress. There is an increased demand for energy to meet the stress, but if the metabolic response is inefficient, then fuel is incompletely oxidized and the byproducts will form.

This knowledge may well be the explanation for something that is becoming better known. Many philosophers and wise people have realized a long and active life by being extremely careful with their diets. They *never* overeat and *always* rise from the table feeling that they could eat more. They are highly selective, choosing only the organic foods that come from natural MN-related sources. They do not succumb to degenerative diseases and are unusually active for their chronologic age.

This relationship of dietary habits to health has been investigated by research in animals. Feeding rats in this way, making sure that their caloric intake is adequate but never excessive, balances their overall nutrient density, and longevity is indeed increased. Even more significantly, old rats behave more like young ones, remaining much more active and interested in their environment. They are correspondingly more playful and project a more attractive animal personality.

Health Foods

The term *health food* is really quite inappropriate. It is more reasonable to think that the proper food for the human is that to which we were adapted and that that is what we should consume as our food. To allocate a special store called a "health food store" is absurd, particularly when it jacks up the price. We shall be discussing this in a later chapter because the rising interest of the public is demanding improved education about the reality of a good diet. There is no such thing as a "health food." Proper food is that which maintains functional well-being of the oxidative machinery which constitutes good health.

If this principle were accepted and acted upon throughout our culture, we would completely solve most of the unnecessary ill-nesses of today. It is very unfortunate that our taste buds on the tongue communicate with those centers in the brain known as the pleasure centers. Hence, the taste factor has become part of our hedonism, and we plunge headlong toward our own slow but sure extinction or, to say the very least, our incredibly poor collective health.

As we have emphasized, the most oxygen-demanding tissue in the body is nervous tissue. The most demanding part of that is the brainstem, the computer. It is now possible for us to see why crib death, described in detail in the last chapter, is really due to malnutrition of an immature and essentially volatile computer. It is therefore, in truth, a nutritional disease. Persist in providing the infant with fuel that "chokes the engine" and we risk the subsequent problems of hyperactivity and school difficulties which haunt us so seriously today. It is extremely obvious that our entire culture, in which hedonistic adventures in food commodities to stimulate brain pleasure centers is the epicenter, is the common denominator of long-term health problems throughout the nation.

Some of my readers will minimize this statement as an over-emphasis; I encounter that reaction frequently. However, I see that our present attitude toward food is a chronically simplistic one. A mother who attempts to feed her family healthy food becomes almost a laughing stock within her own family. She is called a "health nut" by her children, and they groan when she mentions the ingestion of appropriate food.

I have repeatedly encountered this attitude in many different ways. A wife drags her husband into my office. He is reluctant and semi-hostile. Eventually, I will preempt him by saying, "I know that you did not want to see me at all. Your wife dragged you in against your will, and you refer to her as a health nut." Both of them smile as they recognize the scenario. They see the truth, but does it alter the husband's attitude? Sometimes—but only at great cost to my own sanity. It is truly surprising how difficult it is to get people to see the plain, unvarnished truth that food is fuel and that you have to consult the "owner's manual" to see what MN wrote into the specifications.

Why do we stray? Oh, that is so very simple to answer. The food industry will produce what we desire. Hedonism produces a craving for pleasure at all costs. Food is seen as a nuisance to prepare, as well as time-consuming, so we provide ourselves with an endless array of shortcuts. Inevitably, our taste buds become the central factor, since they are over-stimulated by the vast array of goodies which dominate our social existence.

Supplementary vitamins, minerals, and other nutrients, taken in the form of tablets, capsules, and pills, are truly supplementary to the food which should be on the plate. However, using them properly is not by any means a simple task. It requires a knowledge of the biochemistry involved, not the symptoms that the patient has. Make no mistake; they are used as drugs when the dose is increased above the concentration which is found naturally in our organic food. This will be dealt with more fully in a later chapter. It is quite incongruous to have a health food store direct a patient to the purchase of supplements on the basis of symptoms. Supplements are among the most powerful therapeutic weapons that we possess today. They should be used with the greatest respect and care and, in my view, should be prescribed only by a person who is well-educated in the complex biochemistry involved. In the very near future it will not be sufficient for physicians to classify their patients on a clinical basis. They will have to be well-versed in biochemistry, which is presently considered by most of them to be a theoretical exercise that has only a remote connection with nutrition. Slowly this transition is beginning to take place, as the "new medicine," makes its gradual, tenuous advances.

Chapter 10

The Three Circles of Health

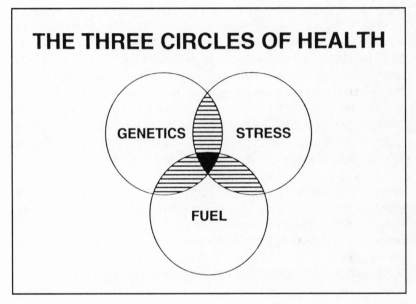

Figure 6.

Figure 6 represents a mathematical approach to analysis of the relationship between the three variables depicted. When used as a method of statistical analysis, it is called Boolean algebra; the degree of overlap between the circles is used to provide a calibration of interaction. We are not, however, presenting this figure for this kind of analytic accuracy. It shows only a qualitative overlap. Note that there is an interaction between any circle with either of the other two. But all three interact at the center. In order to see how this figure can be used to represent *any* clinical situation, we must begin with definitions.

Stress

I constantly find that the word *stress* is used so inaccurately in medicine that it ceases to have any constant meaning. If we look it up in the dictionary it has a number of definitions, but for the purpose of this book we are using it as an engineer would. If an engineer wishes to test the strength of a metal bar, he can apply a stress force. The first evidence that the metal bar is yielding to the stress is seen as stress lines, microscopic cracks in the metal which indicate metal fatigue. Then it begins to bend and may finally fracture. Another example of stress might be heat that is applied to the metal bar. We know that it will expand, and when it cools it will contract.

What is happening, of course, is that the metal bar is adapting to the stress force. Its adaptability depends upon its tensile strength and the nature of its molecular form. On the other hand, glass may shatter when heated and breaks much more easily under mechanical stress. The metal may be viewed as very adaptable, whereas the glass adapts poorly.

Obviously, an engineer is not really interested in the force, other than to calibrate the adaptability of the material that is being stressed. This is precisely how we should view stress in reference to human beings. We are interested in the capacity of an individual to adapt to the physical forces that surround each and every one of us. Because we are complex, live organisms, our adaptability is also extremely complex and so, besides physical stress, we are subjected to mental stress. Unfortunately, for the most part our use of the word *stress* is confined to the mental component. We can, however, divide our stress into these two components: physical stress and mental stress. And on a daily basis we encounter both physical stressors and mental stressors.

Physical Stress

Each of us lives in a dangerous world. Because of a process known as civilization we have lost much of our adaptability to live without artificial assistance. I am always fascinated to see horses and other animals that are left outside on a cold night that would kill me. How do they survive? They adapt, of course. Because of the softening process of civilization, we need clothes and heat in the winter. We are becoming progressively more dependent upon artificial cooling devices in the summer. In short, we are less adaptable.

Examples of Physical Stressors

Heat/Cold
Foreign Chemicals
Light/Dark
Gravity
Microorganisms
Humidity
Barometric Pressure
Trauma

Examples of Mental Stressors

Insult
School
Work (Particularly if disliked)
Marriage
Divorce
Grief

Let me make it clear once again. Stress is induced by the accidental impact of a stressor. It is handled by the brain computer in the same way, whether it be strictly physical or mental. It is a basic adaptive response, and it is automated, not willed.

In an earlier chapter we discussed the way in which our computers handle the impact of stress. The full-blown stress response is the fight-or-flight reflex, developed through the endocrine and autonomic nervous systems. Thus, adapting to stress is a perfectly normal and even an exhilarating experience. It is this contradiction which people find so confusing. How can stress be avoided? Well, of course, it cannot be avoided. Our stress load is the effect of being active in a dangerous world.

Again, to cut through technical discussion and get to the core, I turn to the analogy of the automobile. Its ability to meet its stress load depends completely on the power of the engine. When it comes to a hill, its stress load obviously increases and is proportional to the gradient. If it is unable to climb a given hill, it is because of a combination of two variables: the steepness of the gradient and the failure of engine power. Should we blame the hill? Of course not! It is a normal part of the car's journey which cannot be bypassed. But, on the other hand, even the very best automobile cannot climb a cliff. So there is a point at which a gradient will be too steep.

Take this analogy a little further. Suppose that the car's journey takes it over a mountain range. There is a saddle which the main road scales, the lowest altitude that must be traveled. It is the minimal stress that it has to face. On the saddle, there is a sign post which indicates that there is a scenic route that may be taken. Obviously, this route is optional; it is not a necessary course to take, though the destination may well be the same. Such a scenic route, peppered with steep hills and valleys, may be much more exciting but will also apply a greater degree of stress on the engine and brakes.

In a human life, stress is self-imposed when we take a more exciting job that carries heavy responsibility. Health can break down in some, whereas others meet the challenges with exhilaration. It is to be emphasized that the human engine is just as important as the car engine. It must be maximally efficient in order to take the "scenic route."

Enough of this analogy, though we can use it as a crude map for the conduct of a human life which may be thought of as a journey. The adaptability of an individual is directly proportional to the quality of the metabolism of the whole body, or—as I hope I have sufficiently reiterated—oxidative efficiency. If the stress is great enough, it will be the cliff that we cannot climb. This cliff/stressor could be a severe trauma or an overwhelming infection due to an onslaught by a lethal organism which cannot be overcome by even the best possible immune response. This understanding suggests that all pathogenic organisms are opportunist in character; it is not, therefore, necessary for us to succumb to a large percentage of the infectious challenges that we meet on a day-to-day basis.

Do we have options in life? Of course we do. We might want to take the more exciting "scenic route" and be exhilarated by it. But let us be very clear about one thing: it is imperative that the engine is in the best possible state of health, since the stress is much greater. More fuel will be used, and there will be a greater generation of heat as energy is consumed.

Genetics

Much has appeared in the news lately about genes causing disease. We are told that there is a single gene which causes cystic fibrosis, for example. The gene experts are looking for the gene that causes this disease or that disease. In my opinion, this is a massive waste of our resources and is steadily increasing the cost of medical care. It directs maximal scientific attention to the relative rarities rather than the colossal incidence of common disease. The drive is predicated, of course, on the idea that the faulty gene might be replaced in an affected individual. This is called gene therapy, and cystic fibrosis is a good example of a disease in which this might be accomplished.

The truth, however, is that relatively few diseases are actually governed by the lack of activity of a single gene. Let me emphasize—*lack* of activity. The effect of a single gene disease was illustrated in Chapter 2 when the conditions known as PKU was discussed. It is caused by a defective gene that codes for the synthesis of an enzyme which gives rise to the disease process.

It has never made any sense to me that high-tech science is looking for the gene that causes a given disease. Such a search implies that MN is actually a malignant architect, actually inventing genes that cause disease. It is better to think that the design of the machinery is so complex that an occasional mistake is to be expected and may be passed on to offspring through genetic transmission. I have already pointed out that cellular mechanisms might be perfect but that the mitochondria can be imperfect because of a failure in *their own* gene profile.

But—and this is a big *but*—inheritance is much more complex than that. There was a word used once that has fallen out of fashion in medical discussions: *constitution.* I believe that it explains inheritance much better by taking into account an individual's genetic profile. Just as we have discussed the complex relationship that vitamins have with each other to form a team, genes also work together in a devastatingly complex inter-relationship. When any gene action is missing, it upsets the balance of the genetic profile and has far-reaching effects upon the general well-being of the individual.

I always think of the genetic profile as dictating a constitution which is made up of the sum total of inherited strengths and weaknesses. It is an infinitely complex combination of permutations, which creates a human being who is absolutely and completely unique. Each one of us is so highly individualized by this complex combining process that we can say with confidence that no person has ever existed who is identical to me. No person like me will ever exist in the future.

In considering this complex constitution, think of the relatively common mistake that gives rise to a human being afflicted by what is called Down's syndrome. When I say *mistake,* I am referring to the fact that this syndrome is caused by a phenomenon that occurs at the one-cell stage of development. It is more likely to occur in an older mother, reflecting a loss of efficiency in the mechanism itself. It is, in most cases therefore, not strictly inherited, but represents an accident of nature.

What is important is that such an individual has received one extra chromosome. The reader will remember that a chromosome is somewhat like a wire or rod, upon which the genes are threaded like beads. Each "bead" dictates an inherited characteristic. A person with Down's syndrome therefore has extra genetic machinery, and the constitution is affected by the imbalance that is caused. The personality characteristics of a person with this syndrome are unique, just as they are in people with a normal gene balance. It is better, therefore, to see genetic characteristics as a sum total of genetic shuffling, inherited from a male and a female parent. Each one of us will therefore be born with a constitution which we cannot possibly choose. It is purely an accident of birth which will dictate our strengths and our weaknesses. We can manipulate our characteristics by exercising them, but we can never exceed a final ultimate potential dictated by that accidental shuffling of the genes.

As usual, I am turning to the analogy of the automobile to illustrate the concept of constitution further. We have many automobiles manufactured in the world today. All of them are mass-produced on an assembly line. Imagine that our natural designer, MN, is represented by the original inventor of the automobile, which was very primitive in its early stages of development. We will call this inventor Master Mechanic or MM. (This time, note that our inventor is a male.) He set into motion a series of evolutionary experiments that eventually gave way to the modern, highly sophisticated automobile.

All the automobiles in the world are built on the same *basic* design, but every single one is different in some way. Let's call each automobile company a family. A Chevrolet is going to be similar—although never identical—to another Chevrolet; they have similar design characteristics, and both of them will differ from a Ford. Although each car comes off (is born into) its "family" assembly line, and each one is manipulated in precisely the same automated fashion, we still find that one car performs better than another, and there are cars that are known as "lemons." We can accept that one make of car is generally better than another; being "better" means that it is *more likely* to stand up to the stresses imposed upon it by its owner, and it is therefore more likely to "live longer." But it certainly does not guarantee it. We all know of expensive cars that wear out fast, whereas the supposedly inferior model may outlast it.

Imagine that you have bought a car, brand new and straight off the assembly line. Unbeknown to you, it has an "inherited" weakness in its structure. This characteristic was built into the assembly line design, so all the models have this weakness which has not yet been discovered. Nothing in the car gives the slightest warning to you that this weakness lurks somewhere in its structure. There are three possible events that may occur.

1. You sell the car and never know that it had the inherent weakness. Perhaps the car serves you well for fifteen years. It ages over the years, getting a little rust here and there. It simply "dies" one day, never having indicated a potential for a breakdown. The car had a long and healthy life.

2. One day you are driving the car up a steep hill. You are aware that it has been overheating lately but have done nothing about it. On this occasion, it breaks down and you have to obtain the services of a tow truck. When you get the repair bill, the mechanic tells you that the break occurred because there was a crack in the metal and that is part of a design fault in that model. Knowing the circumstances, you are hardly surprised that the breakdown appeared at a point of structural weakness.

3. On the second day that you owned the car, and without any imposition of undue stress on the car, it breaks down at the hitherto unknown point of weakness.

Transfer this analogy to human beings, and what I am driving at becomes crystal clear. Each of us is derived from a family, and family members are similar but never identical. All the families in the world represent different "models" with different design characteristics, but all are human. In the first scenario, described above, the genetic weakness, though present, never breaks down and the person lives a long healthy life.

To discuss the second scenario, we will choose diabetes as the potential risk built into the genetic profile. We know that families have diabetes popping up in individuals and that there is indeed some kind of inheritance factor. An individual inherits a constitution in which diabetes is a genetically-determined weakness that lurks within the constitution. Perhaps such a person dies at 94 without ever having diabetes, the equivalent of the first automobile-purchasing scenario. Perhaps another individual inherits a similar weakness but is a little bit more at risk. If he is lucky, he may get away with it by following a life which meets only the minimum degree of stress in the journey. On the other hand, if he chooses the "scenic route" which imposes a greater degree of stress, he may have a breakdown and develop diabetes.

Let us imagine such a person who is overworking and unhappy in his job or marriage (or both). One day he develops the flu and the next day he is found to have diabetes. This sequence sometimes occurs after a cold, a head injury, or even the shock of receiving bad news.

It is important to see that *the stress is not the cause of the disease*. It is merely the "straw that broke the camel's back." The breakdown occurs at that point of constitutional weakness that he has inherited. Therefore, we see an unpredictable but very basic relationship between the genetics and the stress. This is the first interaction that we can see in the "three circles of health." It is also easy to see why geneticists cannot find an inheritance pattern in rigid mathematical terms. They do not, and cannot, take into account the second variable, stress.

Let me illustrate this another way by using the disease known as hemophilia for an example. This is a genetically-determined condition where the mechanism is known quite precisely. Affected individuals inherit it in a highly predictable manner which follows Mendelian laws. They have a genetic defect which prevents them from forming a substance in the blood known as anti-hemophilic globulin. Because of this deficiency, they are "bleeders" and trauma is life-threatening. Very well, then this disease is genetic in character and we can close the book on it—right? Wrong—we cannot let it go at that!

It is known that hemophiliacs bleed into their joints more when they are under emotional stress. This relationship can be explained only by understanding the scenario that I have described. What happens, of course, is that the stress impacts upon the computer-driven adaptive responses of the whole individual. The machine— body and mind—is put into a state of heightened activity. Signals go out from the computer to *all* body mechanisms; these signals include an order to "make more anti-hemophilic globulin." This particular order cannot be obeyed because the genetic machinery is unavailable. The increased stress activation therefore finds that point of genetically-determined weakness, and more bleeding results.

It is possible for a genetic weakness of an individual to be so virulent that the breakdown is inevitable. In that case, we have the equivalent of the third car scenario.

Thus, the inheritance pattern, or constitution, of the individual is itself a variable which is unpredictable. I have seen two children within a family, both of whom had diabetes. One developed it at the age of seven months, the other one a few months later. Both were extremely fragile and their doses of insulin were excessively variable. (To anticipate the next part of our discussion of the "three circles of health," I might add that their diseases were much easier to control when they were given regular daily supplements of vitamin B complex. They were not cured, but the doses of insulin became much more predictable. They were less fragile.) In this case, genetics did not require any stress to trigger the disease. The genetics circle in our diagram therefore would be "the big one," altering the balance of the three circles.

Fuel

The third variable in the three circles of health has been labeled *fuel* to remind us that this is what food is meant to be. We have been equipped with a sensory apparatus that connects the tongue to the brain, providing us with a sense of taste. On the surface of the tongue there are groups of cells which make up tiny organs called taste buds. They are sensitive to stimulus which is provided by the molecular constituents of the food that we put into the mouth. It is in the brain that we experience the perception of taste, which gives pleasure when it is good and dislike when it is bad. Why did MN equip us with an apparatus of this nature? If you are a reductionist as I am, you will explain it purely on the basis of incentive. Obviously, food is the only way in which we can satisfy a desire, expressed in the brain, called hunger. If we did not experience the urge of hunger, we would not be in the least interested in going out to forage for food. So this sensory apparatus is given to us in order to stay alive so that we can continue to produce progeny and the continuation of the species.

By eating food, we are refueling; we can turn once again to the analogy of the automobile. We have discussed the inherent weakness of design in the genetics circle and how it relates to the stress circle. How does the fuel circle relate? Imagine that when you bought your new car you did not bother to read the owner's manual. So you have never discovered the nature of the fuel that you should purchase and therefore you have been putting in leaded gasoline when it should have been unleaded. Such an error will lead to breakdown of the catalytic converter. You might say that the car has developed "diabetes."

Should the breakdown take place on a hill, would you blame the "genetic weakness" in the car, the "stress" of the hill, or the nature of the fuel? Quite obviously, all three factors are involved, and the breakdown would have been less likely to occur if the three factors had not interrelated. However, if you examine the situation a little more closely, there is actually only one variable that you can control—the fuel.

This is the way that human disease behaves. In continuing the discussion of diabetes, we have discussed its relationship with stress. However, nearly everybody is aware of the association of diabetes with diet. In fact, most people are aware that the disease can be controlled in many patients with diet alone. Few people, however, think of their nutrition as a risk factor in bringing about diabetes in a genetically-prone individual.

The fuel or nutrition circle relates directly to the genetics circle. The only problem is that none of us comes equipped with an owner's manual to tell us the exact nature of food that each one of us uniquely requires on an individual basis. How much zinc do you require? Nobody can tell you the precise need. You can be sure that it is a quantity that is decisively dictated by your own personal, genetically-determined profile. But its requirement increases under stress, just as a car would need to burn more fuel.

Then do you need to be a biochemical genius to be able to take a healthy diet? Emphatically, the answer is *no*. When you consume organic, natural food (granted, a difficult commodity to find these days) and vary the components, you are hedging your bets and consuming a diet with an appropriate nutrient density. Some organic foods will have a nutrient complement that differs from others. A healthy person living on a healthy, organic, home-grown diet with fresh food should not need nutrient supplements.

The whole unfortunate problem is that (1) we are not nearly as healthy as we believe, in a biochemical sense, and (2) our food supply does not provide an adequate nutrient density. Even when we are well, from a symptomatic point of view, we may well require vitamins and minerals in supplementary form. When we are sick, we need large doses of them in supplemental form. This will be discussed in greater detail in a later chapter.

It is to be understood that the sensation of taste has absolutely nothing to do with guiding us toward good nutrition. In fact, unfortunately, the very opposite is true. The sensation of taste stimulates the pleasure-sensitive cells in the brain. Then why were we given a sense of taste if it beguiles us? I always try to answer that in a natural perspective. We were designed to derive pleasure, or satisfaction, from the process of eating food and slaking thirst. The fact is, however, that our food was presented to us in a natural setting and that is what we ate for thousands of years during prehistory. We were, in fact, adapted to the variety of naturally occurring foods that MN provided. They were probably sampled by trial and error, so that the poisonous plants and animals were remembered. It is only in recent years that our technological skills have enabled us to create food and drink that has absolutely no nutrient density and relies on stimulation of the tongue to sell it in ever-increasing amounts. Furthermore, as we shall see later, many of them—perhaps all of them—are addictive. When we crave something like coffee, chocolate, or cola, we are addicted. It is the pleasure-craving zones in the brain that dictate a continued satisfaction and create the sensation that we call craving.

Now that we have outlined the skeleton of these extremely complex relationships, we can illustrate the use of the model by examining some cases. It is important to note that you cannot affect genetics at all. Stress, which involves living in a hostile world, is usually fixed for the individual who has made his choices. For example, a divorce might be more stressful than the marriage. A new job may be worse than the old one. Neither can we change the physical events such as weather, geographic locality, and so forth.

Take the case of the gentleman who came to see me with the following story. He had been out in a boat on a lake and dived overboard for a swim. There was a sense of impact as he hit the water and he was, of course, acutely aware of the sudden difference in temperature of the water, contrasted with the warmth of the day. But he was not seriously conscious of any sense of trauma. He swam for only a few minutes and climbed back into the boat without any problem. About an hour later he suddenly was hit by exquisite pain in the back of the neck and radiating up into his head. Even the slightest movement of his head produced something like an electrical jolt, and he described himself as "paralyzed" with pain.

He was admitted to a hospital and, after many tests, he was told that he had fibromyositis. Many people will recognize this diagnosis. It used to be called muscular rheumatism and is generally seen, at least by many physicians, as a trivial problem, the pain of which is exaggerated by the patient. One or more extremely tender knots can be felt in the muscle, sometimes relieved by heat and physical therapy.

What most people, and many physicians, do not know, is that the knot in the muscle represents spasm of a very localized nature within the muscle. This spasm really represents an unusually active increase in muscle action known as *tone*, the state of imminent readiness in which all muscles within the body are maintained. (Tone is clinically evident in the muscles on either side of the vertebral column. If you place your hand on your own back muscles arranged on either side of the spinal column in the lower back, you will feel a ridge of muscle which feels like a steel bar. If this muscle tone were not maintained, the parallel pull of the muscles would be absent and the vertebral column would be much more unstable.) For the purpose of this discussion, it is important to note that this muscle tone is maintained by a constant flow of nervous messages from the brainstem, the computer. In my patient, these knots of muscular tension were caused by the brainstem sending messages to some of the muscle fibers within the neck muscle. Thus, it can be seen why this reaction was related to some kind of physical stress.

After this original spasm, experienced after his immersion in the lake, this man experienced relapses which occurred every three or four months, related to changes in environmental temperature or weather. This case is an example of a stress-induced mechanism; it forces us to be aware that stress is really a physical force. In this case, the computer was overreacting in an abnormal manner. The explanation of his recurrent illnesses was in the biochemistry of cells within the computer. The human body "remembers" its stresses, and the reaction will be reinduced repeatedly by some relatively trivial incident such as a change of weather or barometric pressure. This is much more likely if the computer has been rendered more sensitive by high-calorie malnutrition. Therefore, this situation was directly influenced by the man's diet, coupled with ordinary, everyday stress which is unavoidable. The only treatment to offer is a major improvement in diet, together with nutritional supplements which must be carefully chosen to fit the biochemical needs of this particular individual.

The following case may make the "three circles of health" and their interrelated effects more clear. A number of years ago, I was consulted by the parents of a six-year-old boy. He had sustained a severe head injury, incurring a skull fracture that had required surgery to realign that part of the skull which had been caved in. This was obviously an extremely severe injury, and perhaps he was even lucky to be alive.

When he returned to school he was told by the school nurse to report to her every two weeks for an eye test; she indicated that "people go blind after this kind of injury" and, whether this is correct or not, in this case it was sage advice. About three months later, the nurse noted a rather dramatic change in the child's visual acuity. She referred him to an ophthalmologist, who found that the child had developed mature cataracts in both eyes, an extremely unusual phenomenon in a child. Now comes the interesting part of the story. The ophthalmologist was well aware that childhood cataracts occur in a disease called galactosemia. This requires a little deviation from the story, or the point will be missed.

Milk, as most people know, contains a form of sugar known as lactose. In the intestine, lactose is converted to another form of sugar known as galactose, which must be broken down into glucose by two enzymes. If one of these enzymes is missing from a person's genetically-determined machinery, galactose is not broken down. This substance passes in the blood to the eye, where it is toxic to the lens and causes cataract formation. Each enzyme is inherited from two genes, one from the father and one from the mother, in precisely the same way we described PKU's inheritance pattern in Chapter 2. If a gene is not donated from one of the parents, it means that the parent is a carrier of the disease galactosemia. This carrier state has a one-in-two chance of being passed to the child of this parent, thus creating another carrier state. Neither parent nor child will be affected at all by the presence of this carrier state under usual circumstances because the one "good" gene that each possesses is enough to turn out sufficient enzyme to break down galactose, as long as the machinery is not unduly stressed. Thus, a carrier does not normally develop cataracts and would never have the slightest idea that he is affected. Such a recessive gene inheritance, as it is called, can pass through many generations without any cases of galactosemia appearing in the family.

To continue then with the case of this six-year-old boy, the ophthalmologist referred him to me to ascertain whether there was an underlying metabolic condition. There are other diseases similar to galactosemia which cause cataracts in children, all of them genetically determined. It was my job to ascertain whether any of these conditions existed.

It turned out, after special tests had been performed, that this child was a carrier for one of the forms of galactosemia. The treatment is to withdraw galactose from the diet. By far and away the greatest source of this sugar is from lactose in milk, although other foods do contain modest amounts of it. I have already indicated that a carrier of this disease normally does not develop the disease, so classical genetics tells us that the cataracts in this particular child must not be related to either of the two forms of galactosemia.

I puzzled over this case for some time. I knew of the physician, known for his special knowledge of this disease, who had performed the tests on this child that proved him to be a carrier. I called him and asked whether a carrier ever expressed the disease in partial form. He told me that he did not think so, and no investigator had reported it. To me, it seemed to be too much of a coincidence, and I sat down with the parents to discuss the nature of the child's diet. I found that it was the usual kind of junk-ridden diet that I have come to expect in American children. What was particularly important was the fact that he drank enormous quantities of milk, of which he was inordinately fond. Most people are not aware that a child, and even some adults, can become addicted to milk. It is deliberately made to be taste-attractive by the industry. We shall say something more about this later. But, for the time being, I am interested in illustrating how the "three circles of health" provide an extraordinarily good, simple model for understanding why and how a disease occurs.

Can an unusual amount of galactose in the diet of a normal person cause cataracts? Nobody has ever introduced such an idea, to my knowledge. However, there is certainly evidence from animal studies. Many years ago, Roger Williams, sometimes referred to as the father of nutritional therapy, carried out some experiments on rats. When he fed normal rats large amounts of galactose, he was able to induce cataracts in the eyes of nearly all of them. He then took another group of rats and gave them exactly the same amount of galactose as the first group received, but they also received large doses of a broad spectrum of vitamins. None of the vitaminized rats developed cataracts. It is pertinent to point out that Williams was unable to treat any cataracts that had already formed by the use of therapeutic vitamins. This study is one of the best pieces of evidence that prevention of disease is far more effective than attempting to cure one that has already made its appearance.

Now let us get back to the story of the child. Observe the situation closely. The parent who delivered the gene to the child (and it could have been either) was completely unaware that this phenomenon existed in the family. There had been no cases of galactosemia in the family, to their knowledge. It is estimated that each human being has an excellent chance of being a carrier of such a recessive gene. It will *never* be expressed in the form of a disease unless that person has a child by a person who is a carrier of the same recessive gene. Literally no one knows that he has such a potential. If one picks a mate by complete chance, the gene permutations and combinations are so great that there is an exceedingly slim possibility of the same recessive gene being present in the other person. But it does occur, and it is why the condition called PKU occurs in an estimated one in ten thousand births. It is also why such diseases are more likely to crop up if parents are related by blood and therefore are more likely to be carriers of the same recessive genes.

Having dealt with the genetics circle, we must see what kind of effect the stress circle might have. It was a very severe injury that the child had suffered, and it required extensive surgery. In Chapter 4, we discussed a situation where another six-year-old child with an inherited defect had his recurrent episodes of cerebellar ataxia triggered by various kinds of physical stress. The expression of the genetic defect was "silent" between his stress-induced episodes. I have no difficulty whatsoever in seeing the injury as a critical stress.

Finally, we find that this unfortunate child consumed large quantities of milk, the galactose from which has to be detoxified by his inherited machinery. Milk was by far and away the most dangerous food for him, but no one knew it. There is no way of proving that the genetic defect played any part whatsoever. Certainly galactose could not be found elevated in the child's urine, the normal way in which the diagnosis of galactosemia is made. I have always maintained, however, that if any one of these three insults had not been present, this child would never have developed cataracts. The trouble with so many aspects of clinical medicine is that proof often is quite impossible; so it is with this case.

It is coincidental overlap of three factors which makes this case a most unusual one. This experience, perhaps above all others, made me develop the simple figure that we have been discussing. I wrote a book called *The Nutritionist's Guide to the Clinical Use of Vitamin B_1*." It contains a whole chapter of case illustrations in which I have tried to classify illnesses in terms of which element is more important—genetics, stress, or nutrition.

When I look at these cases, as I do from time to time, I find it always difficult to decide which of the three is really the most important. In actual fact, it matters very little indeed from a practical standpoint. In the final analysis, none of us can have any effect on our genetically-determined constitution. We did not make the choice of parents. I know that high-tech medicine is becoming excited about genetic engineering. My own view, however, is that it is an exceedingly dangerous way to go. We cannot tell what kind of "echoes" will occur in the genetic profile when an artificial imitation is introduced. Furthermore, it is ruinously expensive.

Can we really make changes in our stress load? Certainly we cannot change the physical facts of life in reference to the environment. I seriously doubt that we will cease to pollute our world, and that pollution is certainly increasing our environmental stress. We are undoubtedly doomed unless we learn to adapt or change our ways. We are left with the third element, nutrition. Now—*that* we can really do something about. That is what the New Medicine is researching. It is a scientific trend that has an ancient lineage and it is certainly going to change the face of scientific medicine dramatically. Its success depends fundamentally upon biochemical knowledge and, as I have said, a clinical diagnosis is quite useless in defining the nuts and bolts mechanics of the disease process.

I must emphasize again that the biochemical lesion is the cause of the disease. All diseases are "psychosomatic" in the sense that the brain is always involved. If we are attacked by an infection, it is the brain that evokes the fever response, and it is chemical reactions in the brain that make us feel ill. A major block to our perspective is failing to see that the biochemical lesion can project different symptoms in different individuals, depending upon their constitutional reaction and the locality of the biochemical lesion within the body. Let me illustrate this by telling of a family in which there was an inherited disease in the father called alpha-1 antitrypsin deficiency. This name is a mouthful, so I will call it ATD. If we take this condition apart and look at it in the light of the physiologic machinery of the body, it begins to make sense. We can also use it to illustrate how the kaleidoscope of disease can operate.

The family was brought to my attention in a curious and extraordinary manner. There were four children, one boy and three girls. The boy was brought to see me because of this strange story. His personality was extremely stable, well-balanced, and secure. At the age of about six years, he had been taken to a dentist and, although the dentist was gentle and did not give him any undue trauma, he became totally hysterical and the dental appointment had to be aborted. Following this incident, there was a complete change of personality in the child. He cried excessively and had nightmares, and there was a huge difference in him, quite disproportionate to the degree of trauma that he had experienced.

I regarded this as being extraordinary. In the orthodox model, the child was a psychiatric case that should have been referred automatically to a child psychiatrist. It was not regarded as a problem within my range of expertise. He needed a specialist. It turned out that I was the specialist—in chemistry! I was still working in the big multi-specialty clinic with its vast medical resources. My work, like that of my colleagues, was constantly under surveillance of my associates, so it is not surprising that each staff physician normally toes the party line. He can be considered to be "brilliant" *only within the current dogma which guides the attempted solution to any disease problem.* A physician who moves away from the current pattern of medical thought risks losing credibility and losing his job. Such a person becomes a medical outcast within the physician community.

I was then in the process of understanding the broader issues of how bad diet affects behavior and personality. I had received a letter from a very old veterinarian who told me that he had been able to induce a condition that he called "fright disease" in dogs, simply by giving them a diet very high in starch. Such dogs, according to this doctor, disappear under the table with their tails between their legs when anyone approaches them. They whine and give very obvious signs that they are afraid. Simply by restoring a normal canine diet, the personality of these dogs could be restored to normal.

Of course, this information reminded me of the change in personality of this child. I knew that thiamin was a frequent deficiency in children taking the standard American diet (is it a coincidence that these initials spell "sad"?) and so I performed a blood test on him that proved that he was indeed thiamin-deficient. Treated with thiamin and other vitamin supplements and an emphasis on appropriate diet, the child's personality was restored to its former state. The "fright disease" disappeared. This was wondrous! Why were we not looking at so many diseases in this light? Try as I might, the more I discussed it with my colleagues the more my credibility waned. I finally shut my mouth and just followed these new leads alone.

The mother in this family was an intelligent and lovely person, and I came to know her and all the family quite well. So my ears pricked up when I learned that her husband had this relatively rare disease, ATD. In order to understand my theme, I have to describe the mechanics of this disease as far as it is understood. Trypsin is an enzyme that digests protein. Its main locality is in the intestine, of course, and it is one of the enzymes produced by the pancreas. But why does it not attack the protein in the pancreas where it is made? It circulates in the blood as well. Why does it not attack the protein in the rest of the body?

We see the endless and incredible wisdom and planning of MN once again. Our bodies make a substance which inhibits the action of trypsin, under the control of a gene inherited from our parents. It is made within cells by a complex process whereby a series of molecules known as sialic acid are added to it. When it has its full complement of sialic acid residues, it becomes active and will neutralize circulating trypsin, thus protecting us from having our own tissues digested by our own machinery!

A condition in which a person lacks this protective mechanism, like the galactosemia that I described, is recessively inherited; a person affected by the disease has to have a double dose of the faulty genes. A person inheriting only one "bad gene" will be a carrier of the disease, capable of passing on the carrier state to his or her children. Such a carrier is known in technical language as a *heterozygote,* whereas a person who has a double dose of the gene and who thereby has the disease, is known as a *homozygote.*

A homozygous person for the trait is unable to make the inhibitor of his own trypsin. The disease process is related to the fact that circulating trypsin damages the person's own protein. The primary manifestations are in the form of chronic lung and/or liver disease and its progressive nature first of all cripples the patient and finally kills. The father of the boy who had the change in personality was homozygous for ATD and was disabled from the disease. However, it meant that he would pass on one of the bad genes to all his children. Thus, all four children were heterozygous, or carriers of the disease. None would have a homozygously affected child unless the marriage partner was similarly affected.

As I have already stated, classical genetics states that the heterozygote of a recessively inherited trait is not expressed clinically. I had all four of the children tested and, as expected, they were all carriers of the ATD gene. My question, as in the case of the child with cataracts, was whether this state might have some untoward effect upon their health. The boy with "fright disease" was the first example, and he had a blood test which had proved him to be deficient in vitamin B_1. All of them had an unusually low energy level. Fatigue was such a part of their individual lives that they had come to expect it as being *normal* for them. All of them responded to vitamin supplements and improvement in their diet. However, the symptoms have been as variable as are their individual personalities. One of the girls, now grown up and living away from the family home, still consults me periodically. She is particularly prone to fatigue and non-specific ailments, suggesting that she is not always able to muster the energy required to meet the day-to-day stress that she encounters as we all do.

Although there is no way to prove my conclusion, I have concluded that the carrier state disturbs the constitutional balance of the individual so that, thus weakened, the body's ability to meet life stresses is impaired. It does not really make a difference whether one calls it an immune failure, an "allergy," or whatever. But it is clear to me that the only way to help such people is by making sure that they understand the true role of nutrition. It may well be that many people have silent heterozygous states within their constitutions which make them more prone to common disorders.

How should we attempt to put this information together in a meaningful way? In the first place, clearly the cause of the disease in the father was related almost exclusively to the genetics circle. Could vitamin supplements help him? They did help him! What about the four children? That is the inevitable $64,000 question. Since all of them were proven obligate carriers and all had unusual health problems, it was impossible for me to ignore the genetics circle as a force. In some way weakened genetically as they were, the stress circle became an important factor that could not be excluded. In the last analysis, however, did this unusual discovery count for anything? Basically, as far as the children were concerned, only the nutrition circle mattered from a therapeutic point of view. Furthermore, that conclusion applies to all cases because we cannot control the genetic element and the stress circle represents a variable which is neither controllable nor predictable.

I see the three circles as a kind of balance mechanism. Inflate the genetics circle, and the balance is shifted. That shift automatically causes the stress circle to come into operation, and the balance is again shifted. How can balance be restored? The answer is to increase the nutrition circle. Can we begin to see a new model for disease emerging?

I shall attempt to summarize what I hope that this book projects. In the first place, each of us survives in a hostile and dangerous world only because we are able to adapt to its infinite variety of challenges. The body, in reductionist terms, is nothing more than a complex machine that carries the brain around. The body has no feeling, no sense, no intelligence of its own. It is a "dumb" instrument which is like a massive orchestra that has to be conducted in order to keep the action together in a coordinated fashion. All of our 100 trillion cells are like citizens in a vast city. Each has to be in communication with its fellows, and all have to obey the rules that are dictated by the computer in the brain. The fact that communication is in a chemical language is not different from the principle that is used by insects.

In order to interpret the language, we have to find the Rosetta stone. This is the real objective of nutritional research.

The idea of "making a diagnosis" in clinical terms is archaic and old-fashioned. Granted, we must try to exclude the possibility of a tumor as a basic cause of a given problem. But I would point out that, if prevention is perfected, we will be able to abolish the formation of tumors. It is possible that even our genetic challenges may be related to environmental influences in some cases. I will recount a story that I experienced which makes me think this way.

In Chapter 2, I described my activities with those rare inherited conditions called inborn errors of metabolism. One of these is PKU, for which, the reader will recall, every infant in the United States is tested, on a purely preventive basis. We established that the incidence of PKU is about one in 10,000 live births, so it is not exactly common; it is also indisputably a genetically-determined condition, and no other influence has any bearing on it. It is an accident of nature.

The screening laboratory in Columbus, upon identifying a positive test for PKU, would often recommend that a physician refer the patient to a large medical center for treatment of this highly specialized problem. I was, therefore, usually consulted for any case that occurred in northeast Ohio. I remember one dramatic fall when I received calls from six different physicians to refer six different infants with PKU. All the calls came within about one month, and they all came from the same geographic area, a major suburb. Consider that this would have to represent the birth of 60,000 infants in order to make the statistics conform to reality. I wondered whether there could actually be an environmental influence causing such an incredible coincidence.

In the following year after this incident, I was participating in a state committee that had been convened in Columbus to consider ways and means of giving preventive genetic counseling throughout the state. Counseling is the only known way of preventing the appearance of genetically-determined diseases, assuming that there is some indication that such a genetic mistake lurks within a family. A blueprint had been proposed and this provided an analysis of all the genetically-determined conditions that were known to have occurred within the state during the previous year.

When we came to a discussion of the number of cases of PKU that had occurred, my six cases created an extremely noticeable and even a startling peak in the graph which had been drawn to show the month-by-month incidence. I suggested that the phenomenon might be looked at in an epidemiologic way, but the idea was summarily dismissed. "After all," the members of the committee said, "we know that PKU is a genetically-determined disease. How could environment have any bearing on its cause?"

I believe that the story illustrates the lack of imagination that so often rules the slow, plodding course of medical science. We basically say that the professor who taught me was a professor, so he must be right. It is little different from the way in which the people of Rome were guided by instruction from the Oracle at Delphi.

The modern Oracle in medicine is the American Medical Association, which provides analysis of what is acceptable and what is unacceptable practice. It may be a protection from fraud in some cases. (If all practitioners were perfectly honest and were truly mindful of the patient's welfare, it probably would not be a necessary evil.) However, the control by the American Medical Association also creates a wonderful way to stifle individual imagination in a physician.

Large numbers of practitioners are using nutrition and nutritional elements as therapeutic tools with remarkable success. They are certainly not going to turn their backs on this exciting and rewarding methodology. They desire the Model-T to become the Cadillac. All that remains is to go forward with its development. This book is dedicated to providing a rational explanation of why it works.

Chapter 11

What Is the Correct Fuel?

In recent years we have been bombarded with opinion—mixed with pseudo-science and a touch of real science—concerning various aspects of our diet. It is only lately that people have begun to look seriously at the quality of our food in relation to preservation of health. Our inattention to our food is amazing when you consider how careful we are to put the right fuel into our cars. Because we have not thought of our bodies as machines, we have assumed that the nature of our food is of little importance as long as we are hunger-satisfied.

I have taken great pains to point out that Americans are suffering from overeating, a phenomenon that has been called gluttony—one of the seven deadly sins—in the past. It is ironic that one-third of the world population suffers from the ill health of overeating while two-thirds suffer from the effects of under-eating. No wonder the ancient Chinese invented the philosophy of Yin and Yang to represent the unwanted extremes.

High-calorie malnutrition affects us quite differently than does starvation. It has always seemed to me to be extraordinary that the people who die of starvation seem to just waste away and disappear, almost without a whimper. In the early stages, of course, hunger drives them to desperate measures, but finally they seem to become quiescent and passive.

People who suffer from high-calorie malnutrition, however, behave differently. The major effect is in the central nervous system which, because of the "choked engine" mechanism, becomes more irritable. The normal patterns of behavior become grossly exaggerated. For example, a type-A person—who is compulsive and drives himself hard yet is in the normal range of personalities—becomes an exaggerated type A and becomes much more difficult to deal with. One can say that the "balance" of the mind, which dictates a given personality and will largely predict the behavior of an individual, will tilt and the dominant aspect will become magnified. Thus, a person who is relatively prone to anger will have that anger triggered more easily and the anger itself will be magnified. Someone who is susceptible to depression as a normal reaction to a given stimulus will have a magnified state of depression which is out of proportion to the stimulus.

I have long been convinced, as have others, that most violent crime could be eliminated by good nutrition. Alexander Schauss wrote *Diet, Crime and Delinquency* in 1980, providing massive evidence for this conclusion, which has been largely ignored. In his book, he reported that in 1977 Barbara Reed, Chief Probation Officer in Cuyahoga Falls Municipal Probation Department in Ohio, outlined her experience with 318 offenders to the U.S. Senate Select Committee on Nutrition and Human Needs. Of the ones that "required attention to diet and vitamin needs," none had been back in court for further trouble when they had remained on a nutritional diet.

It is absolutely vital to our civilization, and indeed to our survival, that we should be aware of how susceptible the human brain is to the quality of our nutrient intake. It all boils down to computer input, the nature of the data processing that takes place in the computer, and the executive output. Executive output to the body which is unbalanced, excessive, or muted will be maladaptive.

Unfortunately, our pleasure-loving brains are easily stimulated through the taste buds. Our entire modern culture is set against us in this respect. Every social event, every holiday, and every commemoration is celebrated with taste-stimulating food and drink. Candy is given to schoolchildren as a reward, and the teacher believes that anyone prohibiting a child from receiving such a reward is a mean-minded individual, a killjoy.

Perhaps then, in consideration of what is a good diet in this modern age, we should begin by discussing what is *bad* about it and the reason. We will begin with a consideration of the single most destructive nutritional "drug" that we ingest by the hundreds of pounds—sugar.

Why Is Sugar Bad?

Here we run into a problem that is naturally confusing to most people. It is true that glucose, the simplest sugar, is the major fuel of the body and particularly the brain. Then how can it possibly be bad? The answer requires a basic understanding of some simple chemistry and physiology—how the machine works.

First, sugar is *never* found in nature in its free state. It is invariably "locked up" in a fruit, a stem, a leaf, or a root. For example, there are about 1½ to 2 teaspoons of sugar in about two pounds of beetroot. Can you imagine anyone wanting to consume two pounds of beetroot in one sitting? We were designed by MN to eat fruit whole. The seeds were supposed to pass through the intestine and be dropped in a locality far removed from the fruit tree. Thus, the tree's procreation is dependent upon the animal eating its fruit. This, in the wisdom of MN, is the reason the fruit is so attractive in both appearance and taste. It is the "come-on" of MN.

The major difference between fruit juice and the whole fruit is the fiber that makes up the structure of the fruit. The sugar in fruit is fructose, which is dissolved in the juice. Therefore, the juice that you squeeze from a fruit is simply a dilute solution of sugar; for that reason fruit juice tastes sweet. Without the modifying effect of fiber, fructose is quickly converted to glucose and absorbed into the bloodstream, just as is *any* simple sugar, whether it be ingested in the form of chocolate, candy, sweets, or exotic deserts. The rapid rise in blood sugar now signals the computer in exactly the same way as a drug does. I have known people who recognize that they get "a high" from taking sugar and that high is the reason for their addiction to it.

Let me make it as clear as possible. The stimulus to the brain is through the taste buds and through the rapid absorption of sugar into the bloodstream. Sugar is indeed addictive and many heroin addicts have stated that discontinuing ingestion of sugar is as difficult as conquering the heroin habit. This may well be the mechanism by which the sweetener aspartame operates. If a person has become addicted to sugar, the input to the computer is established. Now, when that person takes aspartame, the same signal is received from the tongue. Thus, when the makers of aspartame performed an experiment in which they wanted to test whether it produced untoward effects, they gave the sweetener in a gelatin capsule. This of course, bypassed the route by which the untoward effect would be generated, and they missed the point.

What have been the untoward effects of aspartame? All kinds of neurological problems, including migraine. What is the mechanism of migraine? An autonomic nervous system effect on the vascular supply of the scalp or the brain, instigated by a trigger-happy or irritable computer. This effect is, of course, exactly the same as what might be produced by a drug. In other words, sugar and aspartame and other sweeteners act as drugs which stimulate the pleasure centers of the brain. It may not be directly related to the molecular chemistry of the agent at all, a fact that would explain why no untoward effect is experienced by ingesting it in a capsule which bypasses the taste buds on the tongue.

I have already indicated that sugar is brain fuel. Why then should we be concerned about its harmful effect? You have to turn back once again to the wisdom of MN. Sugar in nature is invariably surrounded by fiber which makes up the skeletal structure of the fruit, leaf, root, or stem of the plant. When ingested in this manner, as intended by MN, the fiber modifies the absorption of sugar from the intestine and slows it down. Thus, a slow increase in blood sugar follows and gives the brain a gentle stimulus that sets into motion the machinery which will cause the sugar to become stored in liver cells as glycogen. Glycogen acts as a fuel storage tank; when the body or brain is called to action, glycogen is converted back into glucose and is then processed through the citric acid cycle to form fuel, as already explained.

If a simple sugar, as opposed to a complex carbohydrate such as starch, is ingested without the natural modifying influence of fiber, it is rapidly absorbed from the intestine and blood sugar also increases rapidly. This sudden, high concentration will stimulate the brain computer, thus acting as a drug. The machinery for using the sugar lags behind and may go into overdrive, depending upon how addicted the individual is. By overdrive, I mean that there may be a significant discharge of insulin, causing the blood sugar to decrease rapidly. It may overshoot and cause a state of abnormally low blood sugar, referred to as hypoglycemia.

It can be seen, therefore, that hypoglycemia is actually *caused* by consuming sugar. Spells of hypoglycemic faintness, sweating, and dizziness can be immediately reversed by taking some sugar! The point is really an obvious one: it is a vicious circle which is being established. Sugar causes the system to become maladapted, leading to hypoglycemia which is relieved by taking sugar which causes more hypoglycemia.

Many adolescents today are excessively irritable, have extraordinarily rude behavioral characteristics, and complain of a whole host of physical symptoms. All these symptoms are due to excessively overactive brain computers. Not that such symptoms are volitional. They are driven by that part of the brain which is reflex. If the condition is bad enough, they may even become so violent that they are literally carrying out the equivalent of sleepwalking. One of the bits of encapsulated wisdom is the concept of "seeing red" in association with an outburst of anger which may or may not be accompanied by violent physical actions. This describes a kind of "red curtain" that the individual sees, causing, as it were, cognitive blindness. The computer, the "primitive man within," takes over and governs the behavior. Violence may be committed without the person being *cognitively* aware of the actions performed.

Many of these adolescents consume carbonated beverages, some of which contain huge amounts of caffeine and incredible amounts of sugar. If they are investigated by means of a glucose tolerance curve, the tracing that is drawn from the glucose concentrations plotted on a graph will not uncommonly be flat. Let me explain this a little further. Most people are familiar with a glucose tolerance curve. It is a laboratory test designed to see how a person metabolizes sugar. After a fasting blood sugar is drawn, the patient receives a dose of glucose. Blood is drawn at intervals of a half-hour and one-hour, and then after five hours. The blood sugar concentrations are then plotted on a graph. A typical, normal glucose tolerance curve is seen in Figure 7. Notice that the time scale is in hours and the blood sugar is back to the fasting concentration in two hours. Figure 7 also shows a flat glucose tolerance curve. The concentrations are similar throughout the curve.

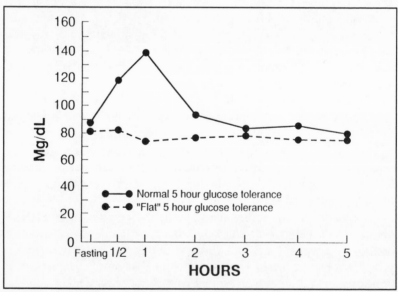

Figure 7. A normal pattern for a 5-hour glucose tolerance curve is contrasted with a "flat" response, in which the blood sugar appears to remain the same throughout the test.

I was very puzzled by the flat curves which I kept seeing in adolescent patients when they were tested in this manner. They were usually suffering from various kinds of behavior problems. One day, when I obtained a flat curve from one of these patients, I repeated the tolerance. However, instead of taking the first blood analysis half an hour after ingestion of glucose, I measured blood sugar every ten minutes. What happened is shown in Figure 8. Notice that the blood sugar rose very rapidly to a peak at twenty minutes and that it had returned to the fasting level at thirty minutes. I refer to this in the figure as an accelerated curve. The dotted line demonstrates that if I had ordered the conventional glucose tolerance test, in which the first blood is drawn half an hour after glucose administration, the rise in blood sugar would have been missed.

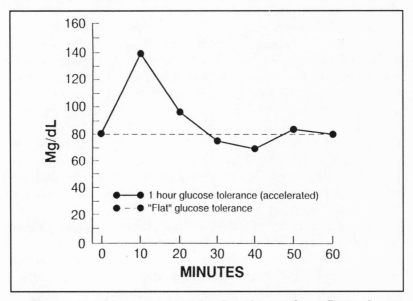

Figure 8. This represents the first hour of a "flat" glucose tolerance. Note that the time scale covers 1 hour only and that the peak glucose concentration is seen only 10 minutes after ingestion of sugar. Glucose concentration is back to the fasting level at 30 minutes.

I carried out several of these tolerance tests in adolescents when they had a flat conventional study. In each case, I saw the same phenomenon. How do I try to explain it? Well, I think that it is caused by the patient's system being unusually sensitive to a raised blood sugar. The blood sugar signals the brain computer, which then sends a fast signal to the pancreas, resulting in a rapid release of insulin, which brings the blood sugar quickly back to normal. It is a *hyperactive nervous system* response, mediated through the computer. In some cases, the reaction is so exaggerated that there will be an abnormal fall in the blood sugar into the hypoglycemic range.

From this observation, it can easily be understood that taking sugar in the diet leads to hypersensitivity in the computer, which makes the individual much more susceptible to any form of *stress,* using that word in its widest sense. For example, an adolescent may be asked to go and clean his room. The request itself is normally repugnant to any adolescent. However, in the adolescent with the trigger-happy computer, caused by diet of junk food, the reaction may be in the form of a temper tantrum.

I have seen one young man who reflexed and dove through a plate glass window. Another one put his fist through a window. Another individual tore the radio out of the dashboard of his car when he was held up at a traffic light. This kind of behavior is evidence of an excessively reactive nervous system which induces automatic, and therefore involuntary, activity.

Some years ago, I found that the veterinary literature often provides extraordinary insights into human illness. I became deeply interested in a particular disease in cows which had been studied in depth by veterinary scientists. I visited two different veterinary research centers in pursuing their knowledge. I happened to learn about Cuban molasses disease from one of the researchers.

The sugar industry in Cuba produced molasses, a heavy liquid which is almost all concentrated sugar. The farmers were using this as a source of high-calorie food for their cows, and the liquid was run into a trough in the cow bier. The concept was, of course, that a high-calorie food of this nature would fatten the animals. The cows, however, were developing a peculiar neurological disease which had mystified the veterinarians in Cuba. An affected animal that walked toward a wall or the side of a barn would be apparently unable to avoid the collision. As soon as its snout came into contact with the wall, the animal would remain "frozen" in that position, unable to move away. As the disease progressed, the animal would eventually go into convulsions and die. British veterinarians solved the problem in an absurdly simple manner. They mixed the molasses with grass or hay, the normal food for cows. One can hardly extrapolate this information to the completely different digestive system of the human. But this much is clear: the grass, in some way, modified the cow's digestion and absorption of sugar. There is absolutely no question but that fiber is as vital in human digestion and that its effect goes far beyond providing residual bulk in the large bowel to encourage normal bowel movement. There are, in fact, many different fibers that we take in with our food, and nutritional research has found that their various activities are extremely complex. It is fiber which has some modifying influence on the intestinal absorption of fruit sugar. This is the reason that fresh fruit can be eaten freely, whereas fruit juice squeezed out of the fruit and drunk as a tasty liquid will frequently contribute to the excessive sugar intake of most Americans.

What often happens is quite simple. A mother becomes aware that soft drinks, particularly colas, cause her children to become bad-tempered and irritable. So she stops buying them. Now she has to provide an alternative and is under the impression that fruit juice is a "health drink." She believes that this can be provided to slake the inordinate thirst of the youngsters which has been primarily induced by soft drinks, and a jug is always available in the fridge. The irritability of the children does not change, and she then draws an obvious conclusion. Since fruit juice is "natural" and contains "lots of vitamin C," it is "good for you" and could not possibly cause irritability and bad behavior. The secondary conclusion that she may come to is that the soft drinks were not the cause of the behavioral problem in the first place. Unfortunately, vitamin C in fruit juice disappears, and the child drinks a sweet-tasting, delicious liquid with no nutritional value other than that of the natural sugar from the fruit. It matters not whether it is artificially unsweetened as the label on the carton announces.

Milk

I have dealt with milk in relation to a child who was a carrier for galactosemia. This is a relative rarity, though it is possible that galactose can be upsetting to normal children when milk is consumed in large amounts. Be that as it may, milk has a profoundly bad effect on many children. Common symptoms are constant nasal congestion, often referred to as "allergies," other respiratory symptoms such as reflex "nervous" cough, and frequently hyperactivity, attention deficit, and even learning disabilities.

It is quite extraordinary how much milk is being consumed by children. It can be recorded frequently in *quarts* per day. What is it about milk that is potentially harmful? Is it not equated with "motherhood and apple pie"? Is it not the best source of calcium for growing bones? These aphorisms are misleading and are heavily encouraged by the industry. The cliché "drink more milk" has long been equated with good health. So how can a physician or a nutritionist have the affrontery to suggest that it is potentially harmful? Indeed, it is my invariable practice to exclude milk and fruit juice from the daily diet of children, along with the soft drinks and all sugar-containing fluids, particularly those with food dyes in them, if the child is hyperactive or has other similar problems. It is quite striking what rapid improvement often occurs, whether the problem be frequent infections or behavioral difficulties.

I reason in this way: is milk of any sort a normal food for a child equipped with teeth? The answer, of course, is that milk is an interim food provided by a mother for her infant. This fact applies to all species of mammals, and it seems incongruous that we have made the milk of another species a staple food in our diet. Furthermore, have carefully labeled it a "health food (drink)."

Consider once again the fact that homo sapiens was adapted to naturally-occurring organic food. Do you really think that adult cave men suckled on the teats of wild animals, let alone cows? Milking of cows is a very recent event in our natural history, arising from the domestication of animals in the process of bringing in agriculture. Raw milk, as obtained from a cow, may be perfectly satisfactory, if the cow is certified and so forth, even though its worth is still only as a basic interim food for calves until they can eat grass! In the world of today, however, we have to follow the milk through processing, which alters the picture very considerably. Processing is performed essentially to give the milk longer shelf-life and sterility. One of the major things that is done to it is homogenization; the fat globules are mechanically broken down so that they no longer rise to the top of the container as cream. These tiny fat globules can pass through the intestinal wall and carry with them the chemical molecules associated with modern farming. This means, of course, that drugs such as antibiotics administered to the cow can be ingested with the milk. Milk also contains a substance known as xanthine oxidase, an enzyme which can have untoward effects on human oxidative metabolism.

Fat

Most people today know that fat, which is a normal part of our diet, comes in various forms which are designated as saturated, monounsaturated and polyunsaturated. *Saturation* refers to the carbon chains that make up the chemical nature of the fat, and we do not need to discuss the highly complex details. From a dietary point of view, it is sufficient to know that saturated fat is almost always solid, whereas unsaturated fats are oils. Most of our saturated fat comes from animal sources. In the world of today, animals are deliberately fattened to yield a better dollar value in the market. In order to do this, they are given hormones and antibiotics, and these substances become sequestered into the fat of the animal before it is butchered. We used to value steaks by the "marbling" in the muscle of the animal. Most people are now aware, however, that ingestion of excessive fat in this manner is bad for our body chemistry and has undoubtedly been responsible for an enormous amount of disease, particularly of the cardiovascular system.

Should we be eating meat at all? All you have to do to answer the question of appropriate food for any animal is to look at its teeth. The human dental construction is clearly that of an omnivore, which means that both meat and vegetable sources are normal in our diet. So I go back to our pre-history to try to understand this question in relation to our modern diet. We were hunter-gatherers, which means that we hunted animals in groups and gathered the available vegetable material. For eons of time, we were adapted to this kind of natural food, which was always organic in nature.

The animals that we killed fed on the untainted vegetable material that we also consumed, and drank the pure water from the streams and rivers. Thus, their meat was not artificially fattened and the fat was not adulterated with antibiotics and hormones. Fish was, of course, an extremely important part of our diet and still is. Cold water fish are particularly important, as they supply us with an oil that enables us to build a vital part of the immune defense system. The only problem is that our sources of fish are entirely different. The fish come to us from long distances and are frozen.

It is not possible and neither is it necessary to return to our ancestral state. The cave man lived a short and brutish life. He died from starvation, frostbite, and animal predators and certainly not from overeating. But we need to understand the principles of diet to which we were forcibly exposed and to which we became adapted. Our genetic inheritance has not altered since that time. It is interesting to contemplate that these ancestors had much the same biologic equipment that we have today and would have had the intelligence to do all the clever things that modern man does, if he had had the knowledge.

Let's return to the analogy of the log fire; I pointed out that a newly-lit camp fire would produce little heat energy until the fire had caught and was burning vigorously. There are two ways in which a camper can accelerate this. He can blow into the fire, which is a simple way of increasing the local oxygen concentration, or he can put an inflammable liquid such as kerosene on it.

Fat is an extremely high-calorie fuel; I have likened it to pouring an inflammable liquid onto a fire. Thus, a high-fat intake with insufficient oxidative power to burn it is a good way to "choke the engine." This analogy may well explain why excess saturated fat in the diet is associated with a higher incidence of cancer. It simply causes loss of oxidative metabolic efficiency, either by this "choking" mechanism or by giving rise to increased formation of free oxygen radicals, which I have likened to sparks from a fire. We now know that poor control of free oxygen radical formation is a potent cause of cancer and creates a link between a high-fat diet and its increased incidence. It is also linked with cardiovascular disease and many other conditions, particularly in older age groups where we would expect greater loss of efficiency in the metabolic "engines."

Polyunsaturated fats are a different story. In a previous chapter we discussed the production of the important tissue hormones known as prostaglandins. They are formed from two *essential* polyunsaturated fats which are collectively known as vitamin F. The vitamin nomenclature simply states their role as being vital to life. So, at least we must have enough vitamin F, just as we require the whole array of essential substances. There are many polyunsaturated fatty acids that we take in with our diet, but only two of them are used for this essential construction. The rest are used as fuel and, although they are not needed in enormous amounts, they are not essential. These oils come from nuts and seeds and often do not figure high on the average menu, so it is not surprising that there is widespread vitamin F deficiency in the American population. This deficiency results in a whole variety of diseases, including a number of skin afflictions and common conditions such as asthma. Again I would like to emphasize that this reasoning, leading to the treatment of many different conditions with the same kind of treatment, offends the present accepted medical model. But the fault lies in the model; it is essentially wrong. We have to start thinking seriously about the biochemical cause of a disease and not worry so much about the nature of the clinical expression.

Cholesterol

Everything is related to balance, the finely tuned middle-of-the-road between Yin and Yang. We know now that high cholesterol in the blood is much less important than the fine tuning of its fractions. Cholesterol is essential to life and is synthesized in the liver. Only a relatively small fraction of it comes from diet and much mythology has been woven around it. It is used by the body to make a large variety of steroid hormones, those vital messengers released by glands on cue from the computer, which enable us to adapt. The cholesterol level in the blood reflects the supply economics of the balance between its production and its utilization. If there is an increased need for synthesis of hormones for an adaptive response, the supply from the liver must meet that demand. The concentration in the blood merely reflects the state of the cholesterol reservoir.

A high cholesterol may indicate under-utilization, as in a state of thyroid deficiency, or over-production. A low cholesterol may suggest either under-production or over-utilization, as in an excessive response to stress. The concentration of cholesterol in the blood therefore indicates a state of metabolism which *may* provide an index for disease potential, but does not provide a diagnostic label by itself. It has to be interpreted in much the same way as a low oil level in the sump of a car may indicate why the engine is overheating.

There is no doubt, therefore, that a high cholesterol is a metabolic indicator for disease potential, but so is a low cholesterol. In fact, it may be that a low cholesterol is more threatening than a high one, a phenomenon which is rarely discussed with patients in the clinic. Let us take an example from real life.

When I worked at the big clinic, I had a friend who was chief of the laboratory division. He told me of an occasional disaster that he had witnessed. A patient would go for major surgery, the nature of the operation not specified. After surgery, during the subsequent week, the patient's blood cholesterol would start to decrease sharply and death would follow. Although it is uncertain what happens in a situation like this, the cholesterol has to be an important indicator and I interpret it as follows.

Surgeons seldom fully take into account the nature of the biochemical mechanisms that lead to structural changes which then lead to surgery. It can be said that surgery, however brilliant the surgeon and however necessary the operation, is an admission of medical failure. It can hardly be said that MN designed the human body so wonderfully that we should have to remove organs that contribute to its function in order to "cure" it of disease. It is a self-repairing machine, and surgery spells out clearly that the self-repair mechanisms have failed. Anyway, a patient may go to surgery already weakened by the biochemical disorder which was the forerunner. Surgery is enormously stressful, no matter how one looks at it. If we return to the "three circles of health" and name surgery as a member of the "stress" circle, it is easy to see that the balance of the figure is severely distorted. This will cause the machine to go into a state of alarm, requiring huge stores of energy to be used. The steroid hormones, notably cortisone, must be produced in large amounts as part of the endocrine response to the stress. The strain on the cholesterol supply may be too great and the organism unable to keep it up to meet the demand. In such a case, it is not the falling cholesterol concentration that kills the patient. It is a metabolic collapse which is registered most dramatically by the falling cholesterol as its indicator. It is also easy to see that if the nutritional reserves of the patient are appropriately tended, the supply would be able to cope with the surgical stress (or any other form of stress) much better. We would be bringing the "three circles of health" back into balance.

There is absolutely no reason for a patient to be operated on without ensuring that the requisite nutrients are readily available. Even in an emergency, an intravenous infusion of a large variety of vitamin and mineral supplements would go a long way in taking much of the danger from the trauma of the operation. In fact, any illness would benefit from such an approach, and I invariably treat conditions such as viral infections by this method. There is no point in giving an antibiotic to a patient with an infection which does not respond to it. It only alters the general ecology of the normal defense mechanisms and therefore does more harm than good. It is always quite sickening to me that a patient admitted to a hospital for an elective procedure has his vitamin supplements denied to him. This is a time when he needs them more than ever. It is a gruesome reflection of the low place that vitamins and minerals have been given in the general conception of modern "scientific" medicine.

Cholesterol Fractions

It is worth repeating that in recent years it has been found that cholesterol is usually not an indicator of disease by itself if it is within reasonably wide margins of concentration. As most people now know, cholesterol is carried in the blood by substances known as lipoproteins. They are classified by their density, so they are known as high (HDL), low (LDL), and very low (VLDL) density lipoproteins. It is the relationship between these fractions that is now considered to be a good indicator of disease risk. There should be a *balance* between the HDL and LDL, and in good health the HDL should be relatively high and the LDL relatively low. These are sometimes known as the "good" and the "bad," but as the Chinese said about Yin and Yang, the balance is made up of a piece of each. Therefore they are not good or bad; they are simply part of the whole.

An easy way of telling whether this ratio represents a state of health is to divide the total cholesterol by the HDL. The ratio should be somewhere between 3 and 5. But, what does it mean? Is cholesterol a disease-producer? We have seen that it is an essential ingredient of our complex adaptive reactions. These phenomena are merely indicators. But what do they indicate? Well, they tell us a great deal about the state of oxidative metabolism, and that is the bottom line.

We now know that oxygen attacks fats in the body, including cholesterol. But it is the free oxygen radical species that do this attacking, so they must be quenched as they form, like the sparks from the fire. Certain forms of oxidized cholesterol contribute to the damage in atherosclerosis. Cholesterol, in its proper balance, is not the cause of cardiovascular disease. Even if it tends to be high, it is still the balance that is the important factor to be noted.

The VLDL largely reflects triglycerides, another form of circulating fat. This substance tends to increase in concentration when sugar, pastry, and "goodies" figure high in the diet. Although there are inheritance factors in both the cholesterol and triglyceride story, diet is by far and away the most important factor in how they are influenced. Obviously, the laboratory becomes an exceedingly important tool in obtaining this information. However, I wish to emphasize that interpretation is all-important. Many people are obtaining blood cholesterol concentrations and then not understanding what they mean or what changes, if any, that they need to make in their lifestyles.

On several occasions I have seen patients, often young adults, who have *low* cholesterol. When I tell them this piece of information, they are pleased because they have been brainwashed with the concept of high cholesterol as the danger. They are under the impression that the lower, the better. Naturally, they are puzzled when I tell them that this is bad and, in the long haul, may be more threatening as a potential disease marker. When diet is corrected and they take selected nutrients, their health improves and the cholesterol rises into the normal, balanced range. The HDL increases and the LDL decreases as part of this important balance.

Although nothing is said about it in the medical literature, there is some circumstantial evidence that the fasting blood cholesterol should be about twice that of the fasting triglycerides. Triglyceride concentration is much more affected by food, so measuring this must be in the fasting state. Here again, we see an important ratio which governs a *balance*.

Another laboratory marker which has been introduced is a substance known as lipoprotein (a). Most physicians now know that a marked increase in the blood of this substance is another risk factor which is independent of the other lipoproteins that we have been discussing. It is a strong indicator of a potential for cardiovascular disease and, when elevated, is one of the phenomena that is most likely to be associated with heart attack in a person under fifty-five years of age. Dr. Linus Pauling, one of the great biochemists of the 20th century, has now published evidence that this substance is very importantly related to long-term, chronic deficiency of vitamin C. He and his clinical colleague have found that the increased lipoprotein (a) decreases in some of the patients whom they have treated with vitamin C. This may become an important way of detecting this kind of deficiency which Pauling maintains is extremely common in America.

Protein

Protein occurs in both animal and vegetable material and is made up of chains of amino acids. Some of these amino acids are known to be essential to life because the body cannot make them from simpler substances. When we ingest protein in our diet, it is digested and broken down in the bowel by digestive enzymes into the amino acids which are its component parts. There are two basic protein classes, known as first and second class. First class protein contains the three aromatic amino acids, tryptophan, tyrosine, and phenylalanine, not found in second class protein. Most first class protein comes from animal sources, though nuts, beans and certain seeds provide the same protein nutritional value as meat. For this reason, people who consume vegetarian diet need to be aware that it is incomplete unless first class protein is included. Most vegetable protein is second class and is therefore an incomplete source of protein nutrition.

Under the impression that taking amino acids, which are the constituents of protein and which our digestive system is designed to handle, would be no different from consuming protein, many people are buying various amino acids from the health food store. This misconception can be dangerous, and people need to understand that a considerable number of amino acids have biologic effects which are equivalent to the ingestion of drugs. Some amino acids, for example, act as neurotransmitters, the chemical messengers of the nervous system and may therefore be capable of producing unpredictable symptoms in some people.

A recent study, sponsored by the Food and Drug Administration, has listed the biologic effects which are exerted by each of the amino acids. As many people are aware, for example, tryptophan has a sedative action, can be helpful in inducing sleep at night, and can have a beneficial effect on nervousness. It may be that they will eventually be prescription items. As a physician, I rarely prescribe them because of their unpredictability. Incidentally, the widely publicized disaster—in which a large number of people were affected by an illness which was lethal in some cases—which struck a few years ago when a toxic contaminant was found in synthetic tryptophan produced by one Japanese manufacturer was not related to the tryptophan itself. In this incident, a contaminant was to blame, and there is no reason to conclude that tryptophan, as an essential amino acid, was the cause. The result of the incident, however, was the FDA's withdrawal of all forms of tryptophan from health food stores and the classification of it as a substance available only through prescription. It is largely because of this disastrous situation with contaminated tryptophan that the amino acids were scrutinized carefully as a class of potentially therapeutic substances.

Non-Caloric Nutrients

We have established that our food is designed to provide us with the fuel that must be burned (the equivalent of gasoline) and vitamins and minerals (the equivalent of spark plugs). Vitamins and minerals are therefore non-caloric.

It has become fashionable but inaccurate to question which vitamin or which mineral should be used to cure which disease. You will sometimes find that a given vitamin is said to be good for a specific disease. When I was spending a great deal of time learning about the physiologic actions of all the known vitamins, I was struck by the fact that in resource material each vitamin was discussed in two sections. The first section dealt with its role in the biochemistry of the body. The second section described the symptoms that are seen when that particular vitamin is lacking in the diet.

I tried to memorize these symptoms so that I could recognize in patients deficiencies of particular vitamins. The first thing that I noted was the overlap. Each specific deficiency gave rise to a series of symptoms which were essentially similar in nature, no matter which vitamin was missing. Three classic deficiency diseases were described: scurvy, due to lack of vitamin C; pellagra, due to lack of niacin; and beriberi, due to lack of thiamin.

I wondered how it would be possible to recognize a given deficiency by an identification of the symptoms when there was so much overlap. Furthermore, I read that experimental withdrawal of thiamin, for example, did not cause beriberi! It caused a set of "psychological" and neurological symptoms, but it did not cause the thoroughly described picture of a person who was malnourished from eating a staple diet of white rice. The overall nature of the diet as a complex whole obviously gave rise to a *spectrum* of deficiency, although the exact nature of the deficiency could not be diagnosed by the clinical expression of symptoms. The current trend—the writing of whole books which use the present disease classification and which indicate the vitamins that should be used to treat a particular disease—is misguided because each disease is really not specific in nature at all. A given biochemical lesion, induced by a poor nutritional balance, will express itself in one individual in one way and in an entirely different way in someone else. It depends upon the particular part of the biologic system that is affected, the genetically-determined constitution of the person, and the degree of stress to which that person is currently exposed.

Thus, when patients ask me what vitamin they should be taking for a particular symptom or diagnosis, I simply say that I do not know. An attempt must be made by trial and error, based to a large extent on the experience of the prescribing nutritionist. There are many surprises for us all, and some of the answers come from an ever-widening experience, coupled with a knowledge of the biochemistry involved. Let me give an example from my own experience.

Some years ago, I was asked to see a young, severely retarded adult. He had seizures for which a neurologist had attempted to treat him by drugs. These efforts, as efforts to treat seizures so often are, were only partly successful. His mother was particularly interested in his overall health and the possible use of vitamins. Could I help him or even cure him?

One of the interesting clinical problems was a dreadful rash, or dermatitis, that had affected the patient's scrotum and thighs for a very long time. His mother had taken him to different dermatologists. A biopsy of the skin had shown a "non-specific" dermatitis and absolutely no treatment had been effective. I was struck by the fact that this rash had the appearance of the dermatitis that occurs in classic pellagra, the deficiency disease due to niacin deficiency. I actually prescribed large doses of vitamin B_6, for two reasons. In the first place, this vitamin has been often linked with successful treatment of seizures, though there is no very good way of recognizing the association except by a trial use of the vitamin. In the second place—and this is the crux of the story—niacin is made in the body by a biochemical pathway that depends upon vitamin B_6. I considered that I might be able to kill two birds with one stone, so to speak.

Several things happened which were extraordinary in light of how futile his previous treatment had been. First, the dermatitis cleared up completely, without a trace of its former presence. Secondly, the patient became calmer in his daily life. And thirdly, he put on weight and looked better in his general appearance. Can you imagine the benefit experienced, by not only the patient but also his mother, who took meticulous care of him virtually on a twenty-four-hour basis?

Well—was I right in my approach? The proof of the pudding is always in the eating. I had beneficially affected my patient, even though he was not cured. I know now, of course, that many different nutrients over a long period of time would have continued his benefits in a host of ways. But, using this as an illustration, did he actually have pellagra? If the dermatitis cleared up, then it was the right vitamin, but that is the *wrong* vitamin for pellagra according to the book. Since niacin is made in the body as I mentioned above, it is not strictly a vitamin. Its synthesis depends upon a series of reactions, some crucial ones of which require vitamin B_6 as a cofactor. What I had been able to accomplish, therefore, was an acceleration of niacin production by stimulating the pathway from which it is made biologically.

Perhaps the reader can see now why I have no intention of providing a do-it-yourself section here in describing the clinical use of vitamins and minerals. I must emphasize that the bottom line, in explaining the clinical projection of vitamin and/or mineral deficiency, is the fact that it *decreases efficiency of oxidative metabolism.* I cannot stress this fact enough. The various tissues in the body have different needs for oxygen which depend upon their metabolic rate. The brain, and particularly the computer in the brain, is the most oxygen-requiring tissue. The next most oxygen-requiring tissue is the heart. So it is hardly surprising that the classic picture of beriberi is that of *either* heart disease *or* brain disease or a combination of *both*. Beriberi is really a disease where oxidative efficiency has declined on the left side of the bell-shaped curve which we examined earlier.

Why have we been constructed in a way which makes us so susceptible to the effects of a given nutrient? How is it that an amino acid, a constituent of protein which is an essential part of our diet, when administered singly affects the nervous system so much? When protein is digested, that amino acid is released along with all the other amino acids which make up its structure. What is the difference?

I believe that we simply have to go back to the rules that were set long ago by MN. We were designed to eat the whole food, not parts of it. We were designed to consume the food that grew out of the earth and the constituents of which make up the essential substance of our own bodies. If we look at the human body in its wondrous structure, it is a truly marvelous but incredibly fragile machine. Boil us down to our essential, physical ingredients, and we are little more than water and a handful of minerals worth somewhere between two and three dollars on the open market. We are too clever for our own good and not apparently bright enough to see that we must fit in with the great design or take the ultimate consequences.

This country, for about 150 years, had the best nutrition in the world. Anthropologists have taught us that man adapts to his environment constitutionally, and we are amongst the largest and best-developed humans on earth as a result of that long period of adaptation. After World War II, however, there was a major change in our food supply. Dismembered foods, messed around with by a dollar-greedy industry, appeared in colorful cardboard boxes which make up the vast increase in trash. Convenience and taste stimulation became the guiding factors, becoming embroiled into our extremely hedonistic culture. Having adapted to the superb nutrition of yesteryear, it is not surprising that our health is suffering a chronic setback when our diet is deteriorating at an accelerated rate. Genetically, we were geared to a high-nutrient density and what we get today is nutrient-poor.

It is a story which nearly everyone who thinks at all will easily recognize. And it is seemingly a hopeless battle which may be already lost. Can we possibly change? Certainly the industry can be changed only by the pressures of the marketplace and the demands of consumers. It is much the same as the appalling junk that is projected from our television sets. As long as we buy it, we will certainly have it available.

One might say that the sickness in our society is the culture itself—not a very new phenomenon in the history of homo sapiens. We destroy ourselves as we enjoy doing it, never connecting the payoff with what we did to ourselves in the first place. The dinosaurs lasted 200 million years, and we call them stupid because we believe that they had small brains unlike the "super-brains" that we believe ourselves to possess. How is it, then, that we can be so stupid? If we do, indeed, possess such a brain, how is it that individuals can rise to such great heights of intellectual and emotional marvels and yet collectively we threaten complete and abject failure as a species? Perhaps, even worse, we threaten to be failures in the stewardship of the world that we have apparently inherited and subjugated. It is a conundrum of enormous consequence to our future as a species, and there are very few signs of real change.

I was very impressed years ago by a trip on a boat on Lake Como. It was an incredibly beautiful day; blue skies were punctuated by clouds that concentrated in large billowing masses over the mountains and the peaceful Italian villages were picture-perfect. An Italian family, sitting in front of us, had evidently brought their lunch. They unpacked the food and, without a single glance, threw their trash over the side of the boat into their beautiful lake. As with the contrasts in a symphony, the contrasts in what I was viewing underlined the beauty of the scene. The stupid and thoughtless act only accentuated the beauty of the surroundings, like a discord suddenly erupting after a lyrical passage of music. It left me with a deep impression of complete irreversibility in the collective personality of the species. It does not take much of a search today to find evidence of this. All you have to do is to visit a particularly beautiful tourist area anywhere, particularly after a public holiday. The trash left behind is always humongous. It is this basic personality defect which affects our attitude toward our world in general. It insinuates itself deeply into the way in which we indulge our convenience for something as essential as an appropriate fuel supply—our basic nutrition.

The patients who come to my office almost always come for one of two reasons. Either they have read a great deal about nutrition and its benefits to health, or they are absolutely fed up with the way that they have been treated unsuccessfully by orthodox, scientific, allopathic medicine. They are thus ready to view the model that I am presenting in this book. Even then, it is a tremendously hard transition for them, though they believe the will to be there. Imagine how difficult it is for a would-be patient to accept this transition "cold turkey" upon coming to see me, not knowing that I have an entirely different approach from "ordinary" physicians.

One of my interesting recurring experiences is treating an unwilling adolescent brought in by a parent, sometimes both parents. The adolescent is usually totally resistant to the suggestion that his nutrition is appalling and that it is causing his allergies, as well as his recurrent diarrhea, chest pain, fatigue, insomnia, and even his jagged personality which no one except his peers can tolerate.

The teenager refers to the parent or parents as "a health nut," so I try to preempt him. I say, "You came unwillingly, dragged in by your mother, didn't you?" Often there is a whimsical smile of recognition; then, I let him have it with "both barrels." I have concluded that being polite and "professional" is often a pure waste of time for both the patient and myself. Occasionally, my bluntness drives someone away, but if I do have a victory, it is a sweet one.

I remember one nice young man who was the son of a very fine lawyer. His nutrition was the American average, and I pointed out to him that he had white spots on his fingernails, the absolute hallmark of marginal malnutrition. He took me seriously and did alter his ways to some degree. He went back to school and looked at his classmate's fingernails. One of his classmates, the son of a physician, had the white nail spots and my patient pointed them out. The boy went home and asked his father whether his white nail spots indicated nutritional deficiency. His father said that it was nonsense and dismissed it as an indicator of anything, revealing the lack of the slightest interest in nutrition that is frequently shown by physicians.

I am fascinated by the people who come back for second visits after being advised to discontinue coffee, chocolate, sweets, tobacco, milk, fruit juice, or whatever is their particular addiction. I ask them how they are getting on with the withdrawal. Often I get the reply, with a kind of smile to suggest that I, the physician, will be pleased, "I am working at it." I point out that their low dose is now often as harmful as or even more harmful than their original intake. Furthermore, they are not at all affecting me as their advisor. They are simply shortchanging themselves.

I remember a delightful gentleman who came to see me because he was repeatedly sick with many different things. He was an alcoholic, a member of AA. He had been "dry" for several years and was justifiably pleased with himself. The only problem was that he had substituted the alcohol with sixteen cups of coffee a day! I told him that he had to quit coffee. He remonstrated, saying that he was unable to do it. He was actually successful, however, and later told me that it was the hardest thing that he had ever done. He went to sleep in his office, became excessively sleepy driving his car, and had the most appalling headaches. Was it worth it? Well, all I can say is that I never see him now. He does not need me. But then, he does not need any other physician either: he is well.

I remember a similar situation which involved a woman who suffered from chronic fatigue and many other symptoms that made her life miserable. She was advised to withdraw from coffee, of which she was inordinately fond. On her second visit she was sitting in my consulting room awaiting my entry. Although it was winter, the air conditioning had been switched on for the purpose of running a test in an adjacent room. I immediately noticed that it was "freezing" in the room. I apologized and asked her to follow me into another room.

"Oh, doctor," she said, "the temperature of the room is of very little consequence. I don't mind coming to your office at all to tell you what a pleasure it is to feel as well as I do. I haven't felt like this in years." She went on to tell me that her withdrawal from coffee was one of the most agonizing experiences of her life. She had remained on the bed for two or three days, in the fetal position, with a blockbuster headache that "threatened her sanity." After the headache ceased, she began to feel progressively better. Energy increased and all her symptoms ceased.

I have seen this kind of result time and time again. The foundation of treatment is fundamental. It is simply good, well-balanced, organic food, accompanied by vitamin and mineral supplements which have been lacking in the diet, sometimes for years.

The word *organic* is sometimes puzzling to people since we now have the buzz words, *organically grown*. This indicates, of course, how very artificial we have become. That is how all our food should be. Under normal circumstances, an animal, including homo sapiens, eats fresh vegetable material which contains a balance of nutrients, giving it appropriate nutrient density. The evacuation of waste material from the body, recycled to the land from which the vegetables are grown, keeps minerals in the cycle and we consume them again in the vegetables. This cycle has been altered, however. We do not recycle bodily waste in the ground. *We* may require minerals for health, but vegetable material does not require them, so the fertilizers put on the soil do not contain minerals. It is too expensive. Hence, we do not obtain the nutrient density from modern vegetables. This fact virtually guarantees that minerals and vitamins should be ingested as supplements for the proper maintenance of optimum health. Oh sure, we can get by on marginal malnutrition, but it certainly will not provide us with *optimal* health. The modern, orthodox view that a good, well-balanced diet will provide appropriate nutrient density for everyone is completely erroneous. I see dozens of people who do not follow an average "junk food" diet and are very careful to obtain the right foods; they do better than the junk-food junkies—a lot better—but they still get sick, in many cases because their diets are just not sufficient to meet the stresses of modern living.

Addiction

We have already discussed some addictive substances. Why is addiction tragic and what causes it? It is based upon stimulation of the pleasure centers in the computer. Once the cells in that center become accustomed or adapted to the sensory pleasure, they cause a longing or a craving which is very hard to resist, as all addicts know. Anything that causes this craving will give rise to addiction, and I have seen it in many different guises. We can become addicted to anything if it causes pleasure. Hence, a deep craving for sex is really no different, in principle, from a craving for tobacco, chocolate, or coffee.

Withdrawal from *any* addictive substance will result in withdrawal symptoms. These are pretty much the same, no matter what the substance is, but they vary in severity and length of action. The symptoms are appalling and cause a person to think of virtually nothing else. They are, to all intents and purposes, crippling. The devilish thing is that taking a dose of the addictive substance abolishes withdrawal symptoms. No wonder it is so hard to do. But—there *is* no short cut, no easy way out. The way to become free of the scourge is to stay away from it, often for a lifetime but certainly for a long time.

Coffee is a well-known addiction, and many people are completely amazed by the strength and virulence of the headaches that they experience during withdrawal. Why do these symptoms develop? It is, I think, because the computer is maladapted to the sensory input. All kinds of autonomic nervous system mischief accrues if the computer becomes erratic in its electro-chemical behavior. We would never become addicted to anything unless exposed to it. Alcoholics, though they are born with the constitutionally predisposed system which easily creates addiction, would never become alcoholics unless exposed to alcohol. An addictive tendency in a woman is accentuated in the premenstrual week, and this is when craving for chocolate or salt is tremendously increased.

Sometimes, the ingestion of the addictive substance may cause a harshly adverse effect. A patient of mine was addicted to chocolate, an extremely common phenomenon. But she was also exquisitely sensitive to it. One evening, she craved it until it was driving her "out of her mind." Knowing that she had to resist it, she thought that she would get some carob, since that was a "naturally occurring substance." She awakened at 2AM with the worst attack of dysautonomia that she had ever experienced.

Tobacco is one of the worst of the addictive drugs. (Also, we now know that passive smoke, that exhaled by the smoker, is dangerous to other people.) Nicotine is a well-known substance that has long been used in animal experiments to poison the nervous system. One of its most dangerous effects is that it encourages the production of free oxygen radicals. The result is a rapid but inefficient metabolism, so the victim does not gain weight. As soon as the person stops smoking, there is often a considerable weight gain because the metabolism remains inefficient but slows down. The calories taken in with food are not used as fuel, but are diverted and stored as fat, like an overflow into a reserve fuel tank.

There is really only one effective way to beat addiction—to quit "cold turkey." When a gradual withdrawal is attempted, the individual may become increasingly sensitive to the substance. Neither should there be a substitute, as when the alcoholic patient exchanges alcohol for coffee in his withdrawal. It is of great interest to me that a big pot of coffee is provided at meetings of Alcoholics Anonymous. The coffee may have some effect in maintaining a "dry" state as far as alcohol is concerned, but you can be sure that the overall health of the clients suffers, at least in some cases.

I teamed up with some colleagues two years ago in order to carry out an experiment on people that were crippled by alcoholism. They were in a "drying-out" residential institution and were therefore a captive audience. They were receiving psychologic counseling and a supervised diet. We wished to find out whether there was any improvement in their progress if they also received a supplement of fat-soluble thiamin, described in an earlier chapter. There was a definite difference which was documented in a statistical analysis of their symptom improvement. Other experiments of a similar nature have shown that nutritional supplements of this nature have definitely helped the process of withdrawal in those who genuinely wish to do it.

Nutrition and Symptoms

Like other physicians who work in this field of therapeutic nutrition, I often have a truly enormous credibility gap with patients. We have been taught that a specific symptom or set of symptoms is used to attempt to delineate the disease, which we then name. It is very difficult for people to grasp the simple fact that a symptom is really nonspecific in the majority of instances. Let me try to provide an example. Abdominal pain might be caused by an inflamed appendix. Much more commonly, however, it is caused by some effect in the nervous system. The patient associates abdominal pain with disease in the abdomen. The pain, arising in the nervous system, is referred to the abdomen as its source, misleading us in its message.

One difficult and recurring problem is "my sinuses." This is also frequently referred to as "my allergies" or "my post-nasal drip" or "vasomotor rhinitis," depending upon what the patient has been told. I invariably ask patients whether they have nasal congestion, and about 75 percent of the patients that I see answer in the affirmative. Then I ask whether it is constant or intermittent. I find that it is intermittent in the majority of cases and that it is worse in the morning. Now—here is where the credibility gap comes in. I try to point out that mucus production is reflex and is "ordered" by the brain computer. It indicates that the nervous reflex between sinuses (or nose) and brain is accentuated; it is a function of circadian rhythm, and is therefore worse in the morning. But then, I try to point out that the reflex activity is *caused* by intake of coffee, sugar, or whatever is the food substance that is creating the trigger-happy computer.

It is a veritable labor of Hercules to get such a point across to the average individual. Imagine what it is like when the patient walks confidently in "just for an antibiotic for my sinuses." I say that it is not a sinus infection and that it is not even an infection—yet! "It is an irritable computer, due to your intake of sugar and coffee," I say. The air of disbelief is quite impenetrable sometimes, and the explanation is necessarily lengthy. But consider—if I comply with the patient's request, coming from assumptions which are wrong but nonetheless confidently accepted, I do more harm than good. It is, of course, much easier to comply. Anybody can write a prescription for an antibiotic.

How much more difficult it is for a mother to accept the fact that the chocolate that a child had at 4PM is responsible for the night terror that he has at 2AM the next morning. How much more difficult it is for parents to accept the fact that their child's diet is responsible for his temper tantrums and attention deficit in school. We are simply not geared to hearing that our behavior and our physiology are directly related to what we eat and, more particularly, what we drink.

Craving

Craving a particular substance is, to all intents and purposes, synonymous with addiction. How can we beat it, assuming of course that we desire to? Food should contain the six different taste stimulants. These are sweet, sour, bitter, salt, pungent, and astringent. But the sweet stimulus should come from a natural source and be accompanied by the other flavors. Sour, bitter, and salt come from fruit and vegetables and pungent comes from spices, an ancient principle of good cuisine. Astringent taste comes from beans and legumes.

There is a tendency for people to think that *good cuisine* means being fancy. What it really means is that food preparation should be artistic and fun to do, not a chore as we think of it today. By using a variety of organic foods, we "hedge our bets" in terms of picking up the array of nutrients that we require. Mixing the flavors gives us a sense of enjoyment, and the food should be eaten in the company of those whom we love.

I was blessed with four wonderful children who have a remark-able personality for a mother. When they were growing up, we did several things that were of extraordinary benefit. Soft drinks were never present except when they had birthday parties and then there was plenty. We had family dinner every evening, no matter what activity was involved, and we had no television for ten years until they grew to the age of reason and discretion. My children, now all grown and married, remember these things with great pleasure. The loving relationships were simply part of their lifestyle and nothing got out of hand or disproportionate. We never had the slightest problem with beating the drug thing, because artificial stimulation was not a required substitute.

I shall close this chapter by saying that the trick to living in peace and harmony is the art of balance. This applies to our relationships with others, and there is no doubt at all that the family unit is by far and away the most important place to nurture children so that they grow to be decent human beings. The family table and the food that is set upon it is a vital part of that family life. In my view, there is no substitute.

Chapter 12

How Does the Laboratory Help?

Throughout this book, I have attempted to show that the present medical model is creakingly inadequate for the widespread problems of disease and illness that we are facing today. We are becoming progressively less and less able to adapt to the self-imposed stresses of our own civilization. I have tried to show that disease is nothing more than evidence of an energy deficit, a breakdown in the ability to use oxygen efficiently in the process of oxidative metabolism. Then what about the laboratory which is conventionally supposed to provide us with a proof of diagnosis?

First, let us see how the laboratory is used in conventional medicine. Physicians are trained to take a history. This starts with the patient volunteering his leading symptom or complaint, such as "my knees hurt."

The physician then guides the patient back to the very beginning. He might ask, "When were you last quite well?" or "Was that your first indication of trouble?" A detailed account on a month-to-month or year-by-year basis is then extracted in a chronological order. It is often during the taking of this history that the patient provides the most important clues. By the end of the history, the physician should have a pretty good "mind's eye" picture of the problem. This is what any physician will do whether he is conventional or not.

The next step is to carry out a physical examination. Whereas the history looks for symptoms, which are the complaints given by the patient, the physical exam looks for signs, which are the phenomena that are observed by the physician himself. If there are no physical signs, he may already be thinking that the symptoms described by the patient are *functional*. This word has become virtually synonymous with *non-disease*. Finding a physical sign encourages the physician to think that the patient has a "real disease."

Imagine that the physician has discovered that the patient has an enlarged liver. The next phase is to discuss what is called a differential diagnosis, which means that the whole range of conditions which give rise to an enlarged liver must be considered. Tests are developed around this discovery, and that is where the laboratory fits in. It is supposed to differentiate between all the various diseases that cause an enlarged liver and, hopefully, clinch the final diagnosis. An appropriate name can now be given to the disease. This process of exclusion is known as a "work-up." The idea now is that the physician applies the appropriate treatment, if known. In many instances, this is quite unknown and is usually quite empirical. A textbook of medicine adds a section on treatment after it has completed the detailed description of how the diagnosis is made. It will often state that "such-and-such a drug has been tried with variable success."

It is quite clear from this discussion that the physician is supposed to control the disease actively by some artificial means. No mention is made of the ability of the tissues to heal themselves and how that process may be assisted. Even at the present time, the subject of diet is, at the best, cursory and superficial in a standard textbook of medicine. This is truly amazing when we have so much evidence that nutrition is the most important of all.

Alternative, nutritionally-related medicine diverges sharply from conventional medicine at an early point in this process. After the history, I begin to classify the symptoms in my mind as to whether they are due to imbalance in the autonomic nervous system or whether the endocrine system is involved in a general way. Then, I try to conclude from the clinical history, physical exam, and diet history what kind of a biochemical abnormality I should expect. Is it likely to be hypo- or hyper-oxidative metabolic inefficiency? I am already thinking about the kind of nutrient supplementation program the patient is likely to need.

At this point I use the laboratory to attempt to identify the underlying biochemical *cause* of the symptoms and signs that have given rise conventionally to a named disease. I am not concerned at all about the name of the disease, which I regard as an artificial classification. The bottom line is the nature of the deviant chemistry in the areas of the body where it is operating. I have already pointed out that the brain is most susceptible to oxidative metabolic inefficiency. So the nervous system is invariably involved in multiple ways, no matter what disease terminology is used. People with the "mental disease" known as schizophrenia also have physical or somatic symptoms, and people who have a typical "physical" disease also have mental symptoms.

The human body is essentially a fuel-burning machine that consumes oxygen in the process of delivering energy to its component parts, the cells. Each of our 100 trillion cells is a unit of function. The combination of their individual effect constitutes the final outcome, which is termed *behavior*. Physical is just as mental as mental is physical, for the common denominator is chemistry, giving rise to electricity. Each person is a complex "black box" that operates on thousands of chemical reactions taking place every second of their existence, twenty-four hours a day.

It can be said, at this stage, that the laboratory is still a relatively crude tool. The many complex tests that have been invented do not tell us, for the most part, about the true, underlying nature of deviant biochemical cause. In so many ways, we fail to get to the root of the tree, even though the tree may be visible. Let me illustrate.

A person tells a physician that he does not feel well. The physician, having arrived at a provisional clinical diagnosis, now asks the laboratory for confirmation. The laboratory data, if abnormal, confirms that the patient is indeed sick, but does not identify the *biochemical* cause. The physician then tells the patient that he is sick.

The patient might well be forgiven if he reminds the physician that he told him that in the first place! Most patients are not really interested in the Latin name that might be applied to the peculiar constellation of symptoms and signs that he brings to the clinic. In most instances, the name serves only to frighten the patient even more, an attitude of mind which is completely foreign to the healing process. For example, the word *cancer* is a virtual death sentence to many because they *know* that it is an incurable disease. The beauty of nutritional medicine is that it is always aimed at supporting the patient's own efforts to reestablish homeostasis. It never attempts to control the disease.

We must be aware of the reaction of the conventional physician if the laboratory tests are all normal. The conclusion is, necessarily, in our present usual and customary state of the art, that the patient has a "non-disease." The whole constellation of complaints is regarded as functional and is either treated with a tranquilizing drug or referred to the psychiatrist's couch. My interpretation of *functional* is that the brain computer coordination of adaptive responses to both exogenous and endogenous stimuli is deviant. Whether this is revealed in purely mental terms (such as delusions, depression, exaggerated mood swings, or panic attacks) or whether it is in physical terms (such as constipation alternating with diarrhea) does not matter at all. The common denominator is chemistry.

The Preventive Laboratory

I have repeatedly taxed my laboratory colleagues with the fact that the laboratory largely fails to give me the information that I seek on behalf of my patients. What *is* the information that I require? In a nutshell, I want to know two things:

1. Whether the patient's illness is due to dysfunctional chemistry on the left side, the right side, or both sides of the bell-shaped curve depicting oxidative metabolism.

2. If an oxidant or anti-oxidant deficiency exists, what are the specific nutritional culprits?

Remember our analogy of the cathedral roof? The oxidants, of which there are a great number, constitute one side of the roof; the anti-oxidants make up the other side and create a balance which keeps the roof in a stable position. I want to know which of the girders in the basic structure of the roof are lacking or are weakened. This creates a riddle of great complexity. At present we can count at least forty major nutrients that make up the girders that enable the oxidative process to operate, and that is probably just for openers. How can the biochemical mechanisms that are dependent upon these vitamins and minerals be identified?

General Tests

All medical laboratories perform a huge number of tests. As everyone knows only too well, all these tests are extremely expensive because they rely on sophisticated technology. The machines are so complex and so dependent upon electronics that they break down relatively easily and have to be serviced. Their accuracy has to be repeatedly tested to avoid false results, and they are very expensive to purchase.

As most people are aware, the old days of a test performed by hand under the care of a skilled technician have gone. The technicians are more diversified in their skills and have to have considerable knowledge in operating electronically-dependent machines, including computers. The number of laboratory tests that are performed automatically is legion. It is essentially a "fishing expedition." By that, I mean that the physician has absolutely no clue at all about the biochemical problem from his initial impact with the patient. He may have formed a basic idea as to whether it is an oxidative or an anti-oxidative deficiency, but even that is far from being sophisticated. Thus, he has to throw a net out in order to attempt to catch a fish. If there is no fish there, there is obviously no catch. But he may also throw the net into the wrong part of the lake.

Of course, the physician can always start nutrient supplements empirically on a trial-and-error basis; in fact, many people are already doing that for themselves, purchasing supplements from a health food store. But we are talking about ways and means of identifying the biochemical problem accurately and quickly, as well as inexpensively, and being able to prescribe the precise supplement formula tailored to the needs of the individual.

The main part of the "fishing expedition" is a comprehensive, automated blood test called a SMAC. The patient's blood is fed into a machine programmed to deliver answers on a tremendous spectrum of tests, and the answers are printed out. If the tests were done singly, the cost would be prohibitive. Any one of these test results, when abnormal, tells the physician that something in the patient's chemical balance is deviant. A general impression can be gained of the degree of deviation that is represented, but it is by no means specific.

I certainly do not wish to give a negative slant to this. An enormous amount of information can be garnered. However, it is imperative to understand that the facts have to be interpreted. They do not stand alone as something that can be corrected by the application of a carefully selected drug or nutrient. Occasionally, a patient asks for his "lab tests" under the impression that they will be self-explanatory. They may not even be interpreted in the same way by two different physicians, particularly if one of the physicians is orthodox in his thinking.

One of the best examples of this discrepancy is the interpretation of a deviant blood cholesterol. For the most part, both physicians and their patients are apt to judge a blood cholesterol as being abnormal only when it is too high. However, as we had already seen, it can also be too low; it should be governed by the Yin and Yang balance of the "middle road." The balance of its fractions, the so-called "good" (HDL) and "bad" (LDL) is even more important. However, in order to interpret these values, a considerable knowledge of biochemistry is required in order to apply a nutrient supplement prescription. It is not just a matter of prescribing the latest anti-cholesterol drug which does nothing for the primary cause of the elevation.

It is even more complex when the blood triglycerides have to be considered. There are other very basic and very important facts that are revealed by a scan of this comprehensive study. However, I stress again that the information is a Rosetta stone which requires translation.

I often employ my automobile analogy in discussions with my patients. The owner of the car drives it into a station where a "car doctor" checks out the fundamental functions of the car. He applies a number of tests to ascertain where the problem is, starting with a clinical history. That means that the driver must explain the symptoms. Perhaps a light on the instrument panel has lit, indicating that something is wrong. That has a certain degree of specificity in that it may be the light that indicates overheating. The next step, of course, is to do some very simple tests such as checking the oil.

Note that a human being has a driver, to which I have repeatedly referred as the computer. The body has engines to burn fuel and the equivalent of a transmission to enable the appropriate use of energy delivered by those engines. A physician must use the general laboratory tests to get a basic indication of how well those engines are running. Preventive medicine is much like a weather forecast. We are recognizing more and more risk factors from the general laboratory survey. We can give a prediction of the chances of disease, but it is necessarily crude and certainly cannot indicate when a breakdown is likely to occur, or even whether it will. Remember my former discussion in the "three circles of health." The laboratory tests merely indicate that the running characteristics of the engines are below par. Thus, a stress event such as an infection, trauma, or bad news may precipitate the breakdown which we call disease.

Let me give an example of such a phenomenon. I have an elderly patient, in his late seventies. As long ago as 1989, his bone marrow had shown a situation which indicated that he might contract the lethal disease multiple myelomatosis at any time. This is a condition in which the functions of the bone marrow go haywire, and it behaves exactly like a cancerous state. He knew this, of course, and came to see me to find out whether nutritional components might stave off the evil day. Over the next several years, using nutrients which are known to affect the health of the blood-producing apparatus, he maintained a status quo and remained in excellent health. Then he developed the flu while in Florida, and, when he returned to Ohio, his blood hemoglobin had dropped to 6.9 grams/d1. This condition is a profound anemia, demanding a blood transfusion. Naturally, I thought that the flu had kicked him over into the full-blown disease that we had dreaded for years. Amazingly, we found that his bone marrow was still in exactly the same state as it had been in 1989; he did not have the fulminating disease that we had expected. The specialist who attended him was surprised and had to accept the fact that the sudden drop in hemoglobin was a "check" caused by the flu virus.

How do I see this in terms of the model that I am trying to project in this book? It is really quite simple. This gentleman has a bone marrow which has been recognized for years as being in a state of metastable equilibrium. All the specialists who have had anything to do with his case have expected the inevitable change that would spell death. We can say that this state was governed by an inherent genetic weakness that had emerged in his later years. This is the genetics circle. The status quo had been maintained by the use of nutrients that had kept the potentially sick marrow from crossing the line to severe illness—the nutrition circle. Along came the stress of the viral attack which caused the bone marrow to become non-productive, but *without kicking him over into full blooded disease.* It is an attack/defend situation, and this patient's system had "duked it out" with the attacking agent without a complete breakdown.

There were two things in his favor. The first was that he had been taking the nutrients. The second was his indomitable spirit and complete certainty that he was in good hands, a very formidable shield in any disease.

Just as we have to judge the possibility of breakdown in a car, we have to take in the tensile strength of the individual parts of the body machinery, thus coming out with a forecast. By recognizing that optimum nutrition is essential for optimal engine-running characteristics, we are able to perceive the importance of nutrition. We can, in fact, begin to glimpse the nuts and bolts of the paradigm shift mentioned earlier. Now, we must begin to look to the laboratory to provide us with a greater degree of specificity.

Hair Analysis

Most nutritionally-oriented preventive physicians are performing hair analyses on their patients. It is sometimes puzzling to the patient, particularly when orthodox medicine has often castigated it as a scam. Sometimes, when a patient asks the purpose of the test, I simply reply that it is to estimate "mineral balance," a poor answer which many people find even more confusing. So let me begin by saying something about this test.

Each cell in the human body is, as we have emphasized, a unit of function. It is a one-celled animal in its own right. As it works, it contributes its unique functional ability to that of the body/mind mechanisms of the whole organism. I have tried to indicate how each of these cells is turned on and off by the chemistry of the nervous system in its constant reactions with each cell. Cellular function depends upon a constant biochemical "chatter" in a complex chemical language. So the ultimate cell mechanism depends upon a fundamental *balance* between ions, particularly magnesium, calcium, sodium, and potassium. Hence, there are numerical ratios which can be derived if we know the individual concentrations of each of these elements. They provide us with a concept of balance which becomes the means by which we can derive a basic idea of how cells are functioning.

A hair, growing out of the scalp, is produced by live cells. True, the hair itself is not alive. It grows indefinitely and is frequently discarded and replaced by a new one. The general appearance of the hair provides a splendid indication of health of a person. When you see it dry and "lifeless," like a section of a haystack, it indicates poor biochemical health. When it has a beautiful metallic sheen, reflecting light, it indicates a healthy scalp chemistry. Of course, that generalization is crude and nonspecific, but it is one of the factors that we take in automatically when we judge the health of a person whom we meet casually. Hair analysis provides a reflection of the cellular biochemistry that was going on at the time when the hair was being formed within the follicle. It is "frozen" in time and is therefore a stable representation of the elements that make up the nuts and bolts of cellular function. True, it gives a picture in the past, not the immediate present, but we can generally assume that it has not changed that much in the short time since that part of the hair shaft grew.

There are two primary facts that can be obtained from mineral analysis of hair. The first is that there is a balance between ions. Two examples are the balance between calcium and magnesium and the balance between sodium and potassium. The concentration of one, divided by the other, provides a ratio. These ratios give important clues about the way the cells of the patient are functioning, and understanding them requires basic scientific knowledge of considerable complexity. I will return to this concept shortly.

The second basic fact is in reference to intoxication by heavy metals. Aluminum, lead, cadmium, arsenic, and mercury are the five that are usually measured. We Americans live in a modern, industrial environment, and these heavy metals are ubiquitous. We now know, from work that was done in England, that they inevitably accumulate in our hair as we grow older. They are, in fact, partially responsible for the slow attenuation of our biochemical mechanisms which cause gradual loss of efficiency on our cells. Thus, they are an integral part of the aging process, even when we maintain an optimal degree of oxidative metabolic efficiency. If one of them accumulates at a greater rate than average, it may be because that individual has a greater exposure, perhaps related to occupation. Or, it may be related to loss of oxidative efficiency which *permits* accelerated accumulation in the presence of an average or normal environmental exposure. The test does not identify what could be called poisoning in the majority of cases, but it is an extremely useful screening device and may well detect true poisoning.

We now know that lead in children is poisonous at much lower concentrations than previously realized. Thus, in a political sense, we increased the numbers of lead-intoxicated children by edict. This is of major importance since it has been at last realized that lead impairs mental function, even in much smaller doses than had been previously believed. Hair analysis is by far and away the cheapest and easiest way of screening for this potential disaster.

Another dangerous metal is mercury; ingested from industrial sources and also from mercury amalgam fillings in our teeth, it can be an important source of symptoms. Aluminum is another important toxic metal. In a recent survey of aluminum concentrations in water supplies in England, it was found that there was an increase in the incidence of Alzheimer's disease in the population in direct proportion to the concentration of aluminum in the water supply. Screening for these heavy metals in the present industrial age, without any other expectation from the test, would justify the use of hair analysis.

Sometimes hair analysis indicates a concentration of heavy metal which may not be sufficient to give rise to explicit symptoms that are generally recognized yet is higher than it should be. I refer to it as a "toxic burden" and suggest to the patient that it is an important phenomenon to take notice of. More efficient metabolism may enable the burdened cells to detoxify themselves. For example, a supplement of thiamin has been shown to reverse the symptoms of lead poisoning in a cow.

Now, let us turn back to ratios. I will provide one example of how a ratio of sodium to potassium can reflect the phenomenon of fatigue, but without giving explicit evidence of the true, underlying clinical cause of the fatigue. Each cell in the body requires a concentration of potassium which is relatively higher than the corresponding concentration of sodium. This is so important that each cell will donate a significant amount of its energy budget to pumping potassium into the interior of the cell and pumping sodium out. These pumps are biochemical in nature, of course, and are located within the cell membrane. If they begin to fail because there is insufficient energy available to maintain them, the potassium concentration falls and the sodium rises. This undesirable ratio provides an indication that the cell is fatigued. If enough cells within the body are fatigued in this way, the net effect for the individual may well be a *sense of fatigue*, the most common symptom that I encounter in my practice.

It should be noted that the relatively high sodium does not indicate that the patient is taking too much dietary sodium. Neither does the low potassium indicate potassium deficiency in the diet. Basically, it tells us that the cell pumps are not as efficient as they should be, and that is all. This may *suggest* certain lines of thinking about the underlying cause of the loss of efficiency. Staying away from dietary sodium and taking a supplement rich in potassium undoubtedly helps, but I want to make it very clear that this kind of result does not give a clear mandate for nutritional supplementation.

If a patient comes in to see me because of fatigue, and I find this change in the hair analysis, I explain that the patient is suffering unusual fatigue because there is loss of efficiency in energy metabolism. Indeed, that is all that the result shows, and I believe that we have to be very cautious in the interpretation of the facts. I could go on and discuss other ratios in a similar context. In my opinion, their interpretation is a skill possessed only by those that understand the chemistry which is revealed. It is therefore totally out of the scope of a book written for the layman. In fact, many physicians are not conversant with these biochemical implications, simply because they are not in general use in modern standard medicine.

Some very important research has shown that hair analysis can give us information about the personality of an individual. An investigator wanted to find out whether this technique would help to differentiate between violent and non-violent criminals who were incarcerated in jail. One of the findings was that the violent criminals tended to have much more copper in the hair than non-violent prisoners. A high copper concentration makes the nervous system more irritable, so it is not too difficult to see the association. Of course, it does not mean that a person with high copper in the hair is a violent criminal. It can, however, be said that such a person is more likely to be irritable and poorly adapted to environmental stimulus. There is every reason to believe that the most important advances in the interpretation of hair analysis will come from pattern recognition, probably with the aid of a computer.

Direct Tests for Nutrient Deficiency

By this time, the reader might well conclude that laboratory tests are virtually useless in determining the exact nature of illness. When a patient goes to a physician and says that he is sick, the laboratory tests may confirm that he is indeed sick, without giving a lead as to the exact biochemical problem. Conclusions have to be drawn from inference, by knowing the connection between the abnormality and its underlying cause. For example, the blood cholesterol might be abnormally high or abnormally low, both being indicators of disease risk, but not necessarily indicative of the actual presence of disease.

The physician faces the patient with the results of a series of tests. Conventionally, these will identify a specific disease entity such as rheumatoid arthritis. In actual fact, they confirm that the patient has something wrong but do not cast any light at all on the underlying reason—*in a biochemical sense.*

Thus, it is fair to ask whether any tests performed by a modern medical laboratory provide a high degree of recognition of a nutrient need. For example, does a blood concentration of a specific vitamin or mineral provide such information? The answer is almost unequivocally in the negative. As I have already indicated, high concentrations of a given vitamin such as thiamin, folate, or B_{12} are extremely misleading. They indicate that something is biochemically wrong with their use by the body but do not offer a clue as to how to correct it. For this reason, I rarely request assays of vitamins in blood. It is true, of course, that if a person is truly starving, that vitamin and/or mineral concentrations may well be low, but that is not the kind of malnutrition that we are dealing with in America. Again, we have to rely on additional knowledge about the essential chemistry involved.

Biologic Saturation Tests

I have already indicated that vitamins and minerals are cofactors to enzymes, and the enzymes do not work without them. A biologic saturation test depends, therefore, on this basic principle. You will recall that a given substance, which we will call a substrate, is acted upon by an enzyme, which converts the substrate to a product. This process is illustrated by the simple equation:

$$\textbf{Substrate + Enzyme + Cofactor(s)} \rightarrow \textbf{Product}$$

In some cases, where an enzyme carries out its function in a blood cell, it is possible to measure the rate at which the product (P) is produced by placing the blood in a test tube. The amount of P that is produced per unit volume of blood per minute can then be calibrated. Now a cofactor can be added to the reaction and the test repeated. If the amount of P is increased significantly, it is a measure of the need for that cofactor.

There are several such tests which provide indication of such a biologic deficiency. Thiamin, vitamin B6, and riboflavin, all members of the vitamin B complex, and selenium deficiency can be identified this way. The problem is that a physician has no specific knowledge of which deficiency is likely to be present because the symptoms of each deficiency are quite similar. All four tests could be run, in a "fishing expedition," and it would be largely a question of chance as to whether one of these tests would indicate the nature of the nutrient deficiency. To perform all of them on speculation would be extremely expensive, and I use them only when I suspect that one of these deficiencies *might* be present, based upon the clinical situation. This judgment requires experience.

Oh sure, there are small clinical clues which can be picked up by the physician who is experienced in the relationships between disease and marginal malnutrition. That physician may say that he *suspects* a given deficiency from such a clue, but he cannot make a definitive judgment. For example, white spots on the nails are a very important and easily observed clue, which frequently gives rise to the suspicion that the person is deficient in zinc or vitamin B6 or both. But it is not a guarantee. The white spots are created when the fingernail is being produced, and each spot represents a deficiency of pigment. They are thus stress-related, and there is a temporary failure of pigment production which marks the stress incident.

Each of the biologic saturation tests gives information about only one nutrient. For a test to be administered, there should be some clinical suspicion of deficiency of that nutrient. For many years, I have used a blood test called transketolase, which tests for the deficiency of thiamin. A person who is addicted to sugar and has a range of symptoms which indicate abnormal autonomic function is a good candidate for such a test, and I have found it to be a useful way of showing the patient that such a nutrient deficiency exists.

New methods are in the process of development, and there is little doubt that the laboratory will become a much more important means of identifying the nutrient combinations required for each individual. Some physicians, using a technique known as kinesiology, and others using homeopathic methods, maintain that they can identify the needed nutrient or nutrients by recognizing their "electrical harmony" with the tested patient. This may or may not be true and is not in general use with most nutritionally-oriented physicians. Unfortunately, in the state of our present knowledge, the best way to determine a given nutrient deficiency is to suspect it and then give it to the patient on clinical trial. There is certainly some overlap in the actions of these various vital substances, and it is worth remembering that each one is a catalyst acting as a "spark plug" in the orchestration of efficient oxidation. Each one represents a girder in the cathedral roof.

For example, several years ago, a classroom experiment was performed on a class of children who were all hyperactive. They were there specifically because they could not be handled in association with normal children. The investigator divided the class into two halves and gave one half a supplement of thiamin. The other half received vitamin B_6 (pyridoxine). About 20 percent of each group responded to their respective supplements. The investigator then took the thiamin "failures" and treated them with pyridoxine, while the pyridoxine "failures" were treated with thiamin. Again, about 20 percent of each group responded. The remainder of the class did not respond to either of these vitamin supplements.

Let me remind the reader once again that the theme of this book is that *the biology of the body is governed solely by how efficiently it uses oxygen.* Thus, a purely empirical approach with thiamin and pyridoxine bore fruit. The remainder of the children did not have a different kind of disease, since they were all classified as hyperactive. They had a loss of efficiency in oxidative metabolism that was related to *other* nutrient deficiencies. The future of the laboratory must be directed toward the elusive characterization of oxidative efficiency.

A most important laboratory development is required (and is in the process of being researched)—the ability to detect pathology related to free radicals. This is a highly technical field and is outside the scope of my essential message. As I have already explained, it is also closely related to efficient *utilization of oxygen.* The production of free radicals in excess indicates that oxygen is not being used for the synthesis of ATP, to be stored as energy, meaning that efficiency automatically declines. The free radicals themselves produce damage, so there is essentially a double effect on tissues.

Summary

I have tried throughout this book to provide a picture of the paradigm shift which nutritional medicine represents. The last paradigm shift was the discovery of germs as causes of disease. This one is, in my view, even more important. For the most part, a good defense system in the body will automatically keep the dangerous microorganisms at bay. Thus the importance of the germ is transcended in the priorities which must be applied to our fight against disease.

In my daily life as a physician, I find that describing this paradigm shift is extremely difficult on a person-to-person basis. It is time-consuming and demands that the patient take a completely new view of disease and health, not an easy switch to make for anyone, let alone in a consulting room. Even those patients who come to me specifically for nutritional therapy want to know which nutrient must be used to treat this or that disease. I try to tell them that the disease, as a specifically named constellation of symptoms and signs, does not matter at all.

It is easy to understand that my response will cause an immediate sense of confusion. I often find that the patient will take on a kind of glazed look in the eyes, and I know that my words are being heard but not understood. This reaction occurs, of course, because we have all been educated in the classification of disease as it fills in-numerable textbooks of medicine. Pains in joints, for example, invariably are regarded as being some form of arthritis, and the patient desires to know not only whether it *is* arthritis, but what sub-classification applies.

I try to tell them that the conditions of the body are as mental as diseases of the mind are physical, that the human body is made up of 100 trillion units (cells) that operate on biochemical and electrical principles. Medical classification has "cut off the patient's head." Everything above the neck is called mental, and everything below it is physical. When there is a combination of mental and physical symptoms, the condition is called psychosomatic, particularly if there are no laboratory tests that signify cellular damage. No reason is given for the patient's experience of pain, aches, heart palpitations, diarrhea/constipation, and many other symptoms, other than "it is in your head," a statement which is automatically interpreted by the patient as an accusation of fraud.

I try to get patients thinking along with me. I ask them whether they think that glaucoma is a disease of the eye. This seems like a rather stupid question since the answer is "Of course it is!" I tell them that it is really a condition in which the eye has become a target of confused autonomic system reflexes. Arthritis is not a disease of the joints. It is a condition in which the joints have become a target of the disordered brain/body signaling relationship. It is not in the least surprising that physical changes in organs occur when the confused messages pour out from a disregulated computer and nervous system.

There is a condition called reflex sympathetic dystrophy. Here is how it develops. A patient—let us take a fourteen-year-old girl as an example—knocks her ankle against a table leg. It is not a severe injury. Next morning, the ankle is swollen and painful and it may not be at all associated by the girl with the trivial injury of the day before. She, and particularly her parents, will rule out the injury as being too slight to cause this kind of effect. During the subsequent days and weeks, she finds that the pain and swelling do not resolve, and she notices that her foot and lower leg change color. Sometimes they are white and sometimes reddened as though inflamed. If the condition is not recognized for what it really is, a diagnosis of some form of arthritis is often made. In a child, it might well be called mono-articular juvenile rheumatoid arthritis (JRA). In some cases, there will ultimately be a change, known as Sudeck's atrophy, in one or more of the ankle bones. This will almost certainly clinch the diagnosis of JRA if the real problem is not understood.

Why is this phenomenon known as reflex sympathetic dystrophy? Because the autonomic nervous system which controls the caliber of blood vessels to the extremity has gone out of balance. This imbalance is triggered by the injury, but not literally *caused* by it. It is the light switch which causes the light to go on. Why does it occur? Because the balance is relatively fragile, and a poor diet, with lots of junk food, may be the underlying cause. But imagine this situation! What a devastating effect from a trivial injury! How utterly misleading it is unless a person is introduced to the condition and knows what she is actually dealing with! It must be seen as a cross-relationship between the nervous system and the target organs which it controls. It is *not* psychosomatic in the traditional sense, which would suggest, in psychologic terms, that this fourteen-year-old child "unconsciously does not want to go to school." It is an unequivocal misinterpretation of the reality unless we see it in a holistic sense as a biochemical, mind/body phenomenon.

Another example: there is a condition known as reflex cephalalgia (RC), a ghastly name to give to anything because it implies something far more devastating than it really is. Leading from the heart to the brain is an artery, known as the carotid artery, in each side of the neck. In close association with this artery is a network of autonomic nerves. Because of their position, they are relatively close to the skin surface and may be involved in a blunt injury in the same way that the girl's leg bumped the table.

Let us take a typical patient with RC, a twenty-three-year-old man. He strikes the right side of his neck against a wooden post while riding a motorcycle. He does not lose consciousness and sustains only superficial bruises. Some swelling and tenderness persists for several weeks. About two months after the accident, he begins to experience severe headaches over the right temple and forehead, associated with profuse sweating over the same area. Similar headaches occur subsequently six to eight times a month, accompanied by nausea, blurred vision in the right eye, and photophobia.

In this patient, the injury produced an imbalance in the autonomic nervous system, and the migraine-like headaches were, in essence, similar to a true migraine—also autonomic in character. So we understand that the young man had a headache which was triggered by the injury, similar to yet different from the headache of true migraine. In actuality both situations have a common, underlying cause in that both are due to an instability in the functions of the autonomic nervous system. Something of a stressful nature, either psychological or physical, can kick it off. In orthodox medicine, the diet history is rarely considered in detail, and very few physicians will ask the patient how many soft drinks are consumed in the course of a day. I know, however, that this may be (and usually is) the most important cause of the instability in the first place. So-called diet drinks are one of the chief culprits, because aspartame is a substance that has a very great effect on the de-stabilization process.

People come to my office, knowing that I use nutrition and nutritional supplements almost exclusively, and ask me whether nutrition will help such-and-such a disease. My answer is invariably the same: *I do not treat disease!* Sometimes, this response stuns the questioner. The implication is the unspoken question of what on earth I am doing then. I explain that I treat people; and that I am trying to build a temple to health, not a temple to disease, as some of our major medical institutions are doing. I try to get across the notion that nutrition is the basic route by which all disease is treated *using the principle that the patient heals his or her own disease*. The body is a self-repairing machine.

It is worth remembering that the ancient Chinese paid their physicians only when they were well. The moment that they became sick, they stopped paying. It was an obvious advantage to both physician and patient to remain well. Such an idea, however, does not work today because so many would either fake the illness or complain in trivial terms. This is what happened in the British National Health scheme. As a family physician at that time, I was overwhelmed with triviality. About 10 percent of my practice gave rise to 90 percent of the work.

But to get back to the subject at hand. What do I mean by "treating people?" I see each human being as an individual who must be in adaptive equilibrium with the environment. The environment is, virtually by definition, cruelly hostile. Our MN is not kind and solicitous in human terms. She is an incredibly hard taskmaster who wants to know whether we are truly fit to survive. She has developed diverse ways of testing that adaptive fitness by surrounding us with microorganisms that are ready to attack us. In that sense, *all* disease-causing microorganisms are opportunist in character. There is no such thing as automatic infection. There is always an attack-and-defense situation. Thus, fitness really and truly depends upon energy metabolism in sufficient supply to run the machinery of the body, assuming that the machinery is complete and intact.

If we use traditional nomenclature, all disease is "psychosomatic," even a case of the flu virus. Fever is caused by mechanisms controlled by the brain; it is a standard defense measure. I reason that ill feeling is also defensive, since it causes the patient to go to bed and seek rest. It is thus inappropriate to reduce the fever artificially with a pharmaceutical such as aspirin. The patient *feels* better, but there is a certain loss of defensive attributes which result in a potential for prolonging the battle between the virus and the host that is being attacked by it.

By developing this theme to its full potential, we have an entirely new model for disease which is vastly superior to that which we presently use. I often tell patients that if the model that we propose were an automobile, it would be in the stage of the Model-T, the forerunner of the modern sophisticated automobile, and it too will develop into a sophisticated, well-running model.

Modern orthodox medicine often does serious damage to the patient, completely contrary to the Hippocratic Oath, which requires that a physician swears that he will do no harm. If the treatment is worse than the disease, then we should be doing nothing at all. Nutritional treatment is almost completely harm-proof and tackles the underlying, biochemical causes. It does not merely treat symptoms. It does not fit with the impatience of many people, however, because it does not give instant relief. In fact, as we have discussed, it may make the initial symptoms much worse before they begin to get better. It takes weeks or months before the patient is able to appreciate the brunt of the benefits, and it is a testing time for the physician/patient relationship.

I am fully aware of the reductionist principles that I have stated. Some people will question the validity because they are unable to accept that we are a mass of whirling electrons and complex chemical reactions. They have been taught that there is something called the human spirit and that we have a soul which is immortal. I do not contest that. I do not know what the human spirit is and whether we do or do not have an immortal soul. In fact, I am seeking to service the physical machinery which enables us to survive as intact human beings. Since the machinery is electrical and chemical in nature, I know of absolutely no method that will enhance that other than putting the best possible fuel into the cellular engine.

One of the best ways that the interaction between the lower and upper brain is seen is in the development of children. When a baby is born, he is run solely by a computer. The cognitive brain is there, but it is not yet a functional entity. The bladder fills with urine and empties automatically, and the characteristic crying is automated. Indeed, the infants who are unfortunately born with only a stump of brain will cry and suck and will be ostensibly completely normal infants for a short while. Temper tantrums are produced by the computer. They are not strictly cognitive, although the child may well know that he is doing it and why. It is usually for some trivial desire such as requesting a candy which is refused.

I tell parents that temper tantrums are produced by the automatic brain and that cognitive awareness is a process which we refer to as maturation. Are temper tantrums normal? Of course they are—up to a certain poorly defined age. If they continue beyond that age or are unusually frequent or violent, they swing into a bracket that is increasingly abnormal. However, it must be understood that it is a normal neurotransmitter reaction *with the volume turned up.* Is it therefore truly abnormal? In a sense, it is not, since it is a normal activity which is poorly controlled by the more sophisticated brain which should not permit the reaction in a mature individual. Hyperactivity falls into the same bracket, since activity is a normal trait in children. *Hyper*activity is activity, a normal mechanism—again, with the volume turned up.

Maturation is an electro-chemical process whereby the brain is gradually "finished off" as the child grows. The process is, of course, normal, as expressed in the Bible: "When I was a child, I spoke as a child, I understood as a child, I thought as a child. But when I became a man I put away childish things." Temper tantrums that persist represent the hallmark of maturational failure. When nutrients are used, this maturation accelerates and gradually catches up with the child's chronologic age. Often, the first sign of genuine improvement is that the child will apologize for a temper tantrum. The cognitive brain is beginning to perceive the child in a more appropriate light from a chronologic standpoint and is accelerating the process of brain integration which is the way in which the child will develop into an adult human being.

Nutritional delinquency, by which I mean high-calorie malnutrition, has a powerful effect on this maturational process. It seems to slow it down or stop it and makes the automatic brain computer more and more irritable. Violence is a phenomenon which is undoubtedly related to this; I am convinced, in fact, that the reason for widespread violence in America is rooted in high-calorie malnutrition in many cases.

I am well aware that I am repeating myself in this final chapter. I am doing so because the principles involved represent a dramatic shift in the thought process as to how we perceive ourselves in health and disease. I have come to realize that most of the diseases that we suffer are self-inflicted. It is exquisitely difficult for people to be aware that a tiny morsel of chocolate can undo them if they are one of those unfortunate people who are highly sensitive to that substance. When I ask patients whether they have discontinued coffee which, for them, spells disaster to their health, they reply, "No, not completely, but I'm working on it!" It is extraordinarily difficult to get people to understand the basic principles. They believe that cutting down on something will make them feel better if they are addicted, whereas they may feel worse. They are familiar with the fact that contact with a few tiny grains of dust will cause them to have an allergic reaction, but they are unable to translate that into chocolate or sugar sensitivity. The approach that says that if more is bad, less is better, is in fact misleading when considering withdrawal from an addictive substance. Only "cold turkey" will suffice.

The present orthodox medical approach is one that depends on very concrete, structural thinking. For example, a person with acute low-back pain which radiates down the leg is regarded as having a "pinched nerve." A more sophisticated diagnosis might be discitis, a slipped disc, or a degenerate disc. Then why does it respond in most cases to an intravenous injection of a drug called colchicine that is extracted from colchicum, the yellow crocus? It is because it is much more complex than a mere mechanical process. It involves inflammatory changes that are induced by biochemical reactions. Low-back pain, suffered by thousands of people, is triggered by mental stress as often as it is by physical stress. The "three circles of health" tells us why.

There are presently two basic points of view relative to nutritional medicine. The first, and most common, is a complete resistance to the whole concept. If nutrition were so beneficial, these people say, why is it not in common use? Why have the big university hospital and the modern medical mecca not accepted it and used it? Surely, the mavericks who are using it must be charlatans. It is true that it does seem much too simple. After all, we have wrapped medicine in such an aura of mystery and scientific jargon that it takes a trained medical man to understand the language. But just sit down quietly and think about it as a principle, and you can see that we must behave like the horticulturist who *feeds* his plants to keep them well!

The second point of view is that nutrition and nutrients are powerful therapeutic agents. But most of the people who are adherents to that point of view operate on what I refer to as "the old medical model"; this model indicates that certain constellations of symptoms and signs constitute a given disease which is named. My point of view goes a stage further. It indicates that the naming of the disease is fruitless unless its mechanism is understood in biochemical terms. You cannot name a disease and then assess which nutrient is valuable in treating that particular disease. You have to assess the symptoms and signs in terms of how the brain/body adaptive mechanisms are failing or over-reacting, and the biochemical delinquency that is responsible. Organic disease, in which a specific organ or set of organs is damaged, is frequently the end point of functional imbalance which may have been present for years.

A female patient, for example, has all the symptoms and signs of PMS. In traditional medicine, this condition is either treated as a non-disease or it is treated as a neurosis or functional problem. She sees a physician who is personable, sympathetic, and kind but does not understand the brain/body relationship which is the cause. He may see it as a gynecological disorder, only because the symptoms are inextricably related to the menstrual cycle. She is treated for twenty years by the physician, and he tries her on various drugs to modify or remove the symptoms. She is grateful and has a sincere appreciation of what her physician does for her to alleviate the problem. When she has episodes of diarrhea, they are regarded as a bowel symptoms and she may be referred to a gastro-enterologist. If she complains of heart palpitations, she may be referred to a cardiologist because the symptom is relative to heart function.

It is clear that both physician and patient are quite satisfied that everything possible is being done for this unfortunate situation and both are happy with the status quo. However, one day she sees her physician because she has detected a lump in her breast. A diagnosis of cancer is made, and she is treated accordingly. The patient is intelligent and perceptive, and she starts wondering whether her twenty years of treatment for PMS have any bearing on her development of cancer. She goes back to her trusted physician and asks this question. The answer that she gets is that there is no relationship.

My view is quite different. There is *every* reason to believe that the twenty years of ineffectual treatment for PMS would be the forerunner of the "real disease," which gets the feared name of cancer. The body, for all those years, was subjected to a bombardment of highly maladaptive orders from the brain. The consumption of energy under those conditions is extraordinarily high, and wear and tear on the body is a twenty-four-hours-a-day phenomenon. Cancer is a disease of the whole organism. It is not a localized thing in the breast, although the breast tissue might be considered the target. The cancer itself is merely the tip of the iceberg. Perhaps the most malignant assaults on that unfortunate lady's physiology might be the birth-control pill (which might well have been used in the treatment of PMS), chocolate, sugar, tobacco smoke, margarine, excessive saturated fat and soft drinks—in short, our culture!

It is for these many reasons that I believe nutritional medicine to be the mandatory medicine of the next century. It is extremely effective, particularly in the early stages of disease, where modern orthodoxy fails miserably. Its preventive approach is a guaranteed benefit; and, last but not least, it is economically effective. By turning our attention collectively to this renaissance, we could save billions of dollars. Surgery would be reduced drastically, and operations such as surgical bypass would be regarded as a primitive assault.

From a pure common-sense point of view, many people know these facts already. But, as in all revolutions, turf battles that must be fought will be humongous. Since our government has had the wisdom to develop an Office of Alternative Medicine, we can at least believe that our politicians are stirred in this direction.

I fervently hope that readers of this book will perceive the importance of a paradigm shift in thought that is required in order to see the value of nutritional medicine and all its alternative medicine relatives. It is certainly here to stay, and my belief is that it will gradually replace the present use of allopathic medicine. If we succeed, a new vista of health is at hand, and the role of physicians will change dramatically. Health will not be seen as something that you can place in the hands of someone else, upon whose skill that fragile phenomenon depends; rather, it will be seen that we control for ourselves, a self-preserved prerogative.

About the Author

Derrick Lonsdale, M.D., is a specialist in nutrition and preventive medicine. He has practiced medicine since 1948, graduating from London University. He has been in family practice, was a medical officer in the Royal Canadian Air Force, did a residency in pediatrics at Cleveland Clinic, and was a staff member in pediatrics and head of the Section of Biochemical Genetics at Cleveland Clinic. Since 1982, he has practiced nutritional medicine at the Preventive Medicine Group in Cleveland. He is also editor of the *Journal of Advancement in Medicine*, the official journal of the American College of Advancement in Medicine. Dr. Lonsdale lives in Strongsville, Ohio.

Hampton Roads Publishing Company
publishes books on a variety of subjects,
including metaphysics, health, alternative medicine,
visionary fiction, and other related topics.
For a copy of our latest catalog, call toll-free,
(800) 766-8009, or send your name and address to:

Hampton Roads Publishing Company, Inc.
134 Burgess Lane
Charlottesville, VA 22902